THE MEMOIRS OF
FIELD-MARSHAL
WILHELM KEITEL

THE MEMOIRS OF
FIELD-MARSHAL
WILHELM KEITEL

Edited with an
introduction and epilogue by
WALTER GORLITZ

Translated by
DAVID IRVING

New introduction by
EARL ZIEMKE

Cooper Square Press

First Cooper Square Press edition 2000

This Cooper Square Press paperback edition of *The Memoirs of Field-Marhsal Wilhelm Keitel* is an unabridged republication of the edition first published in New York in 1966, with the addition of a new introduction by Earl Ziemke.

The Memoirs of Field-Marshal Keitel
Copyright © 1961 by Musterschmnidt-Verlag, Göttigen, Germany

English translation by David Irving
Copyright © 1965 by William Kimber and Co., Limited

New introduction
Copyright © 2000 by Earl Ziemke

Published by Cooper Square Press
An Imprint of the Rowman & Littlefield Publishing Group
150 Fifth Avenue, Suite 911
New York, New York 10011

Distributed by National Book Network

Library of Congress Cataloging-in-Publication Data
Keitel, Wilhelm, 1882–1946.
    [Generalfeldmarschall Keitel, Verbrecher oder Offizier? English]
    The memoirs of Field-Marshal Wilhelm Keitel : Chief of the German High Command, 1938–1945 / edited with an introduction and epilogue by Walter Gorlitz ; new introduction by Earl Ziemke.— 1st Cooper Square Press ed.
    p. cm.
    Rev. translation of: Generalfeldmarschall Keitel, Verbrecher oder Offizier?
    Includes index.
    ISBN 0-8154-1072-7 (pbk : alk. paper)
    1. Keitel, Wilhelm, 1882–1946. 2. Germany. Wehrmacht Oberkommando—Biography. 3. Generals—Germany—Biography. I. Görlitz, Walter, 1913– II. Title.
DD247.K42 A3 2000
940.54'0092—dc21
[B]
                        00-056999

CONTENTS

PUBLISHER'S NOTE

The Memoirs of Field-Marshal Keitel were written in manuscript in prison at Nuremberg, beginning on 1st September, 1946. The original is in the possession of the Keitel family. His narrative covering the years 1933 to 1938 is included in the German edition, but in this English edition Keitel's life up to 1937 is dealt with in the editor's introduction which contains many extracts from Keitel's own account of those years. The translation of the memoirs themselves here begins with 1937, on page 35. On the other hand, some passages from the original manuscript which were not included in the German edition appear in this translation, as for example the description of the Munich crisis and the planning discussions for the invasion of Britain.

The *Führer*'s Shield Bearer

On October 6, 1945, prosecutors at the Nuremberg International Military Tribunal indicted twenty-four "major war criminals" on a possible four counts: waging a war of aggression (in various forms); conspiracy to wage a war of aggression; violations of the laws or customs of war; murder, extermination, enslavement, and other inhumane acts against civilian populations. The prisoner Wilhelm Keitel was one of fourteen charged on all counts, and after seeing the specific charges, he was convinced he would be found guilty in every instance. As the officer who had been closest to Adolf Hitler in the military chain of command, he decided at the outset therefore to accept full legal responsibility before the court and to appeal to the judgment of history for ethical and moral remission in the *Memoirs*, which he wrote in his spare time during the year of the trial. The *Memoirs* also had a second objective, namely, to refute what he considered to be slanderous opinions of himself widely held and expressed by his military colleagues during the war and in the court.

The part of Field-Marshal Wilhelm Keitel's life with which the *Memoirs* is concerned begins in October 1935 when he, fifty-five years old and a major general (U.S. equivalent, brigadier general), became head of the Armed Forces Office in the German Defense Ministry. He was then in the thirty-fifth year of an atypical military career. In fact, he would all along rather have been a farmer and, having recently inherited his family's farm, was on the verge of taking retirement. The Armed Forces Office would give broader scope to the two characteristics that had sustained his progress thus far—rigid devotion to duty and a voracious appetite for work—but its future was in doubt. The defense minister, Field-Marshal Werner von Blomberg, whom Adolf Hitler had also named commander in chief of the Armed Forces, had instituted it as an embryo armed forces high command in the Defense Ministry. The army, navy, and air force high commands regarded it as a politically motivated encroachment on their spheres of responsibility. Blomberg was not disposed to challenge the service commanders in chief, particularly since one of them, Hermann Göring, was Hitler's deputy and successor designate.

Keitel, as always, strove mightily to carry out his mission, but was frustrated at every turn and soon became enmeshed in a comic-opera sort of affair without a happy ending. In January 1938, Blomberg, then fifty-nine years old, with Hitler as his best man, married a much younger woman who was subsequently found to have a record with the Berlin police morals squad. To avoid the embarrassment of having the news become public knowledge, Hitler gave Blomberg a world tour as a "wedding present," abolished the Defense Ministry, made himself commander in chief of the Armed Forces, and renamed the Armed Forces Office the High Command of the Armed Forces. To placate the service commands, he assured them that Keitel, whom he appointed chief (*not* commander in chief) of the Armed Forces High Command, would not be his deputy or chief of staff; would have no authority to issue orders to the service commands; and would be solely concerned with the routine administrative matters that had formerly been the defense minister's responsibility. By and large, Hitler kept his word, probably because, having soon advanced himself to supreme commander of the Armed Forces, he did not propose to delegate any of his power. He subsequently established a small operations staff that was nominally subordinate to Keitel but responsible only to himself. Its chief, General Alfred Jodl, although always one grade below Keitel, functioned independently as Hitler's personal chief of staff.

Except as a dream, the Blomberg affair terminated the idea of a unified armed forces command; however, the subsequent reorganization lifted Keitel, in the tables of organization at least, to the military position closest to Hitler. Although Keitel could not give orders, he also did not take orders from anyone other than Hitler. In less than three years, Keitel rose four grades, from the lowest to the highest general officer rank, field-marshal. The call of duty was clear and the farm no longer a viable alternative.

The anomalies of his position continued unabated: although he could not exercise it, he was at the absolute center of power. On March 12, 1938, a week after Keitel's appointment, Hitler summoned him to Berchtesgaden, where the *Führer* was engaged in bullying Austrian Chancellor Kurt von Schuschnigg into surrendering his country. Keitel did not participate in the negotiations, only in the lunch and coffee breaks when nothing substantive was discussed.

Nevertheless, he says, "It dawned upon me during the course of this day that . . . I was by my very presence acting as a means to an end, my very first major rôle in life." (p. 57) Thereafter, he was a silent presence at Hitler's meetings with foreign leaders, accompanied Hitler whenever he traveled, and throughout the war attended Hitler's twice-a-day situation conferences at which he was seldom called upon to speak. Of the signing of the armistice with France on June 22, 1940, he says, "That day was the climax of my career as a soldier." (p. 114) He saw it as "the hour of our revenge for Versailles" (p.112), but was apparently most stirred by Hitler's having allowed him to act as the master of ceremonies.

His proximity to Hitler did not result in close association. Keitel was concerned with infrastructure, personnel, armament, and other bureaucratic aspects of armed forces development with which Hitler did not wish to be bothered. Those were, in fact, very large responsibilities with respect to which his silent attendance on Hitler was, for the most part, a waste of time, but one that was flattering and that, as Keitel saw it, provided a further opportunity to demonstrate his capacity for work. Recognizing operational and strategic planning to be beyond him, he was content to let Jodl become Hitler's advisor in those areas.

On July 19, 1940, Hitler recognized his generals' contributions to the victory in the Low Countries and France with promotions and decorations. Keitel received the marshal's baton and the Knight's Cross of the Iron Cross. Both were customarily awarded only for achievements on the field of battle. Keitel was pleased to have them, he says, but embarrassed as well, since he had no part either in the planning or execution other than occasionally delivering messages from Hitler to the commanding generals.

The victory over France permanently dispelled any doubts Keitel may have had about Hitler's qualifications as a war leader. Henceforth, content to be his *Führer*'s shield bearer, he took his mission to be to support Hitler without question in all circumstances—in other words, to provide an unimpeded scope for Hitler's genius. Keitel's abiding concern was the services' refusal to accept full unification and their insistence on immediate access to Hitler, which he saw as giving them opportunities to claim credit for Hitler's successes and to blame him for their failures. The use throughout the *Memoirs* of "War Office" as a synonym for "Army High Command" is, no doubt, meant to put the Army High Command, in his opinion, in its proper place as a subordinate office of the Armed Forces High Command.

The war had sharpened the divisions in the command structure.

In the field headquarters Keitel and Jodl took their meals with Hitler, which gave them an advantage over the service chiefs, who saw Hitler only by appointment. A shared concern with operations brought Jodl closer to Hitler than Keitel; however, like Keitel, he always supported Hitler's views as soon as they became known. Jodl also had no authority to issue orders outside his own bailiwick. The occupation of Norway and Denmark (May–June 1940) was the only operation independently managed by the Armed Forces Operations Staff, mainly because the operation was small enough to be organized and executed by an army corps staff borrowed from the army. The composition of *Führer* directives (strategic directives Hitler issued to initiate planning and preparation for major operations) was the Armed Forces Operations Staff's principal task. These organizational peculiarities presented opportunities to meddle in the service commands' conduct of operations, which Jodl frequently exploited and Keitel generally tolerated. As a result, only Hitler could make final decisions, which suited him exactly.

In late July 1940, Hitler put another kink in the chain of command: he set the army General Staff to work on planning an invasion of the Soviet Union and gave the army exclusive responsibility for the eastern front that would ensue. But he did not change the procedure with regard to the *Führer* directives; consequently, when he and Jodl issued his directive for what was to be called Operation BARBAROSSA, they found that the army was too far along with an altogether different plan to change without having to delay its start. (The army proposed to strike toward Moscow, Hitler toward Leningrad and Kiev). Hitler allowed the army to proceed, but—even though Jodl supported the army plan—the *Führer* put the army on notice to expect a switch to his plan after the operation started. Consequently, the army went into the Soviet Union with two incompatible objectives: to defeat the Soviet forces forward of Moscow or to seize Leningrad and the natural resources of the Ukraine and the Caucasus.

Keitel's treatment of the BARBAROSSA Plan and its failure is apparently a compulsive display of loyalty to Hitler. He traces the process of the 1941 summer campaign through several stages by means of which the army generals "shipwrecked Hitler's great strategic master plan" (p. 151) at the gates of Moscow. He proposes a study to determine how the Hitler plan might have fared if it had not been sabotaged by the generals—and thinks its chances would have been greatly improved.

He also sees a profound misjudgment of Hitler in the assumption made in the indictment that the invasion of the Soviet Union was an

4

act of unprovoked aggression. From Hitler's November 1940 meeting with the Soviet foreign minister, Vyacheslav Molotov, at which Keitel was present in his window-dressing role, he concludes that Hitler delayed the invasion until mid-1941 because he was seeking a peaceful solution, whereas, the German dictator's sole concern was to avoid the Russian winter. He also contends that Hitler's primary motive was to forestall Germany's encirclement by the Soviet Union and the Western powers, and was hence defensive. By way of proof Keitel claims that the deployment for BARBAROSSA was not begun until March 31, 1941. In his position, it could hardly have escaped him that the majority of the troops were in fact deployed gradually between August 1940 and January 1941.

All in all, he fails to mount a credible defense of Hitler and manages to demolish what was to have been the keystone of his and Jodl's defense at Nuremberg: a contention that BARBAROSSA was a preventive strike and therefore a legal act of war. At one point he told the court he had attempted to persuade Hitler not to launch the attack because it was unnecessary—Germany was already benefiting mightily from its semi-alliance with the Soviet Union; war in the East would have overextended the German forces. Further on, he states that Soviet strength discovered after the operation began convinced him that "Stalin" would have been ready to attack "within a year or two" but for "our preventive war on Russia" (p. 131). The court was not convinced by the idea of a fortuitous preventive attack.

On March 30, 1941, Hitler told the 250 or so highest-ranking officers that war with the Soviet Union would be a fight to the death between two incompatible ideologies and would therefore have to be conducted without regard for the laws and customs of war. Hitler then formulated—and Keitel subsequently formally promulgated—two decrees, later to be known as the BARBAROSSA Order and the Commissar Order. The first gave soldiers immunity from trial for offenses against Soviet civilians. The second denied Soviet military commissars (political officers) the right to prisoner-of-war status and required that all those captured be summarily shot. In the *Memoirs* Keitel appears to have believed that the Commissar Order and the BARBAROSSA Order—there called "the Order on Liability for Court Martial in Soviet Territories" (p. 137)—should not have been put in writing and that he did so only at the behest of the Army High Command. However, his main concern seems to have been with keeping the orders secret, not with their illegality. Later, he signed agreements giving SS extermination squads authority to operate in occupied Soviet territory. As the war progressed, he issued various *Führer* orders specifying the same treatment for captured commandos, parachutists, and members of resistance movements in Western Europe as was applied to the commissars.

In December 1941, when the onslaught of winter froze the German advance in its tracks and Soviet forces mounted a counterattack, Hitler abolished the post of army commander in chief and assumed the duties himself. Thereafter, the chief of the Army General Staff reported directly to him. But Hitler also retained the Armed Forces Operations Staff and continued to issue *Führer* directives through it. The hierarchical and structural change lost the Army its independence. The chief of the General Staff, Franz Halder, a colonel general, had to represent the army while a grade lower in rank than Keitel and the other service chiefs.

The plan for the 1942 summer campaign was entirely Hitler's. In it he reverted to his original assumption that the Soviet Union could be defeated by seizing its resources—specifically the Caucasus oil fields. In the execution of his strategy he again divided his forces by sending one army group due east toward Stalingrad and another due south toward the oil fields on the Caspian Sea, thereby ensuring that he could not give either the required support to reach its objective. In August, when the southern army group became stalled in the mountains, Hitler, having no army commander in chief other than himself with whom to find fault, sent Jodl to take the army group commander, Field-Marshal Wilhelm List, to task. When Jodl reported List had performed as well as could be expected, Hitler dismissed List, berated Keitel for having recommended List for the command, and thereafter took his meals alone. Hitler also dismissed Halder, who had supported List; and he granted the request of Halder's replacement, General of Infantry Kurt Zeitzler, that Keitel and Jodl henceforth be excluded altogether from eastern front affairs. The German dictator also proposed to get rid of Jodl as soon as Colonel General Friedrich Paulus could be released from command of the drive toward Stalingrad. On January 31, 1943, Paulus surrendered at Stalingrad. By then, Keitel's and Jodl's "betrayals" were beginning to look relatively insignificant to Hitler, and they stayed on in their respective positions to the end.

After Keitel's commentary on the Stalingrad battle, a lengthy break occurs in the *Memoirs*. On September 29, 1946, he had been found guilty and sentenced to death on all four counts. Since he had refused to appeal the verdict, he could not expect to complete his account of the last two years and four months of the war. He decided to focus on the part of the war in which he apparently believed he had proved himself worthy of his rank—and of the *Führer*'s trust. On the afternoon of his fifty-sixth birthday, April 20, 1945, Hitler admitted for the first time that he had lost the war. Although one road was still open to southern Bavaria, where his vacation home at Berchtesgaden had been equipped to serve as a headquarters, Hitler declared he would remain in Berlin to the end. Keitel and Jodl swore they would stay with him. By evening the *Führer*'s spirits had risen, and he was talking about organizing a counterattack. On the 23rd, Keitel, Jodl, and the Armed Forces Operations Staff went out of Berlin to coordinate counterattacks from the west and north. Two days later, the Soviet forces closed an encirclement around Berlin. Communication with Hitler thereafter became too uncertain to permit his retaining command; and Keitel—for the first time in the war—found himself in a position of active command. He knew it was high time to surrender but imagined that somehow he could improve the situation by rescuing Hitler. The army commands on the scene considered that notion absurd; nevertheless, Keitel threatened and bullied them into compliance. In the *Memoirs* he expresses no doubt regarding the correctness of his actions and narrates the final events with a degree of verve not seen in earlier chapters.

On the night of April 29, finally having recognized that his term as Hitler's shieldbearer had reached its end, Keitel told Hitler that the relief operation had failed. On May 1 he learned that Hitler had committed suicide and had named Grand Admiral Karl Doenitz to be president (chief of state) and supreme commander in chief. Doenitz, having expected something of the sort, had been in contact with Keitel for several days, but had been very careful not to assume any authority. As soon as he knew Hitler was dead, Doenitz wanted to order the army group on the eastern front closest to Germany, about a million men, to begin retreating immediately. But he made a mistake that Hitler would never have made in such a situation: he consulted Keitel, who advised him not to let the troops abandon prepared positions until they could conduct an orderly retreat. As a result, the army group lost about a week's time and then had only forty-eight hours in which to avoid capture. Doenitz sent Keitel back to Berlin on May 8. The unconditional surrender instrument had already been signed in Reims early on the morning of the 7th, and the 8th was V-E Day everywhere but in the Soviet Union. Josef Stalin insisted on a second signing in Berlin, which occurred at midnight on the 8th. Keitel was proud of having secured a twelve-hour grace period after they received notice of the surrender terms for the remaining troops on the eastern front.

Introduction

At Nuremberg, Keitel symbolically resumed the role of the *Führer*'s shieldbearer, voicing only disappointment that Hitler had not chosen to stay to answer for himself. Ironically, in the *Memoirs* he provided enough evidence both to get himself hanged and to prove him to have been a less-than-convincing example of the dyed-in-the-wool war criminal. On the other hand, whether he established an entitlement to the remission he sought, or refuted the low opinion in which he was widely held, is at best doubtful.

Earl F. Ziemke
Athens, Georgia
May 2000

Earl F. Ziemke, a research professor of history of at the University of Georgia, is the author of *Moscow to Stalingrad: Decision in the East, Stalingrad to Berlin: The German Defeat in the East,* and *The German Northern Theater of Operations, 1940–1945.*

PART I

The Background and Career
of
Field-Marshal Keitel

1

The Background and Career of
Field-Marshal Keitel
1882—1946
by
Walter Görlitz

HE photographs of Field-Marshal Wilhelm Keitel, Chief of
the German Armed Forces High Command, signing the
Instrument of Unconditional Surrender at Karlshorst near
Berlin, show him to have been just the kind of *Junkers* type that the
Western Allies had always made him out to be—a tall, broad-
shouldered man, his face a little haggard but proud and set, and
a monocle firmly screwed into his left eye. At the hour when the
totalitarian regime in Germany finally collapsed he was acknow-
ledging that he was an officer of the old school, although there was
nothing about him characteristic of the make-up of the indomitable
Prussian officer.

Even the skilled American psychologists who analysed and inter-
rogated him during his period of confinement were inclined to see
in him the prototype of the *Junkers*, of the Prussian militarist; perhaps they had never had any real opportunity of making any study
of the *Junkers* class of Prussia. Keitel, in fact, came from an entirely
different *milieu*.

The middle-class Hanoverian Keitel family, a family of land-
owners, came from a region with a marked anti-Prussian tradition:
the field-marshal's grandfather was a Royal Hanoverian crown-
land lessee and was closely connected with the House of Hanover
that Bismarck overthrew. Military tendencies and traditions were
completely alien to the family, and in silent protest against Prussia's
annexation of the kingdom of Hanover in 1866 the grandfather had

11

bought the 600-acre estate of Helmscherode in the Gandersheim district of the duchy of Brunswick in 1871, while still detesting everything that was Prussian: and when his son, the field-marshal's father, served for a year as a volunteer in a regiment of the Prussian Hussars he was strictly forbidden when he came home on leave to cross the threshold of Helmscherode while wearing the hated Prussian uniform.

There is little similarity between a Brunswick estate like Helmscherode and the great manors east of the Elbe; their lords cannot simply be classified as Junkers. Carl Keitel, the field-marshal's father, led a life no more pretentious than that of any well-to-do farmer. In contrast to his son, who was an enthusiastic huntsman and loved horses and riding, he believed in the maxim that a good farmer could never be a huntsman; the two were incompatible. At the bottom of his heart the son wanted nothing more than one day to be able to manage the Helmscherode estate himself; farmer's blood coursed strongly through his veins. He knew a little about agriculture and as the descendant of a long line of crown-land lessees and estate owners he had inherited a talent for organising and administering the affairs of large establishments. Several times Keitel was later to toy with the idea of giving up the soldier's life, but always he heeded what he believed to be his duty, perhaps abetted by the counsels of his ambitious and strong-willed wife.

The obstinacy of his father, who had no intention of relinquishing control over Helmscherode as long as he was of sound body, and the increasing tendency among the landed gentry to take up military careers, particularly after the victorious Franco-Prussian War of 1870–1871, produced the opposite effect.

The heir of Helmscherode, Wilhelm Bodewin Johann Gustav Keitel, born on 22nd September, 1882, became an officer; there is a family story that he was almost in tears as he finally decided to give up all hope of ever being a farmer. There was another reason for the decision, characteristic of the rising generation of middle-class farmers: if one could not be a farmer then the officer's was the only profession appropriate to one's rank. But the officer cadre, in the small northern and central German provinces at least, was of purely Prussian stock. What a comedown it was for a family with such a strong anti-Prussian tradition!

Nothing in his youth and nothing in his early years as an officer gave any hint that the young Keitel was destined to rise to the highest position in the German armed forces, or that it was to bring him such a cruel death. Initially he was a poor scholar, and he improved but little with time. His real interests were hunting, riding and farming at Helmscherode. After taking his school-leaving examination at Göttingen in March 1901 he entered the 46th Lower-Saxon Field Artillery Regiment, with its headquarters and 1st detachment at Wolfenbüttel (Brunswick).

By contrast, the young Lieutenant Keitel was a good and conscientious soldier. As one would expect from his earlier life of eating, drinking, hunting and riding and his enjoyment of good company, he was by no means an ascetic. Even so, he detested frivolity and he loathed extravagant pleasures. When he and his friend Felix Bürkner, the famous show jumper, were posted together to the Military Riding Academy in 1906 they pledged to one another that there would be 'no skylarking and no affairs with women'.

It was said of Keitel during his time as a division commander in Bremen, between 1934 and 1935, that while he naturally used a service car if he drove to official functions, his wife—if she was invited—had to go by tram as they had no car of their own. This strict and extreme correctness was a characteristic of the man. During the war and at the height of the fuel crisis Keitel, the Chief of the Armed Forces High Command, shocked the senior SS officials attending state funerals, by turning up in a modest Volkswagen, while they, the gentlemen with the silver deaths-heads on their caps and the motto: '*Our honour lies in our loyalty*' drove up in enormous and glittering limousines.

In any event, the young Keitel soon came to the attention of his superiors on account of his boundless proficiency. First his name was put up for the command of the demonstration regiment of the Field-Artillery Gunnery School, then there was talk of his being posted as inspecting officer to the training establishment for officer recruits. His then commanding officer disclosed to him that there was a condition attached to the latter posting, and that was that the candidate should be a bachelor. Keitel had a violent quarrel with his superior, and pointed out that he was going to be engaged and was thinking of marrying shortly.

In April 1909 Lieutenant Keitel married Lisa Fontaine, the daughter of a well-to-do estate owner and brewer of Wülfel, near Hanover, a strongly anti-Prussian man to whom his new 'Prussian' son-in-law was initially not a welcome addition to his family.

Lisa Fontaine had many intellectual and artistic interests; in her youth she was very beautiful although standoffish in manner. As far as can be judged from the letters that she left, she was probably the stronger and certainly the more ambitious partner of the marriage; Wilhelm Keitel was just an average officer, whose only secret ambition was to be a farmer and to manage Helmscherode. The marriage, which was blessed with three sons and three daughters, one of whom died tragically of an early and incurable disease, was to endure through all their trials and tribulations. And when the worst hour came, and her husband was sentenced to death by the International Military Tribunal at Nuremberg, Lisa Keitel retained her composure. Of Keitel's sons, all of whom became officers, the eldest married the daughter of Field-Marshal von Blomberg, the Reich War Minister, in whose *démise* Keitel was to be so disastrously yet innocently involved; while the youngest son was later killed in action in Russia.

Perhaps because he respected a man who knew how to speak his mind, Keitel's colonel selected him as his regimental adjutant. In the Prussian-German army this was a position of considerable trust: to the regimental adjutant fell the duty not only of handling personnel matters, but also of formulating the mobilisation measures and much else besides.

But his superiors must have believed Lieutenant Keitel capable of far more than this: during the autumn exercises of the Tenth Corps, of which his regiment was a subordinate formation, the Corps' Chief of Staff Colonel Freiherr von der Wenge, struck up a conversation with him, from which Keitel concluded that he had been earmarked for General Staff duties; it was a belief in which he was not deceived. And so, during the winter of 1913 to 1914, the man who had hated deskwork all his life began, as he himself describes in his early *Memoirs*, to study the 'gray easel' as the handbook for General Staff officers was dubbed by the German Army at that time.

In March 1914 Keitel took part in the Corps' course for current or future General Staff officers; four Army General Staff officers had been detached to the course, including Captains von Stülpnagel and von dem Bussche-Ippenburg, both of whom were later to be influential personalities in the Republican *Reichswehr*. It was Bussche-Ippenburg, the Chief of the Army Personnel Office, a key position in this small republican army, who according to Keitel's early *Memoirs* fetched him in to the organisational department (T–2) of the so-called '*Troop Office*', the disguised agency set up to replace the General Staff forbidden under the Versailles Treaty.

Keitel went to war with the 46th Artillery Regiment, and in September 1914 he was quite seriously wounded in his right forearm

14

by a shell fragment. Among the family papers there is a whole series of letters written by him to his father and father-in-law, and by his wife to her parents; these reveal Keitel's views on this first great and terrible European war. Naturally, he was duty-bound to hope piously for a German victory, but at the same time deep down there was a dejected conviction that, in fact, all they could do now was just grimly hang on. How similar was his attitude to the Second World War! Determined to fulfil his personal obligations, ruled by blind obedience, but with no hopes left of final victory. He served his Head of State, and he continued to serve him even at the Nuremberg Trial, despite his self-confessed inability to fathom this last Supreme Warlord of Germany.

The turning point in his career as an officer, an event which brought little solace to a man so aware of the limits to his own talents, was his posting to the General Staff in 1914; the General Staff was—and had been ever since Moltke—an *élite* among the officers. His contemporary letters show how hard the blow fell on him, and how well he knew that he lacked the mental equipment for this new job; those of his wife show her enormous pride in her husband's appointment.

From the later years of Keitel's employment as a General Staff officer in the higher command echelons of the Republican *Reichswehr* there is sufficient testimony of Keitel's intense nervousness; but we also hear of his immense and insatiable lust for work. His wife's letters during the 'twenties complain bitterly about his frightful nervousness. And later still, during the Second World War, an over-cynical adjutant coined the catchphrase about him: 'See that field-marshal scurrying past, with his adjutant bringing up the rear with measured tread . . .' By then the head of Hitler's military chancellery, promoted to field-marshal against his will (because traditionally one attains that rank only by valour in face of the enemy) Keitel was already a virtuoso in military and war administration, but not, it must be stressed, in war leadership.

We have no testimony on Keitel's attitude towards Kaiser Wilhelm II or the Prussian monarchy by the time the Great War ended, with Keitel a captain and General Staff officer to the naval corps in Flanders. It is interesting to note how, unusually for an Army General Staff officer, he had been given such an opportunity to experiment in promoting the Army's collaboration with the only other branch of the armed forces at the time, the Navy (even though it was only with a naval land force).

For a long time, according to his eldest son, Keitel had a picture of Crown Prince Wilhelm on his writing desk, even at the Reich Defence Ministry. It is not known why he finally removed the picture of this not very worthy heir to the Prussian kings and German Kaisers.

In a letter to his father-in-law on 10th December, 1918, we find Keitel commenting that he wanted now to say goodbye to the officer's profession in the near future 'for all time'. Nevertheless, he stayed on. After a brief period of service in the German frontier guard on the Polish border and a period as General Staff officer to one of the new *Reichswehr* brigades, and after two more years as a lecturer at the Hanover Cavalry School, Keitel was transferred to the Reich Defence Ministry and to the 'Troop Office', the disguised General Staff, being allocated ostensibly to the Army organisational department, T–2. As he told his father in a letter of 23rd January, 1925, he had entered not the T–2 department itself but a 'controlling position' on the immediate staff of the then Chief of the Troop Office, Lieutenant-General Wetzell. In this position Keitel was occupied primarily with questions of how to raise modest reserves— officially forbidden under the Versailles Treaty—for the numerically weak *Reichswehr*; he also dealt with the organisation of paramilitary frontier guard formations to keep watch on the German-Polish border. Other aspects of his new post were of greater importance for the future. In the small 'Troop Office' with its four departments (T–1, operations; T–2, organisation; T–3, foreign armies; and T–4, training) he became very familiar with a number of officers who were later repeatedly to cross his path: Werner von Blomberg, who was later to be Keitel's ultimate superior as Reich War Minister, began as head of the T–4 department and from 1927 to 1929 he was the chief of the Troop Office, in other words the *de facto* Chief of General Staff. Colonel Freiherr von Fritsch was head of the T–1 department. As Commander-in-Chief of the Army in 1935 it was Fritsch who put forward Keitel's name for appointment as Chief of the 'Armed Forces Office', the *Wehrnachtamt*. Colonel von Brauchitsch, later recommended by Keitel as Commander-in-Chief of the Army, was also head of T–4 for a time.

In September 1931 Keitel, head of T–2, and the heads of T–1 and T–4, Major-General Adam and Colonel von Brauchitsch respectively, paid a friendly visit to the Soviet Union; there were at the time extremely cordial relations between the *Reichswehr* and the Red Army, a tradition which already dated back some ten years. There are no records among the field-marshal's papers throwing any light on what military results and experiences were gathered on this trip, but there is a letter he wrote to his father on 29th September, 1931, in which he describes his impressions of the Russian economy and the high status enjoyed in general by the country's army; the strict leadership which was characteristic of the system, and the respect paid to the army, made a deep impression on the German lieutenant-colonel.

During the years after 1930 in which Keitel had been head of the organisational department, the first secret preparations began for raising the so-called A-Army, a reserve army which provided for a tripling in the size of the then Army of seven infantry and three cavalry divisions, in the event either of a national emergency or of the relaxation of the disarmament conditions imposed upon Germany. Even a sworn enemy of Keitel, the now famous Field-Marshal von Manstein, who did not even mention Keitel in his reminiscences on their journey to Russia in 1931, is forced to admit that in his field of military organisation Keitel did the most excellent work.*

On the other hand, in his wife's letters to her mother and sometimes even in Keitel's letters to his father we see mirrored the burden and the turbulence of those dying years of the first German Republic: Lisa Keitel complains frequently about the mountain of desk work heaped upon her husband and about his nervousness—a trait which one would not have credited in such a tall and burly man, but which was a sign of his lack of patience (which equipped him especially poorly for standing up to a man like Hitler). Politics as such are only lightly touched upon. Like most of the so-called good citizens in Germany both the Keitels backed Hindenburg, who had been elected Reich president in 1925; after him they rooted for the apparently so promising and energetic Reich Chancellor Brüning (1931–1932) and finally for Franz von Papen, under whose aegis the army gained rather more breathing space.

It is a matter for regret that we have no comment by Keitel on the most mysterious and significant figure in the then Reich Defence Ministry, General von Schleicher, who was head first of its Central Office and then of the Minister's Office, an officer who from 1932 onwards was Reich Defence Minister, and finally, from December 1932 to 28th January, 1933, the last Reich Chancellor before Hitler. A possible explanation of this lack of Keitel's views on Schleicher can be found in his illness late in the autumn of 1932, when he fell ill with a severe phlebitis of his right leg to which, however, he at first paid no attention, even continuing to walk from his home in

---

* Erich von Manstein, *Aus einem Soldatenleben* (Bonn, 1958), p. 111.

west Berlin to the Defence Ministry building in Bendlerstrasse, clear proof of his stubborn sense of duty. The final result was a thrombosis and pleural embolism, a heart attack and double pneumonia. As his wife fell ill with a heart complaint at the same time, a period of convalescence was ordered for both of them.

During the very months that the head of the T-2 department of the Troop Office lay on his sickbed, initially even calling his subordinates to his bedside for routine briefings and toying all the time with the secret idea of finally writing out his resignation from the service, the fate of democracy in Germany was in the balance; had he still been at work during those months, Keitel would probably have had to declare himself for General von Schleicher, the then Reich Chancellor and Defence Minister.

But he was still at a clinic in the High Tatra mountains in Czechoslovakia on 30th January, 1933, as the president, Field-Marshal von Hindenburg, appointed the Führer of the National Socialist German Worker's Party, Adolf Hitler, the 21st Reich Chancellor of the German Republic. According to Keitel's *Memoirs* the first reaction to the appointment expressed by a man who was after all one of Germany's senior General Staff officers, was remarkably negative. He tells how he was bombarded with questions at Dr. Guhr's clinic at Tatra-Westerheim and again all the way back to Berlin: what would happen now?

> I announced [writes Keitel] that I thought Hitler was *ein Trommler*— a 'drummer' who had met with his great success among the simple people thanks only to the power of his oratory; I said that whether he was really suited to be Reich Chancellor seemed highly questionable to me.

This view was echoed by the marked reserve with which most of the senior *Reichswehr* officers received this new Reich Chancellor, after twenty others had gone before in the eighteen melancholy years of the Weimar Republic. Even so, Hitler was Reich Chancellor and, more significantly for Lieutenant-Colonel Keitel, his one-time superior at the Troop Office, Lieutenant-General von Blomberg, with whom by his own testimony he had been able to get on very well from the outset, and whose departure he had deeply regretted, was now Reich Defence Minister under Hitler:

> Blomberg had in the meantime moved into the Reich Defence Ministry, having been suddenly summoned by the Reich President from Geneva, where he had been leading the German delegation at

the disarmament conference. Behind his appointment were von Reichenau and General von Hindenburg, the Reich President's son. Hitler had known von Reichenau for a long time, as the latter had already—as he himself said—been of great assistance to him during his election tours in East Prussia, when he had captured the province for the Party.

Early in May [1934] the first large-scale General Staff exercises under the new Commander-in-Chief of the Army, Colonel-General Freiherr von Fritsch, took place at Bad Nauheim; von Fritsch had replaced von Hammerstein as C.-in-C. on 1st February. I would like to state here that von Blomberg tried to press the candidacy of Reichenau personally upon the Reich President, even threatening to resign, but the old Hindenburg waved both of them away and appointed Freiherr von Fritsch, without paying the slightest attention to Hitler's endeavours to back Blomberg up in his campaign for Reichenau. Thus, the first attempt at handing over the army to a 'National Socialist' general had failed. When I looked Fritsch up immediately afterwards to congratulate him on his appointment, he said I was the first to do so, and for old time's sake he was particularly glad of that.

The common bond which united Keitel and Blomberg can no longer be traced with any clarity: Blomberg was highly gifted, an intellectual hugely interested in matters of the greatest diversity, towering far above the normal specimens of the Prussian officer corps; Keitel was conscientious, loyal, an outstanding expert in those fields that were his own. Perhaps that was the reason why Blomberg selected him as his closest colleague, especially as this was a time when army expansion was the order of the day and nobody had turned his hand so successfully and so intensively to this problem as Keitel.

After recovering from his illness Keitel hung on for some time in his old office as head of the T–2 department. He saw and spoke to Hitler for the first time at Bad Reichenhall in July 1933—while still head of the organisational department in the Troop Office— at a conference of senior *Sturmabteilung* commanders; the SA—storm detachments—were the National Socialist Party's private army.

One of his wife's letters to her mother, written on 5th July, 1933, describes Keitel's personal impressions of Hitler:

> He has spoken at length with Hitler, he has been up to his cottage, and is full of enthusiasm about him. His eyes were fabulous, and how the man could speak . . . !

Curiously, neither Hitler nor Keitel seems to have recalled this conversation, for later on Keitel suggests that he became acquainted with Hitler only in 1938, while Hitler is reported at the height of the Blomberg–Fritsch crisis to have asked to see 'this General *von* Keitel', whom he obviously did not recall after five years. It can be noted that it was characteristic of Hitler that he automatically assumed that Keitel as a Prussian general had the *von*-prefix of the nobility.

The Bad Reichenhall conference had been called by Hitler to smooth out the frictions extant between the legitimate German army and the para-military Party troops of the SA, problems on which Keitel's *Memoirs* dwell in some detail; his reminiscences from this time as Infantry Commander III with the 3rd infantry division at Potsdam in 1934 throw new light on the background to what has become known as the Night of the Long Knives—the bloody purge of the SA. Keitel takes up a clear frontal stand against the dark intrigues of the SA:

The SA group at Berlin-Brandenburg, commanded by SA-General Ernst—a former apprentice waiter who had been a volunteer despatch rider in the Great War at the age of sixteen—became conspicuous by its intensive activity in my own area [Potsdam] founding new SA units everywhere and trying to establish contacts with *Reichswehr* officers all over my area. Ernst paid several visits on me as well, without my being able to detect what was really behind them. During the summer of 1934 he began to bring the topic of conversation round to our secret [and illegal] arms dumps in my area; he considered them to be in danger because of their inadequate guards, and offered to provide guards for them himself. I thanked him but turned his offer down; at the same time I did shift the location of some of the dumps (machine guns and rifles) because I feared their existence had been betrayed to him. My General Staff officer (Major von Rintelen) and I both smelt rats; we did not trust the SA Group one inch and were highly suspicious of the questionable background of their effusive protestations of friendship.

Von Rintelen had served in the Intelligence Service under Colonel Nicolai [Chief of the Army General Staff's Counterespionage and Intelligence department in the Great War], so he was a trained Intelligence Officer, and I gave him a free hand to exercise his skill on this 'outfit' and take a look behind its scenes. Ostensibly he was just checking back on certain proposals Ernst's people had made. In the meantime we wound up the smaller arms dumps which were not safe from a military point of view, and transferred them to the maintenance workshops at Potsdam.

Von Rintelen was able to throw a lot of light on the goings-on, thanks to their loquacity. While we had no idea of any political plans a man like Röhm might be hatching, we *did* find out that they were trawling for arms for some 'operation' in Berlin at the end of June, and that they were prepared—if necessary—to acquire these by capturing military arms dumps whose location had been betrayed to them.

I drove to Berlin and called at the War Ministry building to speak to von Fritsch, but I did not find him in. I went to Reichenau and then with him to Blomberg, where I reported the Berlin SA Group's secret plans. I was waved coldly away, and told that it was all just imagination: the SA was loyal to the Führer, there was no question of any danger from that quarter. I told him I was not satisfied of that. I ordered von Rintelen to maintain contact and secure further Intelligence on the SA's intentions. In about the second half of June Ernst again called on me, visiting me in my office at Potsdam, accompanied by his adjutant and chief of staff [von Mohrenschildt and Sander respectively]. I called Rintelen in to act as an observer. After all sorts of empty phrases, Ernst again came round to the subject of the arms dumps urging me to entrust him with their custody in locations where there were no military units stationed: he had information, he said, that the communists knew where the dumps were and he feared that they would seize them. I now entered into the act and identified three small country arms dumps to him, which, however, I knew had been evacuated in the meantime. The arrangements for transferring their custody would be worked out in the near future with the director of the arms dumps, and Ernst would then be told of them. Finally, Ernst said goodbye to me, as he was leaving the country for a long voyage at the end of the month, and he named his deputy to me.

With this new information on the *Putsch* plans, Major von Rintelen drove in to Berlin the same day and called on Reichenau at the War Ministry; this unscheduled visit by Ernst was all that the overall picture had lacked to confirm our suspicions. Rintelen was seen by Blomberg, who now began to take it seriously too. He later informed me that he broke the news to Hitler on the same day, and that the latter had replied that he would speak to Röhm about it, although Röhm had been dodging him for some weeks now as Hitler had found it necessary to take him pretty sharply to task over Röhm's ideas on a People's Militia.

The 30th June *Putsch* never happened. Hitler flew straight to Munich from Bad Godesberg where he had received the latest news on the plans being hatched by Röhm. Röhm himself had mustered all his accomplices at Bad Wiessee. Hitler's plane landed at dawn, and he drove in person out to Bad Wiessee, where he caught the nest of conspirators red-handed. Thus one can say that Röhm's plan was thwarted, on the very day of his briefing for the *Putsch*. There never was any *Putsch*. According to the orders seized by Hitler at Bad Wiessee and shown to Blomberg, the *Putsch* was aimed primarily at the Army— that is to say at the *Reichswehr*—and at its officer corps, the bulwarks of reaction. They considered that Hitler had apparently overlooked this step in his revolution, but they would be making up for that now. Even so Hitler was to be allowed to remain as Reich Chancellor: only Blomberg and Fritsch were to be removed—Röhm wanted to assume one of these offices himself.

As far as Röhm's plan was just a matter of reinforcing the army permitted us by the Versailles *Diktat* by means of a large People's Militia on the Swiss model, it was already well known to von Schleicher [the former Reich Chancellor and War Minister]. Röhm had wanted to turn the SA, with its revolutionary officer cadre, mostly comprised of former army officers disgruntled at having been retired and hence hostile to the *Reichswehr*, into a future People's Army of a Yeomanry nature. This could never have functioned alongside the *Reichswehr*, but only against it; it would have meant the elimination of the *Reichswehr*. Röhm knew that Hitler had always rejected these ideas, so he had wanted to force Hitler's hand by confronting him with a *fait accompli*. Unfortunately, General von Schleicher also had a finger in the pie: he always was the cat who could not resist political mice. That was why both Schleicher and his emissary, von Bredow, who was *en route* for Paris with Röhm's proposals to the French government, had to be arrested. I am not aware whether either of them offered armed resistance, and today I am inclined to think they did not. Both were shot.

Von Blomberg kept the list of names of those who were shot in his safe; it recorded seventy-eight names. It is to be regretted that during the Nuremberg Trial the witnesses, even [SA Lieutenant-General] Jüttner, concealed Röhm's real objectives and tried to hush things up. Those who were participants in his plans and fully initiated in them were the highest echelons of the SA leadership corps; the average SA man and the SA officers below the rank of colonel had no idea of them, and probably never did even afterwards.

Nevertheless, what he [Blomberg] said in his telegram of thanks to Hitler is absolutely correct: by Hitler's decisive personal intervention at Bad Wiessee and the steps he took, he had managed to stamp out a smouldering danger before it burst into a conflagration which would have cost a hundred times more lives than it eventually did. Why the guilty parties were not made to stand trial by court martial, but were simply shot, is beyond my comprehension.

This latter comment is characteristic of the field-marshal's ingenuousness. That Hitler had no legal right whatsoever to order these executions without further ado, that this was a clear breach of justice, occurred to neither Blomberg nor Keitel in 1934: they saw only the vague and disturbing outlines of a post-revolutionary SA state looming up ahead, under the figurehead of Röhm. As Field-Marshal von Manstein later wrote:

The more distant those days become from the present, the more people seem inclined to minimise the extent of the danger represented by the SA at the time under the leadership of a man like Röhm; it was a danger not only to the *Reichswehr*, but to the very State itself.

Karl Ernst, the leader of the Berlin SA Group, and his adjutant and chief of staff were both shot on the night of 30th June to 1st July, the Night of the Long Knives, while Ernst Röhm, the Chief of Staff of the SA, was shot early next morning; General Kurt von Schleicher and his wife were murdered that night at their home at Neubabelsberg, and Major-General von Bredow was shot as well.

In the spring of 1934 Keitel's father died and he inherited the estate at Helmscherode for himself. Keitel applied to resign his commission so that he could devote himself wholly to the affairs of the family estate; he wanted his resignation to come into effect on 1st October, 1934. He was called before the Chief of Army Personnel, General Schwedler, who told him that Fritsch was prepared to offer him the command of a division near Helmscherode, and Keitel selected one at Bremen, the 22nd Infantry Division. He withdrew his resignation. 'Such', said Keitel in his *Memoirs*, 'is the force of human destiny.' He was not long in his new command.

At the end of August [1935] I received a telephone call from the commander of the Military District, that the Commander [General von Kluge] wanted me to drive out and meet him at a rendezvous to discuss something very urgent with him. At the time I was at the exercise ground at Ohrdruf; we met nearby and had a quiet conversation *à deux*. He was extremely friendly: he disclosed to me that on 1st October I was to succeed von Reichenau as Chief [of the *Wehrmachtamt*, the Armed Forces Office] in Blomberg's ministry, and that the only other candidate for the post, von Vietinghoff, had been turned down. I was very disturbed, and obviously showed it. He told me further that it was Fritsch who had been behind my nomination and that I ought to bear in mind that this was just as much a vote of confidence from Fritsch as from Blomberg. I begged him to move heaven and earth to prevent my appointment, there was still time for that. Would he tell Fritsch that as a soldier I had never been so happy as I was now as a divisional commander in Bremen; I wanted nothing to do with politics. He promised to do so, and we parted.

On the way back to Bremen from Ohrdruf I stayed for some days at Helmscherode, where my wife was living with our children. She urged me to accept the offer, and not to do anything to prejudice my chances of selection. . . .

Keitel had been on good terms with Fritsch for a long time, and he valued Blomberg as an understanding, intelligent and educated superior. Keitel's ideal was to buttress the position of the Reich War Minister as supreme commander of the armed forces, and to create for him in the Armed Forces Office—and above all in its National Defence Department—an effective joint operations staff controlling all three services. He never considered himself suited either by education or talent for the rôle of a Chief of the Armed Forces General Staff; like Blomberg, he did recognise the need for establishing such a post, but no such post was ever created. Both the army—in the persons of Colonel-General Fritsch and General Ludwig Beck, the latter being Chief of the Troop Office and a leading military theoretician—and the navy stood up in arms against these innovations.

But it was the army that was in the forefront of the protest. General Beck, the chief of the Army General Staff, detached one of his most gifted General Staff officers, the Bavarian Alfred Jodl, to the National Defence Department in the pious hope that Jodl would champion the army's interests. But Jodl, a brilliant thinker, also went over to the new ideas. Beck's abomination of Keitel became deadly, insofar as such a harsh expression can be used of a man as elegant as Beck.

Even more of a problem was how to bring the German Air Force into line: this third and newest branch of the armed forces had as its Commander-in-Chief the former air force captain Hermann Göring, a freshly minted colonel-general enjoying a position of unique political power in his simultaneous capacities as Reich Aviation Minister, Prussian Prime Minister and Commissioner for the Four-Year-Plan, quite apart from being close to Party circles.

Keitel's relationship with Blomberg was amicable but cool and impersonal. They tolerated each other well, they never quarrelled or even disagreed; but between the two there was a lack of any of the personal contact that one would have expected from the long years they had known each other since 1914; Keitel himself always attributed this to the way in which Blomberg withdrew into himself after the death of his wife in the spring of 1932. His relations with von Fritsch, the Commander-in-Chief of the Army, were on the other hand always friendly, warmhearted and trusting. At the latter's initiation, they often spent evenings alone together, talking and reminiscing over a glass of wine.

In 1936 Keitel was promoted to lieutenant-general; the year was occupied very fully with the reconstruction of the German armed forces and brought the highly dramatic days of the German military reoccupation of the Rhineland on 7th March, 1936, upon which Hitler had, says Keitel, decided only a very few days before actually putting it into effect:

It was a highly risky operation, for there was an acute danger of sanctions being imposed by the French. The Western Powers' sharp protests led Blomberg to suggest to Hitler the withdrawal of the three battalions which were our only forces actually to have crossed the Rhine, and which had proceeded as far as Aix-la-Chapelle, Kaiserslautern and Saarbrücken. The second battalion of the 17th Infantry Regiment had entered Saarbrücken and was drilling on the market square while French guns were actually trained on the town. Hitler rejected any idea of withdrawing the battalions: if the enemy attacked they were to fight, and not to give way an inch. Orders to that effect were then issued.

Our three military attachés in London raised the most violent protests. Fritsch and Blomberg lodged renewed complaints with Hitler, but he refused to entertain any idea of yielding to threats. Our Foreign Office received a Note from London demanding assurances that no fortifications would be constructed west of the Rhine, but very much against my advice Blomberg had flown off to Bremen that day. In his absence, the Führer called Fritsch, Neurath [Reich Foreign Secretary] and myself before him. It was the first time—apart from the first occasion on which I had reported to him along with numerous other generals—on which I stood before him. He asked what proposals Fritsch and Neurath had to make for our answer to the Note, and finally he asked me. Up to that point I had only been a silent listener. Upon his asking me, I suggested we answer that for the time being we would construct no permanent fortifications there: we could say that with a perfectly clear conscience, as from technical considerations alone it would take us at least a year to do anything there. The Führer listened calmly to me, and appeared at first to be disinclined to accept my suggestion; then he decided to answer the Note evasively: we would say that we would bear their demand in mind, although we had been entertaining no such plans as we saw no need for them at present. In view of the way we had already commenced the construction of fortifications along the rest of our western frontiers, even if they were only part of a long-term programme designed to last until 1950, nobody recognised better than the French the non-binding subterfuge we were searching for in our terminology.

Neurath was directed to make this answer, and Fritsch and I were dismissed the Führer's presence. That was my first official encounter with Hitler. In the subsequent days the tension relaxed: Hitler had played with fire and won, and against his soldiers' advice he had avoided committing himself in any way. He had shown the stronger nerves and the more highly developed political instinct. Small wonder that he soared in our estimation.

* * *

In 1938 Lieutenant-General Keitel, the then head of the Armed Forces Office, had been recommended to Hitler by the departing Reich War Minister von Blomberg as his new *chef de bureau*. (That is how Blomberg described the position in an official document.) Blomberg could recommend him with a clear conscience. The Armed Forces Office was already a peculiarly hybrid structure: normally Blomberg would have had an under-secretary in his capacity as War Minister and a 'Chief of Staff' in his capacity as Supreme Commander of the Armed Forces; but in an autocratic Führer state with no parliamentary life but only the occasional plebiscites held from time to time, the position of an Under-Secretary of State had lost importance, and even during the years of the Weimar Republic, with its civil Secretaries for Defence, there had been no such office. Informally, the head of the Reich Defence Minister's Central Office had taken over such duties himself.

During the Blomberg era, the ministerial secretariat and the chief of staff's offices were rolled into one. Thus the Armed Forces Office united under one head a strategic planning office, a military command office, the national defence department and numerous other departments handling all the signals, Intelligence and administrative functions of the Ministry as well as its controversial joint armed forces command function. The systematic expansion of the Office to which Keitel aspired was rudely interrupted by Blomberg's overthrow early in 1938, as was the continuous development of its national defence department to a genuine joint 'operations staff' for all three services, army, navy and air force.

Keitel has explained that he never guessed what awaited him as—without any hesitation—he agreed to accept the position Hitler offered him as 'Chief of the Armed Forces High Command' although admittedly he expressed the view that logically the official title should have been '*Chief of Staff* to the High Command of the Armed Forces'. They may have thought that his willpower was not all that strong; but during the Blomberg–Fritsch crisis he pushed through the appointment of his own candidate as Fritsch's successor with surprising obstinacy and with final success.

His candidate was Field-Marshal von Brauchitsch, the product of a Silesian family that had furnished Prussia with a dozen generals over the previous hundred and fifty years; he called him up to Berlin from Leipzig, where for some time he had been in command of the Fourth Army Group. Brauchitsch, brought up in the Corps of Cadets and the Field Artillery Guards, met with the full approval of the other senior generals and above all of the very *Junker*-ish General von Rundstedt; on the other hand his appointment sealed the fate of the outstanding and talented Chief of the General Staff, General Beck. Keitel probably never did have any warm feelings towards this latter officer, and Brauchitsch certainly had no desire to work with the Chief of the General Staff.

Again, Keitel doggedly insisted on the appointment of his brother as Chief of Army Personnel and on the removal from Hitler's entourage of the latter's Army adjutant, the dynamic and self-assured Colonel Hossbach. Hossbach had shamelessly but skilfully upheld the traditions of the Prussian General Staff and championed the ideas of General Beck, who believed that the command of the armed forces was a matter for the old classic General Staff alone. In close collaboration with the Commander-in-Chief of the Army, Keitel hoped to achieve a breakthrough in the front of the other two Commanders-in-Chief, and establish a uniform overall command of the armed forces.

In any event, Keitel's victory over Hitler's own candidate, Reichenau, was a Pyrrhic victory: there is a danger in retrospectively analysing the crisis and the intrigues surrounding Blomberg and Fritsch that one will overlook the fact that at the time Hitler was still by no means the ogre he was to prove himself to be during the war. At the time Hitler had behind him a whole string of diplomatic victories and Keitel himself has very objectively commented on how far simple soldiers could be impressed by such successes.

Keitel thought he knew Brauchitsch well, and he had held him in high regard since the time both of them had been departmental heads in the Troop Office, and both had travelled to the Soviet Union. But though Keitel was in no position to assert himself with Hitler, Brauchitsch was even less well suited to this than he: Brauchitsch was a well-educated and even a sensitive man of the old school.

By his appearance, by his good education, by his bearing as a senior officer and by his mannerisms, Keitel was the complete antithesis to Hitler. Outwardly, Keitel looked like a landed *Junker*: he liked eating well; he did not reject a glass of wine, seldom though one might appear on his own table; he liked to smoke a cigar from time to

27

time, and he was an excellent horseman and an enthusiastic huntsman.

Hitler, on the other hand, was a vegetarian, keeping to a singular and scanty diet; he did not drink, and strongly disapproved of people smoking in his presence (which everybody accordingly avoided as far as possible); he hated horses and regarded the noble hunt as the murder of innocent fauna, upon which subject he was liable to lapse into gross sentimentality in his conversation. The corporal, moreover, was moved by an instinctive mistrust of all senior officers, always dreading that they might not be taking him seriously.

In answer to a questionnaire put to him by his defence counsel, Keitel himself stressed how hard it was to deal with his new superior:

> I was naturally entitled to give voice to my own opinions. But the Führer usually cut me short and told me what *he* thought and what his *own* views were. It was no easy task then to contradict him. Often I was able to make my point only on a later occasion.

Again, Keitel described Hitler's remark whenever he raised any objections:

> I don't know why you are getting so het up about it. You are not answerable for this, the responsibility is mine alone.*

To both Dr. Nelte, his defence counsel, and one of the American interrogators Keitel described how distressed he had been at the tone of Hitler's dealings with him at first. In this respect too, Hitler had been the 'revolutionary' and Keitel the soldier of the old school. Unfortunately this often robbed him of the confidence he needed to stand up against Hitler's methods and blustering—'We looked at things in different ways.' He added that he never gained the impression that Hitler had any real confidence in him; but he considered it his duty to 'sit out' Hitler's attacks on the Officer Corps and on the Army. 'I was,' he commented, 'Hitler's lightning conductor.'

On the other hand, Keitel the soldier was convinced that the man at the pinnacle of the Reich and Armed Forces was possessed of no mean talents; Hitler did indeed have unusual gifts in many fields, disposing over the power of seductive oratory, a copious memory for detail even in military affairs, and tremendous imagination, willpower and audacity. In Keitel's view the traditional loyalty due to the sovereign transferred automatically to this new captain of

---

* Statements made by Keitel in affidavits for his defence counsel; 1/2 (Keitel Orders); and 1/3 (Keitel's relations with Hitler).

Germany's fate; this was the same attachment to the person of the monarch which had for centuries ruled the thinking of the officer corps of every German state. The 'Führer' became unconsciously a kind of *'Ersatz-Kaiser'*. And though the sovereign might be difficult, or behave abnormally and, in the opinion of many, incomprehensibly too, he *was* taboo. To voice criticism of him, either publicly or in private, was dishonourable; one might out of a sense of duty express doubts about the propriety of certain orders issued to one. But once the sovereign had decided upon them, then the officer had a duty to comply with the orders and to associate himself with them.

This creed was not so much a leftover of the Old Prussian *Junkers* era of the eighteenth century, as an expression of the rationalisation of the concept of loyalty that had sprung up in the age of Kaiser Wilhelm. In the case of a leader like Hitler this creed was especially dangerous; but it was nevertheless the creed by which Field-Marshal Keitel abided. There was more to it than that: Hitler had the gift of being able to influence people; it was a gift which he often used upon Keitel, although the field-marshal was in himself a very courageous officer. Inwardly he felt himself defenceless against a man so generously endowed with such enormous powers, the more so as for a long time he was bound to agree that Germany's 'Führer' was assessing individual situations more accurately than were his trained soldiers:

> At the bottom of my heart I was a loyal shield-bearer for Adolf Hitler; my political conviction would have been National Socialist.

That was how Keitel described himself to Colonel Dr. Bohuslav Ecer, of the Czechoslovakian Judge Advocate's Office, in a preliminary interrogation on 3rd August, 1945. But he stressed that earlier, during the Kaiser's Reich and the Weimar Republic, he had had no political inclinations and had taken no part in political activities; so he had not then been a 'Nazi', he added.

On the other hand Keitel does admit that when he was asked about the costs of the German rearmament programme he 'almost fell over backwards' when he learned that on 1st September, 1939, during his first speech of the war, Hitler had put them at 90 milliard Reichsmarks, when in fact they could not have been more than 30 to 40 milliards at most. Such exaggerations and lies were all part of the make-up of this 'Supreme Warlord'. For Keitel, Hitler—both the man and the Führer—was always an enigma. Hitler's suicide at the end of the war and his evasion thereby of the sole responsibility which he had so vehemently and bluntly claimed for himself in his quarrels with Keitel were something that the field-marshal totally failed to comprehend. But even then, at the nadir of his misfortunes, he spurns to cast off his rôle as Hitler's 'shield-bearer', even though he must pay for his loyalty with his life.

* * *

The documents and letters reproduced in this book, in so far as they emanate from the papers left by Field-Marshal Keitel, are derived from two main depositories: firstly, there is the correspondence placed on the file of his Nuremberg defence counsel, Dr. Otto Nelte, and the large numbers of letters written by the field-marshal's wife to her mother, father and father-in-law; the letters have been reproduced verbatim, but for greater readability the normal dotted lines indicating omissions have been left out. Secondly, there are the *Memoirs* and reminiscences written by the field-marshal himself in his cell at Nuremberg, as he awaited sentencing and execution, written without access to any documents or material.

Keitel himself depicted the strain of the last months before his trial and execution in a note on his life, at the end of which he pointed out:

The conditions under which we have been living here for five months now [on remand in the Nuremberg Palace of Justice] are really less than enviable, since I know nothing at all about what has become of my country or my family, and indeed about what is to become of myself. For the last two months we have been permitted to write letters and postcards, but we have received no replies.

That all these circumstances are not without their effect on my health, nerves and frame of mind is self evident. Since May [1945] I have lost two stone in weight, of which I have lost one stone in the last eight weeks here in prison at Nuremberg alone. Now I cannot lose any more.

I can well understand the fact that we soldiers are to be called to account by the Allied military Tribunal and that we have to be kept apart while on remand for investigations, but I find that my being deprived of even the most humble necessities for my cell is a far greater burden to bear than the admittedly wearying interrogations, where every testimony I make—being under oath—has to be carefully weighed.

I mention only a few of the deprivations. From 5.30 pm, or when it grows dark—which at present is considerably earlier than that—one must sit and brood in darkness, because they have taken away my glasses and it is impossible to read even by the glimmer of light coming in from the corridor outside. Secondly, one has only a bunk and a small table, with *no* desk or shelf, and even the wooden chair is taken out. Thirdly, there is nothing to hang or lay one's clothes and underwear on: one is obliged to lay it on the stone floor, so it is impossible to keep one's clothes clean. Fourthly, the window which ventilates the cell and regulates the temperature cannot be operated from inside. Fifthly, one is restricted to ten minutes' exercise in the open air each day.

Those are only the worst deprivations, which seem to go some way beyond what is already a decidedly austere furnishing of a remand prison. The effects of all this on my frame of mind, and the uncertainty over my fate, are gradually taking their toll of my physical and mental capacities.

I must stress that by drawing up this list of reasons for my unchecked physical and mental decline I am *not raising any complaints*, because I have no doubt as to the basically good intentions of my immediate custodians [the Americans] and because I have benefitted personally from the manifold help of the American military surgeons, and I must make my gratitude to them quite plain. But my permanent back pains are physical torture to a man of sixty who is not even permitted a chair with a back to it.

As will be seen from the main body of the *Memoirs*, Keitel had no time to read through or revise his original manuscript and, as one would expect, there are many errors of chronology, spelling and detail, and occasionally sentences without verbs or without endings. Bearing in mind that this is a historical document of the highest importance, the Editor has thought it necessary to amplify the punctuation and occasionally to correct the grammar of the original; and in the English edition the wrong dates and incorrect spelling of names have been corrected, though where there is some doubt about Keitel's exact meaning, this has been noted or the text left uncorrected. On occasion, suggested endings for sentences and explanatory phrases have been inserted by the Editor in square brackets. Keitel's original underlinings have been indicated by italics.

In general, it is astonishing that despite the great mental strain of the weeks between his sentencing and execution the field-marshal should have been capable of writing such a coherent account of his life and description of his *modus operandi* during these decisive years in Germany's history. But perhaps this work was a labour of love for a man who had had perforce to accustom himself to military desk-work in the previous two decades, and it was a diversion too, for it gave him something else for his mind to dwell on. Nobody will claim that the field-marshal was a born writer, nobody will recognise the work of a great historian in his writings. The diction of this, his first and only book, is often cumbersome and involved; possibly he would have altered and re-cast much of it had he had the time to do so.

But if he little valued the prospect of writing a dramatic and colourful account, one can also recall that in his wartime memoranda and written orders he always tried to express what he had to say in a few honest and well-chosen words; it will be well to bear this simplicity in mind, in reading his *Memoirs*.

PART II

The Memoirs
of
Field-Marshal Keitel

2

The Blomberg–Fritsch Crisis, 1938

FOR the winter of 1936 to 1937, Blomberg had ordained that the armed forces were to hold joint manoeuvres: these were to enable us to make a study of the unified control of the armed forces in time of war, and clarify the problems latent in the dispute between us and the Army General Staff; the manoeuvres would put to a severe practical test the relative distributions of authority within the upper echelons of the military structure. As chief of the national defence department, General Jodl directed the manoeuvres in close collaboration with myself. Blomberg, Jodl and myself hoped that they would resolve the conflicting points of view that prevailed, although we fully realised that we were tackling an extremely delicate subject for which we would reap not thanks but charges of treachery from the General Staff; I was fully aware that as the departmental chief responsible for the decisions to hold the manoeuvres I would become a natural object for their enmities: I would be regarded as the spiritual originator of such an innovation [manoeuvres directed by a joint operations staff].

Blomberg held a final conference with his service generals and admirals, in Hitler's presence.* The result was an outburst of unrestricted indignation from the Army General Staff: the cat was out of the bag. As Hitler and Blomberg left the room together, Fritsch forced his way through to me and announced that these plans for high-level control of the Army's operations were insupportable. I believe it was the only time his wrath boiled up so much that he could not refrain from spontaneously venting his anger on me; we never spoke about this incident afterwards. In the eyes of the

* This conference is dealt with separately by Keitel in a note for his Defence Counsel, Dr. Nelte.

General Staff it was quite insupportable for the 'Army Minister' to aspire to exercise a command function; and the Army Directorate [*Heeresleitung*] announced it would refuse to recognise Blomberg's absolute authority over the armed forces. They just would not hear of it. I was too simple, too innocent and too logical to see that by having spoken out for the solution which seemed to me the most obvious one, I had invited such enmities or hung such a millstone round my neck. After all, Blomberg had under Heye been Chief of the Army General Staff—called Troop Office [*Truppenamt*] at the time—and as such he had been a predecessor to Adam and the present office-holder, Beck, with whom my hitherto amicable relations had now been wrecked beyond repair.

I had interviews with Beck that lasted often for hours on end, but none of my endeavours availed me in my efforts either to obtain his sanction for the decrees that Blomberg was about to issue on the unified control of the forces, or to take his objections into account. For example, I visited him several times with the draft of Blomberg's first 'Mobilisation and Battle Directive for the Armed Forces' finally issued in the summer of 1937; I gave him the draft to look over and got it back from him with numerous marginal notes. They were largely of a formal nature, but they clearly betrayed his suppressed annoyance that anybody should dare to issue directives to his Army. When he told me finally that the General Staff had no intention of making any such 'preparations' as those Blomberg demanded on Hitler's insistence, doubtless because of the General Staff's political and strategic assessment of the situation, I altered the word 'prepare' to 'review', a very weak compromise, but one which Blomberg obviously overlooked when he eventually signed the document. Jodl and Zeitzler, his chief of operations, were very indignant at the time about my capitulation to Beck.

In fact, the Army General Staff proceeded to bury the directive in a safe somewhere and took *no* action whatsoever. At the Nuremberg Trials the document has been accorded exaggerated importance, and the accounts Jodl and I have given of its origins have met only with sympathetic disbelief. In actual fact there was no *Otto* contingency plan [*Fall Otto*], no *Green* or *Red* contingencies, but only the most tenuous defence of our frontiers to the east and to the west, and preparations for the evacuation of the endangered frontier areas to the west of the Rhine and the east of the Oder. What we and Blomberg earnestly feared at the time was the possibility of sanctions of which we had become aware from Italy's Abyssinian campaign; they continued to hang over us like the Sword of Damocles all the time that our rearmament programme was still only at the organisational stage; it must be remembered that we no longer had even a seven-division army on a war-footing, as it had been split up throughout the Reich since 1st October, 1935, to provide the nuclei for the formation of the new thirty-six-division army.

At any time our neighbours would have been able to invade our frontiers with impunity and demand our disarmament. Our army disposed over neither tanks nor heavy artillery, and it was still insufficiently equipped with infantry weapons; our navy was of no significance and our air force was still being laboriously built up. Any kind of military intervention would have made light work of us. Nobody knew that better than Hitler, and it was in accordance with these dangers that he had adjusted his foreign policy.

Blomberg's next step in his campaign for closer control over the armed forces was to direct me to prepare military manoeuvres involving the navy and the air force as well. During a Scandinavian voyage aboard the *Grille*, Blomberg defined the objectives of the manoeuvres, which Jodl was to direct. When I later briefed Fritsch [Commander-in-Chief of the Army], as naturally the army would be bearing the lion's share of the manoeuvres, he just smiled sympathetically at the 'war-situation' foreseen and declared that the region of Mecklenburg earmarked for the manoeuvres was quite inadequate. I asked him to select a controlling headquarters staff for the army, and units to reconnoitre the manoeuvre areas. He agreed to both requests, and selected General Halder, the then chief of the training department, to take over command of the headquarters staff. General Beck, the Chief of the General Staff, was naturally far too lofty to lend himself to such a venture, which he regarded as doomed from the start. As I only hovered in the background the whole time and played little part in the laborious preparations and direction of the manoeuvres, I am in some position to pass judgment on them: I would regard the whole venture as having been highly successful; Jodl merits the greatest possible credit for them.

A number of prominent guests had accepted Blomberg's invitation to attend, including [Field-Marshal Sir Edmund] Ironside, the British Chief of Imperial General Staff and his staff, the Italian Head of State Mussolini and his entourage, and missions from various other countries and all the military attachés in Berlin. We showed off our fleet and submarine force for the first time, attacking Swinemünde; we showed our air force bombers in land- and naval-support operations, carrying out high-level and dive-bombing attacks;

and we showed a weak armoured division equipped with light tanks mounting only machine-guns, as at the time we had no heavier models.

Blomberg's guests met for coffee afterwards at the mess on the air force base at Tutow, where we had set up our manoeuvre headquarters during the last days of preparation. General Halder deserves particular credit for the success of this, our first attempt at combined operations, and for their having passed off so smoothly; he mastered his onerous rôle in exemplary fashion and made the biggest contribution to its overall success.

The only note of discord that I was called upon to iron out was the sudden appearance at the *'Blue'* party's headquarters of a special battalion of military correspondents and war reporters raised by the Ministry of Propaganda. [Colonel-General von] Rundstedt's chief of staff threw the gentlemen out with little ceremony, and the result was that they were deeply offended and said they wanted to go home at once. I had to go over there and soothe the party, which was being cared for by an officer provided by my Armed Forces Office anyway, and re-establish the peace between them and Hoepner, the chief of staff concerned, so that the correspondents could resume their activities and obtain the information they wanted.

It was from Tutow that I paid my first visit to Chief-Forester Müller in the Darss peninsula, which had been declared a game reserve and to which Göring had invited me for a shot at a deer in the rutting season. I was very hospitably received, and I at once forged with him what was later to blossom into a warm friendship which brought me many happy hours in the peninsula. Early in October I bagged my deer.

After the armed forces manoeuvres, Mussolini rounded off his visit in Berlin where he was the guest of the Führer. In Berlin there was a parade in his honour, with a mass demonstration that evening at the Reich stadium with first Hitler and then Mussolini addressing the crowd of almost a hundred thousand from the rostrum, the latter speaking in German. The vast crowd broke up in a cloudburst and it rained very heavily, while for almost an hour we tried in vain to reach our motor car so that we could drive home.

On 1st October, [1937] I partially reorganised the Armed Forces Office which by the enforced expansion of its functions had already begun to sprawl in several directions: I grouped what had hitherto been small departments into larger offices and branches, with the creation of an Armed Forces operations office [*Wehrmacht-Führungsamt*], an office for economics and armaments, an Intelligence office with three departments (I—Intelligence service; II—Sabotage, and III—Counter-espionage), to which latter office our foreign department was subordinated.

Finally, I formed from the various branches which had formerly come under the general category 'Inland' a 'General Armed Forces Office'. The offices were headed by generals given great latitude for independent action. This was our first, quite unintentional step towards what was later to become the OKW, the High Command of the Armed Forces, although at the time I had quite different motives for laying these foundations. My own idea, which was in close accordance with Blomberg's line of thinking and to which he fully subscribed, was to distinguish more clearly between his command and his purely ministerial functions so that as Supreme Commander and the ultimate embodiment of military leadership he would have an *Oberkommando der Wehrmacht*, a High Command of the Armed Forces, while in his capacity as Minister he would have a kind of ministerial secretariat; he would then issue his orders and decrees under appropriate letter-headings, one as 'Supreme Commander of the Armed Forces', and the other as 'Reich War Minister'. This second function would to all intents and purposes be transferred to me in all non-basic decisions; I would be a kind of ministerial Under-Secretary of State, while the former office would establish his command function more clearly than hitherto.

In this way one really could prosecute a war: the Armed Forces operations office would acquire a Chief of General Staff in addition to myself, while I relieved the Supreme Commander of the greater part of his ministerial functions. Today I still consider that this solution was the correct one; the Commander-in-Chief of the Army did in fact proceed rather along those lines during the war in as much as he appointed a highly autonomous Commander of the Reserve Army to take over the main burden of the Army's administrative work. It was plain to me that the Supreme Commander of the Armed Forces needed a high-grade operations staff, although only quite a small one, and that the selection of its chief was a question of personality and trustworthiness which should, however, only be dealt with just before or on the outbreak of a war. I myself never had any personal ambitions for this office; I lacked the essential characteristics for it as a result of my military upbringing. Blomberg and I were in close agreement on that score; the reason why no such reorganisation ever took place during the Blomberg regime is well-enough known. The titles one would choose for the offices if such a reorganisation did take place were of marginal importance;

I myself was thinking at the time in terms of 'Chief of the OKW' or 'Quartermaster-General of the Armed Forces'.*

My official contacts with the foreign military attachés were only of a loose and infrequent nature, as was the case with our own attaché office; I was glad that they did not burden me with official visits and, if these were unavoidable, I asked for the head of the Army's attaché office to be present too, as he was familiar with how to handle such snooping around [*Schnüffeleien*]. Only Oshima [the Japanese military attaché] was a frequent and welcome visitor to my office; I looked forward to his visits, as I welcomed the opportunity of gathering information on their war in the Chinese theatre. It was he who told me during an official visit to us at about Christmas 1937 that in his view they could still take Nanking (its capture was imminent) and that they ought then to terminate their war with China by reaching a compromise whatever the cost. He was right, but unfortunately things went the other way as Tokio did not share his views and failed to recognise that war in vast spaces has no end if one is not easily satisfied as a victor, but must continually raise one's sights and try to conquer more.

With the outbreak of the Sino-Japanese War Hitler had finally written off the China policies pursued by Blomberg and Reichenau and had the German military mission recalled from China. Blomberg had prevailed upon Hitler to despatch Reichenau to China in the winter of 1935–1936; our go-between with China was a certain Herr Klein, a former banker and agent for the firm of Otto Wolff. He had built up hopes of very great trade with China whereby they would deliver raw materials for our re-armament programme in return for arms deliveries and the erection of munitions, small-arms and machine-gun factories and arsenals in China. Reichenau had been detailed to visit General von Seeckt out there, to get Herr Klein's contracts with Chiang Kai-shek safely under lock and key and to familiarise himself with China.

All that really was something for Reichenau's political empire-building. While General von Seeckt was indeed the first adviser appointed by the uncrowned emperor of China [i.e. Chiang Kai-shek] he had had to withdraw to the solitude of the mountains for health reasons and he was shortly replaced by General von

* In Keitel's original manuscript there follows lengthy descriptions of the Keitel family's social intercourse in Berlin during 1937, frequently involving meetings with Major-General Oshima, the Japanese military attaché, and Colonel Szymanski, the Polish one; the Field-Marshal believed that he had 'made a good impression' on the French and British ambassadors, André François-Poncet and Sir Nevile Henderson. The whole passage has been omitted by the Editor.

Falkenhausen, the bustling head of the German military mission proper.

Herr Klein's contracts and the agreements signed by Reichenau on behalf of the German War Minister and therefore of the Reich government were never more than bits of paper, even though they did bring us a few shiploads of powdered egg and foodstuffs together with some thousands of tons of antimony, bismuth and other precious metals in scarce supply.

It was left to me to set off our wasted gold investments against the account of our service budget with the Finance Minister. A high Chinese medal, presented on the occasion of a visit paid to Blomberg by the Chinese Minister of Finance, Kung, and his assistants was the sole estate bequeathed to us by our China policies.

The Führer now insisted that we dismantle all the links between our countries, and that included sending home Chiang Kai-shek's son, who was an officer in the Munich infantry regiment and lived with Reichenau, the Commander of Military District VII. The way was thus open for the German-Japanese *rapprochement* to which Hitler now aspired.

Blomberg left me to visit General von Seeckt after his return from China and inform him that the military mission there was to be wound up. General von Seeckt listened wordlessly to my statement, then imparted to me his own views on the situation in China and the Head of State's plans for ending the incipient civil war. He declared that Chiang Kai-shek was the bitterest enemy of communism, and one ought not to overlook that fact. It was the last time I ever saw von Seeckt; he had probably observed that Blomberg avoided meeting him face to face. About six months later we buried him at the military cemetery.*

[*In January* 1938 *the engagement was announced between Field-Marshal Keitel's eldest son, Lieutenant Karl-Heinz Keitel, and Dorothea von Blomberg, one of the War Minister's daughters, with the blessing of both parents. Keitel made no attempt to hide the fact that with the engagement of his son to Blomberg's daughter he was aiming at an entente with his superior, Field-Marshal von Blomberg himself.*]

I never dreamt that Blomberg was now on the lookout for a new wife for himself again; still less did I guess what was to follow. The only thing that had struck me was that twice he had driven out alone in his car to Oberhof, in the Thüringian forest, in civilian

---

* In Keitel's original manuscript there follow lengthy descriptions of family affairs and the business of their Helmscherode estate; these have been omitted, as have other details summarised above, by the Editor.

clothes, just leaving a note for me with his hotel and telephone number in case he was wanted urgently for anything on the telephone. His chief adjutant, Major von der Decken, merely shrugged his shoulders and told me there was nothing he could tell me in detail; he only knew that Blomberg was supposed to be visiting a lady who had broken an ankle skiing over there. I had my own ideas but I did not broach them to anybody, not even to my wife.

In about the middle of December [1937] Ludendorff died after a grave illness; the Führer decreed a state funeral in Munich with an oration delivered by Blomberg as the senior representative of the Services. The Führer had in the meantime ceremoniously promoted Blomberg to *Generalfeldmarschall*, handing him his field-marshal's baton before an audience of senior officers of all three services in the large hall of the War Ministry building.

For our journey to Munich I had ordered a small special train for the field-marshal and ourselves, to which had been coupled the shining new saloon-coach he had just been given by the Führer. We were obliged not only to call for him at Oberhof but to set him down there upon our return from Munich as well. None of us guessed that this was to be his first and last journey in the new coach—he least of all.

Over Christmas, Blomberg's daughters Sibylle and 'Dorle' [i.e. Dorothea] stayed with us while their father celebrated the holiday, again at Oberhof. The picture was growing clearer to me now: he was going to marry again. He confirmed my suspicions confidentially upon his return: he was thinking of a quiet marriage in January. It was true, he admitted, that the lady concerned was from a simple *milieu*, but that was no obstacle to him; in any case he had made up his mind upon this step. He was glad, he said, that his Dorle was engaged to my Karl-Heinz, and he would even like to find some way for our children to get married earlier; he would be giving them a suitable monthly allowance. In any case, it was no disgrace in our modern National Socialist Germany to marry a 'child of the people' and he did not care a hoot for the gossip in so-called society. He had called all his offspring together and discussed the whole matter quite frankly with them, and they had shown great understanding and would lay no obstacles across his path. That was all that either I or my family learned: it was to be some nameless 'child of the people'. A number of odd suspicions did pass through our minds but I hesitated to ask questions if Blomberg himself, whatever his motives, did not choose to discuss the affair.

From his adjutants I learned that the wedding, a civil one, was to take place very privately towards the middle of January, in a hall at the War Ministry building, and that Hitler and Göring had accepted invitations to attend as witnesses. I myself received no invitation to the ceremony, which was not followed by any religious wedding service; probably only the War Minister's three adjutants and—if I am not mistaken—von Friedeburg, a family friend and his former naval adjutant were present. That evening Blomberg left Berlin with the young lady on a honeymoon of which the Press published a photograph taken in Leipzig or Dresden, showing them visiting a zoo, with the couple posing in front of a cage full of monkeys. It struck me as more than tasteless.

Their honeymoon had to be suddenly broken off because Blomberg's aged mother, who was living in Eberswalde with one of her daughters, fell seriously ill with little hope of recovery. Whether or not grief was a contributory factor I do not know; Fräulein [Margarete] von Blomberg, who frequently called on my wife after her mother's death, was wrapped in silence so that I never learned whether her mother had in fact learned any closer details about Blomberg's wife. I went to the funeral of Frau von Blomberg and actually saw the couple standing by the graveside at the cemetery at Eberswalde; the young lady's face was heavily veiled and unrecognisable. On this occasion the condolences usual for the next-of-kin had been forbidden and the couple were the first to vanish; even I was unable to express my sympathy to them.

Towards the end of the month the Chief of Police in Berlin, Count von Helldorf, called on me in my office, having urgently asked for an interview. He was very agitated and began at once to ask me what the young bride had looked like. He found it hard to believe that—apart from the funeral at Eberswalde cemetery—I had not yet set eyes on her, particularly as with the announcement of our children's engagement I was now one of the family. Finally, he pulled out of his pocket a change-of-address registration-card with a passport-style photograph of one Fräulein Erna Gruhn. This police file card reported her move to Blomberg's flat in the Ministry building on Tirpitzufer; it had been sent up to him by her local police station.

The first thing Helldorf wanted to know was whether the photograph was identical with Blomberg's young wife: I was unable to answer the question. Helldorf demanded that I find Blomberg at once and ask him outright about it, as it was vital to establish the truth. I was so taken aback that I telephoned the Minister's outer office at once, to ask whether he was available; I was told that he was not, as he had gone out to Eberswalde to put his late mother's affairs in order. Helldorf listened in to my telephone conversation. Finally he came out with it: the Fräulein Erna Gruhn, who had in her new name as Blomberg's wife checked out with the police authorities where she had lived had in fact a criminal record for immorality. It would be indecorous of me to expand upon the details, which I was able to read for myself on her police record card.

Now I knew why Helldorf was so agitated; I expressed it as my view that Blomberg would certainly dissolve the marriage at once should the identity of his wife be proven beyond doubt. We discussed what our next moves should be: I said I was prepared to show Blomberg her record card next day, although I could not conceal the fact that as his daughter's future father-in-law I would find the matter highly embarrassing. Helldorf, however, refused to let me hang on to the card until next day; he said he would prefer not to let it out of his sight; he wanted to clear the matter up at once. I accordingly referred him to Göring, who as a witness at their wedding had, of course, met and seen the young lady.

Helldorf was immediately all for this solution. I telephoned Göring's office to arrange their interview, and Helldorf went straight round there. I kept turning it all over in my own mind; I was also hoping that I had now been relieved of making the painful disclosure to Blomberg myself, for there could scarcely be any doubt that the Erna Gruhn of the registration card, who had reported her change of address, was von Blomberg's bride. That evening, Helldorf telephoned me and informed me that Göring had immediately confirmed the identity beyond all possible doubt; it was, he said, a calamity of the first order. He said that Göring was going to speak to Blomberg next day about it and he could imagine that it would only be a relief to me not to be exposed to such an embarrassing situation. I had escaped the painful duty only by the merest coincidence, for really I should have been the one.

Göring called on Hitler that same evening, and broke the news to him. He was ordered to inform Blomberg next day about the lady's criminal past. If he was prepared to have the marriage dissolved on the spot they would find some way of avoiding a public scandal; the police officials concerned had on Göring's orders been sworn to secrecy. Blomberg rejected the idea of the annulment suggested to him by Göring on the Führer's instructions; he justified this stand later to me by saying that he was deeply in love with his

44

wife and claimed that had Hitler and Göring only *wanted* to help him he would have been able to stand firm on the 'position he had taken' in the affair. The fact was, however, that neither Hitler nor Göring believed Blomberg's protestations that he had embarked innocently upon this adventure; they were beside themselves with rage at having been exploited as witnesses at his wedding. Both were convinced, as I learned from them later, that Blomberg had wanted to compel them in this way to hush up and stamp out any rumours and after-effects that might follow his step.

I did not speak with Blomberg until that midday, upon his return from seeing first Göring and then the Führer; he was absolutely shattered and near to collapse. He had repeated to the Führer his disinclination to dissolve his marriage, and their long interview had ended with his resignation.

Afterwards Blomberg confided to me that he laid the blame squarely on Göring; if Göring had not entertained hopes of becoming his successor they would very easily have been able to cover up the whole affair with the mantle of true love. He had known all along that his wife had lived loosely in the past, but that was no reason for casting a woman out for ever; in any case, she had for some time now been employed by the Reich Egg Board and earned her keep like that, though her mother was only an ironing-woman.

The Führer had also discussed with him the question of who ought to succeed him; he would be telling me the rest himself. In any case, [Colonel-General] von Fritsch [Commander-in-Chief of the Army] was also on his way out, as serious legal proceedings were pending against him of a kind that could not be set aside; I would be hearing all that from Hitler too. He, Blomberg, had proposed Brauchitsch's name as his successor. He had parted with the Führer on amicable terms, the latter telling him that if ever the hour should come when a war had to be fought, he would be seeing him at his side once again.

I gained the immediate impression that Blomberg was clutching very strongly at these words and saw in them an easy way out. He added that as a field-marshal he would, in the old Prussian tradition, still be 'on call' and continue to draw full pay even though he was for the time being condemned to inactivity. I tried to persuade him to consider once again whether it would not be better to divorce his wife after all, and I reproached him for not having consulted me before taking such a step; I was only a little younger than he, but I would at least have been able to make inquiries about this woman *beforehand*. He waved my remonstrances aside, explaining that he would never have done that even for our children's sake, and I would have to try to understand that. He indignantly rejected the idea of a divorce, as it had been a love-match on both sides, and he would 'rather put a bullet in his head than do that'. Telling me I was to report to the Führer in plain clothes at one o'clock that afternoon he left me standing there in the middle of his office, and rushed out of the room and into his flat with his eyes full of tears.

I was so dazed by the whole situation that before I could leave his room I had to sit down for a while. I had always known how thick-headed and obstinate he was, once he had set his mind on a course of action. And now there was to be a second calamity over Fritsch; what on earth could that be? I was still at a loss to know when I went home for lunch and a change into plain clothes; I could not screw myself up sufficiently to tell my wife anything. Shortly afterwards I was telephoned by Göring in person, and asked to come round to see him as soon as possible; I agreed to do so, and drove round to his flat.

He wanted to know what Blomberg had told me after his interview with the Führer, and who was to be his successor. 'You are the only one in the running for that,' I told him, 'because you probably won't be wanting to take orders from yet another Army general.' This he at once confirmed, saying that there was absolutely no question of his putting up with that. The Fritsch business suddenly occurred to me, and I began to wonder who could be behind it. Göring was telling me that he had known of Blomberg's wedding plans for some time in advance; the lady had wanted to marry some other man, but at Blomberg's request he had been able to persuade the man in question to turn her down by bribing him with a well-paid job abroad; the whole thing had gone off perfectly and the rival was already overseas. In the meantime, Göring had ascertained all the details of the lady's earlier character and he told me everything, but I intend to keep these details to myself even now, even though Mr. Gisevius wagged his tongue about them in the witness box at Nuremberg; no doubt Count von Helldorf was his oracle.

I reported at the Reich Chancellery at five o'clock that afternoon [26th January, 1938] and was at once shown up to Hitler's study. I had only spoken with him once before, on the occasion of our re-occupation of the demilitarised zone, together with Neurath and Fritsch; otherwise I had met Hitler only while accompanying Blomberg, once during a Cabinet meeting on the reform of the penal code, in conjunction with a number of other secretaries of state, and again during a conference with Schacht, the President of the Reichsbank, on the subject of the financing of our rearmament programme. Both of these occasions had been back in 1936. I had not been called upon to speak, but had just sat behind Blomberg taking notes. Hitler knew my name only from reports to him and from the manœuvres of 1935 in which I had commanded an infantry division.

Colonel Hossbach, the Führer's adjutant, had carefully avoided ever permitting me to get through to the Führer, probably to prevent a situation like that arising with Reichenau, who just announced his own arrival or gatecrashed the Führer's dinner-table in the same way as a number of ministers and senior Party officials were generally wont to do. Even later I still attended these functions only when I had been expressly invited by Hitler to attend.

My first impression was that the Führer had certainly been deeply shaken by the Blomberg affair; but *pace* Gisevius he had certainly not suffered a 'nervous breakdown'. He spoke of his great admiration for Blomberg and of his indebtedness to him, but he made no attempt to conceal that it had deeply offended him to have been abused in his position as witness to the wedding. He asked me whether the officer corps would ever have steeled itself to accept such an impossible marriage, whose circumstances would not have remained shrouded for long. I was obliged to agree that they would not; I was aware that in any case there was no love lost on him at least in the Army and no tears would be shed over his departure, although I did not say so. Hitler told me he had given Blomberg a world tour as a wedding present and had expressed the hope that they would stay away from Germany for a year. Blomberg had accepted the offer. Hitler wanted, he said, to discuss the question of a successor with me, and whom did I propose?

My first nomination was Göring, and I told him bluntly the reasons I had for proposing him. Hitler turned him down at once, saying that there was no question of it as he had given Göring the Four Year Plan and he had to hang on to the Air Force as well, as there was nobody better for that than he; anyway, Göring had to gather experience in the affairs of State as his own predestined successor as Führer. I suggested Fritsch next. He crossed to his writing-desk and handed to me an indictment personally signed by Gürtner, the Minister of Justice, charging Fritsch with an offence under Paragraph 175 of the penal code. He informed me that he had had this indictment in his hands for some time already, but had suppressed it up to now as he had not believed the charge. But now that the question of the succession had suddenly and unexpectedly become acute the matter would have to be cleared up, and in these circumstances he could no longer allow things to rest as they were. Besides Gürtner, Göring had also been put in the picture.

I was horrified at the charge: while on the one hand I could not believe Gürtner would have drawn it up without good reason, on the other hand I would never believe that it could be true of Fritsch. I said that either there must be some mistaken identity involved, or else it was sheer slander because I knew Fritsch too well to accept that such an allegation could possibly be well-founded. Hitler ordered me to say nothing to anybody about this; he would have a talk *à deux* with Fritsch next day and suddenly ask him point-blank about it, without warning, and see from his reaction what truth there was in the charge. Then we would be able to look one stage further.

He asked me who I would suggest for Fritsch's successor, and I nominated von Rundstedt first of all. He replied that he valued him very highly and would have accepted him without the least hesitation, despite his hostile attitude towards the National Socialist ideology. No considerations like that would ever have stood in his way, Hitler said, but he was too old for the job; it was a pity that he was not five or ten years younger as his selection would then have been automatic. So I put forward von Brauchitsch's name.

The Führer was silent for a moment, then spontaneously asked 'Why not von Reichenau?' I at once told him what my reasons were: not thorough enough, not a hard worker, a busybody, too superficial, little-loved and a soldier who sought satisfaction for his ambitions more in the political than in the purely military sphere. Hitler admitted that I was right about my last point, but suggested the rest of my assessment had probably been a bit harsh on him. By way of contrast, I recommended Brauchitsch as a 100 per cent soldier, an able organiser and trainer and a leader highly valued by the Army. Hitler told me that he would be speaking with Brauchitsch himself, and that in the meantime our discussion was to remain a close secret; he would speak with Fritsch next day. I was ordered to present myself again on the following afternoon. In the meantime only Blomberg's abdication had been decided upon.

When I called on Hitler next day he was in a high degree of agitation. Fritsch had been with him earlier and had, of course, denied the unnatural offences alleged of him; but he had left a distressed and nervous impression. Quite apart from that they had fetched from prison the witness who had incriminated him and stood him by the entry to the Reich Chancellery building, so that he could get a good look at Fritsch. The man had afterwards confirmed that this was the officer; in other words he claimed to have recognised him again. Fritsch was, said Hitler, thus heavily incriminated and it was impossible for him to remain Commander-in-Chief of the Army; he had for the time being been given leave of absence and confined to his flat. Then Hitler's indignation turned towards Hossbach; this officer, his own personal adjutant, had shamelessly gone behind his back and, despite his having forbidden it, warned Fritsch of what was afoot. Hossbach had broken confidence and he never wanted to see him again; I was to explain this to Hossbach and suggest somebody to take his place immediately. As I had already been commissioned by Blomberg some months before to select from the General Staff a major capable of replacing Hossbach should the latter be required for the front-line posting for which he had been earmarked, I had after considerable thought eventually decided upon Major Schmundt whom I had known well from my T-2 days, and from when he had been my former regimental adjutant at Potsdam. I suggested his name to Hitler and he accepted it. He took over the office a few days later without any kind of initiation, coming to me for this during his early days. It was a thankless duty for me to have to inform Hossbach that he had been dismissed his office without any formal leavetaking.

When I again tried to persuade Hitler to make Göring Blomberg's successor as Supreme Commander of the Armed Forces—I could see no other way out—he rejoined that he had already decided to take over the immediate Supreme Command himself, while I was to remain as his Chief of Staff; I was to be neither allowed nor enabled to desert him at an hour like this. If he eventually found that I was not indispensable in such a position, then he would appoint me Commander-in-Chief of the Army, but until such a time I was to remain at my present post. I unhesitatingly agreed to do so.

That evening I visited Fritsch to place myself at his disposal should he need me. I found him outwardly very calm but obviously deeply embittered about such a disgraceful libel on his person. He showed me his written resignation lying on his desk; it contained a demand to be tried by court martial. I could only agree with him on this point: there was no other way for him to cast off the slur on his character, for the absence of a judicial verdict would be tantamount to a tacit confession of guilt. Hitler appeared at first to disagree, but then he said I was right and he decreed that there should be a trial along the lines I suggested. The Commanders-in-Chief of all three services were appointed to judge the case with Göring as their president and two additional high-ranking professional judges to assist them; Hitler held open his final decision on Fritsch's resignation although there was apparently no longer any intention of reinstating him in his former office; the accusations were sufficient for him to be discredited and cast off in what would appear a perfectly justifiable manner. They had already sufficed for him to be debarred from consideration as Blomberg's successor. Minister Gürtner's indictment, which probably originated with the secret State police [*Gestapo*] authorities, had proved ideal for such a contingency: it had been thawed out for this questionable use only after it had been kept on ice for a considerable time.

During the days that followed, the Führer called in Generals Beck and von Rundstedt, and Grand-Admiral Raeder, in order to discuss the question of Fritsch's successor with these senior officers, too. In addition I spent several hours a day with him. I could see that he still could not give up his idea of having Reichenau; but I remained loyal to my iron conviction and finally my own views prevailed: von Brauchitsch had already been waiting for two days at his hotel by the time I finally summoned him to the Führer's presence. I had personally fetched him from Leipzig where he had been in command of the Fourth Army Group there; my action in doing so had led to a violent quarrel with General Beck, who considered himself to be deputy Commander-in-Chief of the Army and forbade me to take such 'unauthorised' actions again. Von Rundstedt smoothed Beck's ruffled feathers. Now began a series of endless three-cornered discussions: Brauchitsch acknowledged in detail his views on National Socialism, the Church, the expansion and replenishment of the Officer Corps, and so on.* Finally, after our third meeting, on the morning of 4th February, 1938, Hitler rose, spontaneously held out his hand to von Brauchitsch and appointed him Commander-in-Chief of the Army; he thereby opted for Fritsch's total abdication while I myself had advocated only that a temporary substitute should be found for him.

Meanwhile, as I was able to discern from his several telephone calls to me, Dr. Lammers, Head of the Reich Chancellery, was endeavouring to formulate the order for the newly-created position of 'Chief of the OKW'. Finally, we called jointly on Hitler with it

---

* From Keitel's original text it is not clear whether Brauchitsch *expounded* on his own views or *identified* himself with Hitler's; the result was the same.

who signed the order shortly before that evening's Cabinet meeting after making a few alterations in its text. Brauchitsch and I were presented to the members of the Cabinet by Hitler in a short speech, and the other changes being made in the composition of the Cabinet itself (von Neurath, etc.), and the order setting up a Privy Cabinet Council were read out by Lammers. There was no subsequent discussion in the Cabinet.

Hitler left for Berchtesgaden and the Berghof soon afterwards. Not a syllable did he utter to Brauchitsch, the Cabinet or myself about his imminent plans and policies. The only thing that he did intimate to the two of us was that he was making use of the current bad odour left especially abroad by the departure of Blomberg and Fritsch to carry out a major Cabinet reshuffle: he was placing von Neurath at the head of a Privy Cabinet Council in order to ensure that no impression was given of any change of course in our foreign policies.

After the frightful day of Blomberg's resignation I did speak with him once more, on the following day [28th January, 1938]. He handed to me the key to his safe and two large sealed envelopes. One contained the secret Order of the Succession to Hitler, and the other contained Fritsch's memorandum on the command of the Armed Forces, which he had tabled in the spring of 1937, after the manœuvres. It had caused a critical dispute between the two of them at the time, with Blomberg threatening to resign if Fritsch insisted on handing in this memorandum to the Führer; but both of them had been persuaded to change their minds. Apart from these things, he left me nothing, either written or spoken, as he went.

He informed me that he was embarking on a voyage to the Indian Ocean with his wife, but before that he would be staying for some weeks in Italy; even so, he could not keep on the move for a whole year. He planned to write to me in good time to ask for Hitler's consent to his taking up residence in his cottage at Bad Wiessee. He would be putting up half the money for Dorle's wedding, as it was wrong to keep on postponing it any longer.

I have gone to some trouble to write such a detailed account of the whole affair in order that at least *one* truthful version should be committed to paper: the version reproduced by Gisevius and the various other rumours and gossip in the circles frequented by the generals and Party officials are baseless and false. To suggest that the Secret State Police had a finger in the Blomberg affair is demonstrably incorrect. As far as Fritsch was concerned I still believe today

that the charge had been trumped up against him in an intrigue
designed to make his continued tenure of office impossible: I do not
know who was behind it, but it was probably either Himmler or
Heydrich, his evil genius, for it was well known in the SS and in the
Army too that Fritsch was implacably opposed to the military
aspirations entertained by the SS now that the *Sturmabteilung* [Storm
Detachment] had lost its influence.

I must have been in a daze all that first week after 4th February,
with my appointment as Chief of the OKW—the High Command
of the Armed Forces—and certainly I never dreamed that the sword
I had accepted was to prove so double-edged. It is evident from the
notes that Jodl entered in his diary that I can only have given him
the barest outline of events at the time.

Perhaps a speech delivered by Hitler to his Berlin generals before
the Cabinet meeting is worthy of some mention: he announced
tactfully what had occurred and the consequences, and that he had
assumed Supreme Command of the Armed Forces, while a High
Command was to be established with myself at its head. General
von Manstein was the only one to ask whether a 'Chief of the Armed
Forces General Staff' would ever be appointed, to which Hitler
replied that the way was open for that if occasion should arise.

I was fully aware at the time that like a novice monk I was faced
by great hardships, and that I was entering upon a new world,
but on the other hand I was able to comfort myself with the thought
that I could find enough support in my familiar old *Wehrmachtsamt*,
my Armed Forces Office, to do justice to the task allotted me: that
it was virtually insoluble, and that I would become the victim of
Hitler's unbridled dictatorship were things which no human being
could have foreseen. For the execution of his plans, which were
unknown to us, he needed impotent tools unable to inhibit him,
men who would be obedient and faithful to him in the real soldiers'
tradition. How easy it is for all those who are not exposed to the
ball and shot and who do not have to face up to a demon like that
man day after day, to criticise! I do not deny that I made mistakes
as well, perhaps I lost the opportunity of compelling him to adopt
at least some restraint; but in wartime, when everything was at
stake, it was twice as hard. It is my hallowed conviction now that
it would have been equally impossible for any other general even if
he had been far tougher, far more critical and intelligent than I,
to have halted our landslide into misfortune.

Why did Brauchitsch fail to do so? Why did the generals who
have been so ready to term me a complaisant and incompetent

yes-man fail to secure my removal? Was that all that difficult? No, that wasn't it: the truth was that nobody would have been ready to replace me, because each one knew that he would end up just as much a wreck as I.

In view of my candour in my dealings with Brauchitsch it would not have been too difficult for him to have turned Hitler against me or to have awakened his mistrust in me, for in that respect Hitler was more than sensitive and he never failed to follow these things up. I know from Brauchitsch himself that in 1939 [General] Milch, the Secretary of State for Air, was being nominated to replace me. There would certainly have been endeavours from the Army's side to eliminate me as well, had they been able to find even one person prepared to accept my thorny office. But it was more comfortable for them to curse me and to heap all the responsibility on to my shoulders; and nobody was trampled underfoot in any rush to assist me and stand by my side. I myself advised Hitler three times to replace me with von Manstein: the first time was in the autumn of 1939, before our campaign in the west; the second was in December 1941, when Brauchitsch went; and the third time was in September 1942 when his big quarrel with Jodl and myself flared up. But despite his frequently expressed admiration for Manstein's outstanding talents, Hitler obviously feared to take such a step and each time he turned it down; was it sheer indolence on his part of some other unvoiced objection he had to him? I have no idea. Nobody can ever have known how miserable I felt in my new office; perhaps only Jodl does to a certain extent. My admission at the end of my closing speech during the Trial says everything that needs to be said; it shows that at least in retrospect I am wiser than I was at the time.

For myself and for my family, how I wish that I had been granted an upright and honourable soldier's death; why did Fate deny me that on 20th July, 1944, during the attempt on the Führer's life?

3

1938-1940: From Austria to the end of the French Campaign

Nuremberg, 7th September 1946

ON the evening of 4th February, 1938, after his final mono-
logue to the Reich Cabinet, Hitler departed for the
Berghof. Major Schmundt, who had just been appointed
on my recommendation as Hitler's 'chief military adjutant' accompanied him, together with a special army adjutant Captain Engel,
who had been appointed to satisfy von Brauchitsch's own particular
wishes, the latter hoping in this way to establish a direct and, to a
certain extent, personal link with the Supreme Commander. In
addition to Engel there was also a naval adjutant, Commander
Albrecht, and one from the air force, Captain von Below, all three
being subordinated to Schmundt. The need for serving two masters
at the same time, as Hossbach had had to under the Chief of the
General Staff in the past, was thus obviated.

Brauchitsch had failed to comply with Hitler's wishes and recommendation that he surround himself as the new Commander-in-
Chief of the Army only with lieutenants whom he could trust, as for
example Dönitz did in 1943. But only in one instance did Hitler
insist on a change, and that was that there should be another Chief
of the Army General Staff; even so, I witnessed myself how
Brauchitsch argued at great length with him to let him keep Beck
on in office at least until the autumn of 1938 to acquaint him with
his duties and daily responsibilities as the Army's Commander-in-
Chief.

I myself am today convinced that this was Brauchitsch's first big
mistake; his second was his failure to select as his lieutenants only
those upon whom he could completely rely to give him their unconditional support, however little they applauded his appointment

54

as their new Commander-in-Chief. The result was that while the reshuffle which took place on Hitler's orders simultaneously with Brauchitsch's appointment on 4th February, 1938 had in fact been decided upon in many conferences with Hitler before the one I attended, the changes not only failed to serve the interests of the new Commander-in-Chief but occasioned the first damage to [Hitler's] trust both in him and in myself.

A further factor was that to find a new Chief of Army Personnel as a replacement for Schwedler, Brauchitsch had—admittedly on my advice—chosen my own brother whom he knew quite well. All these were only half measures and they did more harm than good; they evoked immediate criticism from the broad mass of the generals. Nobody knows better than Brauchitsch or I how heavy was the burden that he had inherited: Fritsch had enjoyed unlimited respect and admiration, and his shameless hounding had caused a wave of unjustified bitterness. Brauchitsch was harried day and night by Beck and the commanding generals all demanding that he speak out for his predecessor's immediate rehabilitation and reinstatement, insisting on Hitler's promoting him to field-marshal, and the like. At the time the position was that it was brought home pretty bluntly to Brauchitsch that their faith in him was conditional upon his pressing through these demands.

Fritsch's trial had ended with the acquittal everyone had expected. One can thank Göring alone for the masterly way in which, by pitiless cross-examination, he forced the sole prosecution witness, the convict who had earlier sworn that he had had a homosexual *mésalliance* with the accused and allegedly recognised him afterwards in the Reich Chancellery, to admit that he did not even know Colonel-General von Fritsch and that it was all a mix-up over names: his real co-respondent had been a retired cavalry captain, von *Frisch*. The accused was acquitted as his innocence had been proven. But those who had either set this disgraceful trial in motion or exploited the opportunity presented by a possibly entirely fortuitous similarity of names, had succeeded in their secondary objective: the Commander-in-Chief of the Army had been smeared and eliminated from the scene.

Now a demand was raised for the victim's public rehabilitation and promotion to be exacted from Hitler, and the storm broke around Brauchitsch's ears. As I judged the situation, I thought everything should be left to take its time; it was hard for Hitler to admit that he himself had been the victim of deceit or even of an intrigue. All Brauchitsch's endeavours to carry Hitler with him foundered on the sheer impossibility of putting across his point of view. Finally Hitler appointed Fritsch an honorary colonel of the 12th Artillery Regiment, but the generals remained unappeased.

I could see that Brauchitsch was jeopardising what little confidence Hitler still had in him, without on the other hand winning the generals over to his side; in my view this was his second mistake.

I called Brauchitsch's attention to this and advised him for the time being not to sap his prestige in Hitler's eyes any further over this delicate matter. But General Beck, the spiritual leader of the opposition, gave him no peace: he was an agitator, always goading his new master on and finding ready listeners all the time among the other senior generals. Where was the cry: *le roi est mort, vive le roi*? There was no such spirit in the Army, only this pernicious campaign, with all its disastrous consequences. In 1943 Admiral Dönitz as Raeder's successor was to succeed to just such a grievous burden: two military dogmas stood face to face against each other inside the Navy. Dönitz was able to draw the proper conclusions and ruthlessly replaced every one of his senior officers with men he could vouch for, and the result was a 100 per cent success.

I have no doubt whatsoever that after Fritsch's departure, General Beck was the one who strew the largest rocks in the path between Brauchitsch and the Führer. I cannot say what kind of motive led Beck to move into the camp of the 'resistance movement', the first step along the road towards his later high treason, as early as this time: was it his injured vanity? Or his own designs on the office of Commander-in-Chief of the Army?

One thing is certain: nobody did more damage to von Brauchitsch's reputation in the Army and in the Führer's eyes than Beck, together with the deeply embittered Colonel Hossbach and the chief adjutant to the C.-in-C. Army, Lieutenant-Colonel Siewert; they were from Fritsch's old guard, they were the protectors of his interests. For them von Brauchitsch was only a means to an end, but despite my warnings he did not attempt to find a way out of the impasse. I always made excuses for Brauchitsch in Hitler's presence, admittedly not so much out of soldierly discretion or decorum as from my own selfishness, as I could only feel some responsibility towards Hitler for having recommended him. The generals never idolised Brauchitsch as they had idolised Fritsch before him; it was not until they eventually lost Brauchitsch that they recognised the true calibre of the man.

Brauchitsch always acted honourably in his dealings with the Führer and the generals: the War Crimes Trial should not be allowed to conceal this fact. He always wanted to get the best, even from Hitler, but he never knew how to get it. But I deny him any right to impeach me for *my* shortcomings or *my* weakness with Hitler, as I have far more right and reason to say things like that about him; at least neither of us can make any accusations about the other in this respect.

A week after I acceded to my office, I was summoned to the Berghof [at Berchtesgaden] without any reason being given. When I reported to Hitler in his house that February morning [12th February, 1938] he told me he was expecting the Federal Austrian Chancellor, Schuschnigg, within half an hour for a serious talk with him, as the crisis between our brother countries was calling for an intelligent solution. [At the end of January, Viennese Police had raided the headquarters of the Austrian National Socialists and captured incriminating documentary evidence proving they were banking on Hitler's armed intervention in Austria. Hitler dismissed the leader of the Austrian National Socialists, and Schuschnigg was visiting Hitler to try to obtain his assurance of standing by their agreement of 1936.] He had sent for me, he said, only so that Schuschnigg would see a few uniforms around; Reichenau and Sperrle were coming down from Munich, so the significance was certain not to be lost on their guest.

We generals played no part in the conferences and had no inkling of either the objectives or the aims of the talks until Schuschnigg's departure; we were fearfully bored. We were called in only for lunch and again for coffee later that afternoon, joining in the informal conversations then. The then Austrian Foreign Secretary, Guido Schmidt, confirmed all this at the Trial.

Obviously it dawned upon me during the course of the day that —with the other two generals—I was by my very presence acting as a means to an end, my very first major rôle in life. This view was strengthened by Hitler's bellowing for me when Schuschnigg withdrew briefly for private consultations with his Foreign Secretary during the afternoon. I entered Hitler's study just as Schuschnigg was leaving it, and when I asked Hitler what commands he had for me, he replied: 'None at all! Just sit down.' We kept up a short, indifferent conversation for ten minutes, after which I was dismissed from his presence. The effect this had on Schuschnigg has been testified to at the Trial.

I spent that night—the only time in all those years—at the Führer's house; but I had to leave the Berghof in the early hours of the next morning in order to set in motion the various deception tactics agreed upon, in collaboration with Jodl and Canaris. As a result of the agreements that were reached, actual military preparations did not even come into the question and, as I was to apprise the Commander-in-Chief of the Army, at that time even the Führer had no thoughts of a military conflict.

All the greater was our surprise when Hitler's demand for our troops to enter Austria reached us on 10th March. I was summoned to the Reich Chancellery and briefly told that he had formulated this intention because Schuschnigg had without warning announced there would be a plebiscite on the subject of his agreements with Hitler; Hitler interpreted this move as a breach of their agreements, and planned to circumvent it by military action.

I proposed that the Commander-in-Chief of the Army and the Chief of the General Staff should be summoned to receive orders from Hitler direct. It was quite clear to me that Beck would otherwise simply dismiss the whole thing as quite impossible, and I could never report that to the Führer. Brauchitsch was away on an official journey so I called back at the Reich Chancellery, accompanied only by Beck. His objections were summarily brushed aside by Hitler, so he had no alternative but to comply and report back some hours later what troop formations would be ready to enter Austria early on the 12th. Late on 11th March Brauchitsch left the Reich Chancellery building with the final executive order, after it had already been temporarily withheld once during the afternoon.

I reached my home only about eight o'clock that evening and my guests were already awaiting me, among them being by coincidence the Austrian ambassador [Tauschitz] and his military attaché [Major-General Pohl], together with a motley assembly in both uniform and mufti. The invitations had gone out three weeks before, without my even dreaming that 12th March was to be a historic day of the first order. I was shortly able to establish for myself that the Austrian gentlemen were completely at ease and obviously had no idea of what was to happen within a very few hours. It was pure coincidence, but this evening party became the ideal camouflage for our entry into Austria.

The night that followed was sheer purgatory for me: one telephone call followed another from the Army General Staff and from Brauchitsch; finally at about four o'clock in the morning there was a call from the then chief of the military operations staff, General von Viebahn; all adjured me to persuade the Führer to call the

58

operation off. I had no intention of asking this of the Führer even once; of course I promised them I would try, but I called them back a short time later (having made no attempt to contact him) and told each one that he had rejected their protests. This was something of which the Führer never learned; if he had, his verdict on the Army's leadership would have been devastating, a disillusionment I wanted to spare both parties.

At six o'clock on the morning of the 12th, the Führer and I flew out of Berlin: he wanted to take part in the triumphal entry into his Fatherland and personally accompany the troops. We put in our first appearance at the command post of the Commander-in-Chief of the divisions marching into Austria, General von Bock, and he briefed us on the troops' movements and on their entry routes, because the Führer naturally wanted to be there to welcome his troops. It was from here that the memorable telephone conversation with Mussolini took place, the Führer having flown a handwritten letter out to him by an emissary, justifying his actions to him: Mussolini personally telephoned to confirm that he had received it, and congratulated Hitler; there followed then Hitler's memorable phrase—'Duce, I will never forget you for this'—an exclamation which he repeated several times.

At midday we drove through Adolf Hitler's birthplace, Braunau, acclaimed by the townsfolk with an unending roar of welcome. He showed us his school, and his parents' home, and he was visibly deeply moved by it all. We rounded off the evening in Hitler's second native city Linz, on the Danube, having been delayed in every town and village on the way by the advancing troops and the wildly celebrating crowds that packed around us. It was long after dark when we drove into the city together with the Austrian Minister Seyss-Inquart [Federal Chancellor since the 11th] who had joined our party on the outskirts; here, from a balcony of the City Hall, Hitler addressed a vast crowd of people tightly packed into the market square below. The atmosphere of the whole demonstration was electric and excited beyond belief; I had never seen anything like it before and I was deeply impressed. I had thought it unlikely that there would be any shooting or anything like that when our troops entered the country, but a reception like this was something I had never dreamed of. We stayed there all next day, Sunday; he [i.e. Hitler] was greatly preoccupied with the administrative details of the union, and during the afternoon there was a brief march-past by German and Austrian troops in front of the hotel [the Weinzinger Hotel at Linz].

Next day came our grand entry into Vienna, after a midday break at Saint-Pölten. It was not until far into the night that I could get to sleep in our hotel [the Imperial Hotel], where again I had a room giving out onto the street; the dense and thronging crowd below seemed never to tire of roaring and chanting: 'We want to see our Führer! We want to see our Führer!' A military parade by German *and* Austrian troops followed that afternoon, after the Führer's historic speech to the vast crowd gathered in the Castle square, with its closing sentence, 'I announce to the German people that my Austrian fatherland has now returned to the Greater German Reich.' That same evening we flew back from Vienna to Munich: this flight before dusk is the most breathtaking and extraordinary spectacle I have ever witnessed; Hitler saw me in my enchantment, and with tears of joy in his eyes he stammered out to me the bare words: 'All that . . . all that is now German again.'

After a hasty meal in the airport restaurant I flew back to Berlin while it was still dark. That same night I was back in my home. The last few days had been like some vast and incomprehensive dream to me. For the first time I had been an eye-witness of history in the making.

On my arrival [in Berlin] next morning the Chief of my Central Office, Major Kleikamp, received me with the news that General von Viebahn, chief of the military operations staff, had locked himself into the small overnight room I had had fitted out in Blomberg's flat after it fell vacant and was threatening everybody who tried to speak to or see him with a gun. I was to call Jodl in to have a word with me at once, as he wanted to see me as soon as I arrived.

General von Viebahn had been warmly recommended to the Führer as a superlative general staff officer by General von der Schulenburg, the chief of staff of the First World War Army (later Army Group) named '*Deutscher Kronprinz*'; Schulenburg had had him as a captain on his own staff. The Führer had several times suggested to me I ought to take Viebahn into the OKW for its operations staff, as he greatly valued Schulenburg's judgment; the latter was close to Party circles, and a General in the SS and the SA. I also respected him in view of my old connections with him. I knew Viebahn from my personnel office days and had had a lot to do with him earlier, even before 1933. As the office of chief of the military operations staff was free at the time and as I was employing Jodl as chief of the OKW's national defence department, I concurred with the Führer's wishes. At the beginning it had seemed a sound solution to me, as Viebahn was a close friend of Beck's and I had some hopes therefore that he would bridge the gap between Beck and myself and smooth over our differences. But I never could make head or tail of this odd fellow, and Jodl could make even less; in view of the way he had implored me [to hold Hitler back] during the night before our entry into Austria I completely lost confidence in him. During my absence Jodl had had to suffer the most improbable scenes from him. At one time he had been praying out loud and prophesying disaster for us all; then he had gone off into a distracted and brooding silence for several hours on end. Then, when Jodl had finally told him to get a grip on himself, he had locked himself in, refused to let anybody speak to him, and thrown an inkwell against the door.

I called Viebahn in to see me. But now that the spectre of disaster had vanished from before his eyes, he was quite coherent again, and when I advised him to take an immediate rest to convalesce he firmly refused saying that he was perfectly healthy and that he failed to understand what I was getting at. He protested to Jodl for having 'lied' to me about him, whereupon Jodl unceremoniously threw him out of the room. I had the most extraordinary difficulty in getting rid of this mentally sick and hysterical man at all; the War Office refused to take him away from me, and I had to threaten Brauchitsch that I would go to the Führer and demand the man's removal if he was not retired from the OKW. That did some good, but it resulted in a complaint from Viebahn against me for libelling him by my assertion that he was not of sound mind. I was happy to be alone with Jodl once again; this other chief of operations staff was a dreadful broken reed.

On 18th March the end of the Fritsch trial arrived, with the verdict described above. Fritsch retired to the seclusion of a country house that had been built for him some time before on the military training ground at Bergen (near Uelzen), far from man or beast, and the Führer himself announced this to the Berlin generals in an address to them at the Reich Chancellery. He concluded that he had ordered the prosecution witness, whose shameless lying had caused the scandal, to be shot. Some weeks later Canaris told me that the Secret State Police had not complied with the execution order; so it was obvious to me that the witness must have been a hired tool who could hardly be shot as a reward for his deed.

I demanded an immediate clarification of the case from Canaris, to enable me to make a report to the Führer. Canaris begged me not to make any use of what he had told me, as he had only heard it from hearsay himself; he promised to make immediate inquiries of

Heydrich himself. Some days later he told me that the Führer's order had now been executed and I declared myself satisfied. Today I am convinced that Canaris' first report to me was correct and that he had retracted it only for fear of Heydrich and what I would tell Hitler. My faith in Canaris was to cost me dearly later.

The immediate annexation which Hitler had ordered of the Austrian Federal Army and the raising from strongly Reich-German strains of two general-headquarter staffs, together with one armoured, two infantry and two mountain divisions, inflicted a considerable new organisational burden on the War Office as well as signifying that the 36-division programme was being exceeded for the first time. Hitler himself undertook a tour of several garrisons of the new '*Ostmark*' to harangue the recruits and troop units being raised; it was his supreme ambition to raise here exemplary formations in the shortest possible time and in the old Prussian tradition, under the command of selected Reich-German officers; his thoughts were on the Czechs, who had been taken by surprise by the solution of the Austrian problem and whose interest in it could hardly remain purely academic.

On 20th April, together with the Commanders-in-Chief of the three services, I took part for the first time in the Führer's birthday celebrations. Göring, who since Blomberg's departure had been promoted to *Generalfeldmarschall* and was thus the senior ranking C.-in-C., made a short speech voicing the Armed Forces' congratulations; this was followed by the usual handshakes and then we went to view a military parade of all three services in the Tiergarten. At midday we were the Führer's guests at a small banquet.

During the evening, shortly before the Führer's departure for Berchtesgaden, I was called in to see him alone at the Reich Chancellery. There followed the first directive to me (referred to several times at the Trial) to institute preliminary General Staff studies for a conflict with Czechoslovakia. As always, he spoke his thoughts out loud to me, in a little speech: the problem would have to be solved some time, not only because of the way in which the Czech government was oppressing the German population living there but because of the strategically impossible situation that would develop should the time ever come for the big reckoning with the East, and by that he meant not just the Poles but particularly the Bolsheviks. He was absolutely convinced that here would lie the greatest danger to the Reich; western Czechoslovakia would act as a springboard for the Red Army and Air Force, and in no time at all the enemy could be at the gates of Dresden and in the heart of the Reich. While he admitted that he had no intention of unleashing a war on the Czechs of his own accord, yet political constellations might emerge where one would have to strike like lightning.

The instructions issued to me were recorded for posterity in the Schmundt Document, which I have never seen for myself; I took them in without saying a word, but not without some apprehension. I went over the instructions issued to me [with Jodl] next day and we resolved to temporise, while still drafting a formal directive in the required sense; the documents which have been preserved will, together with Jodl's diary entries, show the subsequent course of events. About four weeks later—on Schmundt's insistence—I sent down to the Berghof this first draft of our 'directive' to the War Office; its introduction has often been mentioned: 'It is not my intention to smash Czechoslovakia by military action in the immediate future . . . etc.'

Jodl and I had prudently concealed the matter from the Army General Staff in order, as we thought, to avoid unnecessary alarm. Whether something had indeed leaked out to them—perhaps the Führer had expressed thoughts similarly to Brauchitsch—I do not know. In any event, a comprehensive memorandum emerged, written by Beck, with a first part of a political nature and a second part discussing the balance of military strength and the strategic considerations which would be involved should France intervene in a conflict with the Czechs on account of the French treaty with them.

Brauchitsch called me over to discuss the best way of bringing this memorandum to Hitler's attention. He had learned to proceed more cautiously since Hitler's blunt rejection of the General Staff memorandum on 'Command of the Armed Forces in Time of War', which he had handed to Hitler without my knowledge shortly after taking office.

After I had run briefly through Beck's memorandum on the likely outcome of a war with Czechoslovakia, I advised Brauchitsch not to table its first part on any account, as Hitler would at once reject its political and military arguments out of hand, not even troubling to read the second part at all. We decided for this reason to table only the second part as the Führer really ought to study that. That was how we, in fact, set about it, but the only result was a very sharp protest from Hitler that the data were not objective and that the balance of strength had been depicted far too favourably for the enemy (for example the French armoured fighting vehicles, etc.). It was another disaster for the Army and resulted in a further loss of confidence in Brauchitsch, which I bitterly regretted, even though the Führer did not hold Brauchitsch responsible as much as Beck and the General Staff.

It was at this time that a new note of discord sounded: much to the (justified) rage of the Army, Hitler had commissioned Göring to survey the progress being made in the construction of fortifications in the west, or rather to inspect them. Göring's report to the Führer was one long accusation against the War Office from beginning to end: virtually nothing had been done, he alleged, what had been done was inadequate, and there was barely even the most primitive field defence system, etc. Grossly over-exaggerated though all that was, it *was* true that the whole construction project was still only in embryo; with Blomberg's agreement, the building programme for the concrete structures and larger fortification works had been foreseen as covering a twenty-year span to their completion. Work had been put in hand all along the line, as Blomberg and I had been able to establish during a 1937 drive lasting several days along the whole length of the front, and while they were indeed only isolated beginnings the plans were complete and were shown to us at the time. But now the Führer was bitterly disappointed and he strongly accused the General Staff of sabotaging his requirements: he announced his intention of transferring the construction of fortifications to [Major-General Fritz] Todt, as the Army's engineer troops were incompetent.

The result was renewed ill-feeling on both sides. The Führer must, in my view, have known of the existence of the construction programme and of its planned rate of progress because Blomberg had briefed him about it in the summer of 1937. The truth was that it no longer fitted in with his own private political ambitions; hence his irritation and the intervention.

On 20th May, Czechoslovakia for no reason at all and quite out of the blue announced the temporary mobilisation of her Army, which could only be intended for Germany's edification. Hitler returned to Berlin full of new plans and decisions. He announced he had no intention of accepting this renewed provocation from Czechoslovakia lying down or of letting them get away with it; he demanded we should put ourselves on a war footing as quickly as possible, a demand which found tangible expression in his alteration of the directive's opening sentence to read:

> It is my unalterable decision to smash Czechoslovakia by military action in the near future.

64

The Commander-in-Chief of the Army was at once warned verbally of these new orders, which were then confirmed by the directive itself.

At the same time, the construction of the fortifications in the west—the 'West Wall'—was transferred to Todt, the Inspector-General of Roadbuilding; he was directed to accelerate the construction programme to top speed, in accordance with the military and tactical plans and principles drawn up by the engineer troops, employing for this task the construction squads which had built the autobahns. The target was to build within eighteen months ten thousand concrete structures of every kind from the most massive fortifications down to the smallest bunkers, while by the autumn of 1938 five thousand small bunkers were to have been built to the designs which Hitler himself had drawn up, to afford protection against mortar and heavy shrapnel, mainly concentrated along the sector between Karlsruhe and Aix-la-Chapelle.

After he had issued all the most important orders—resulting in much head-shaking and further denigration of the OKW at the War Office—Hitler witnessed firing trials at Jüterbog where various sizes of concrete structures were subjected to heavy field-howitzer and mortar fire to test the ability of the concrete thicknesses he himself had decreed to withstand the bombardment. Afterwards, in the mess, he addressed the Army's commanding generals who had met to witness the trials; his aim, as he told me, was to counteract with hard and objective criticism the defeatist talk of Beck's memorandum on the military potential of our prospective enemies and of ourselves. His friend von Reichenau, who still enjoyed a close personal friendship with Hitler, had informed him that Brauchitsch had had the Beck memorandum read out to the commanding generals during a conference, and it had left a decidedly unfavourable impression on them; this was clearly Reichenau's own contribution to the campaign against the Commander-in-Chief of the Army: Reichenau and Guderian were vying with each other to see who could denigrate Brauchitsch the more.

The Führer's speech was quite adroit and convincingly revealed certain vulnerable points in the memorandum; in any event it was a cutting criticism of the General Staff and of its Chief in particular, who accordingly applied to resign his office as he 'no longer felt able to guide the training of General Staff officers'. On 30th September Beck was relieved of his office and Halder took his place.

The Commander-in-Chief of the Army requested that Beck be given the command of an Army Group, but the Führer categorically refused: Beck, in his view, had been 'too intellectual' to be Chief of General Staff; Beck was seen as an incorrigible defeatist and an obstacle to his plans, and perhaps above all he was recognised as the evil genius who had so often fouled his relations with Brauchitsch. From what I had seen myself, I was able to concur unreservedly with Hitler's judgment only on this last score.

I wept no tears over Beck in view of the shameless way he had treated me; I was always the first to recognise his great virtues, and I would never have thought him capable of selling his soul to treasonable intriguers as early as 1938, or of being their spiritual leader from that point on. One can seek his motives only in his injured vanity and his abysmal hatred of Hitler; that was why this formerly impeccable officer made common cause with our enemies and stiffened their resolve while awaiting our overthrow, something Beck was impotent to bring about himself. He was no leader, as he was to show as a conspirator by his pathetic behaviour when there was still time to act and when the plot—even though it had gone wrong—demanded a man of action and not the *cunctator* that he has always been; witness his three futile attempts at putting a bullet into his own head while sitting in a chair!

For the War Office and the OKW the summer of 1938 was taken up with preliminary planning for the Czechoslovakian contingency (code-named the *Green* contingency). The difficulties involved in the exercise were primarily of a logistical nature: how could the man-power and equipment of forty incomplete divisions (including Austria's) be assembled for the attack without the least suggestion of mobilisation, which Hitler had expressly forbidden?

The primary method was to hold large-scale 'manœuvres' in Silesia, Saxony and Bavaria, with the successive call-up of several age-groups of reservists without releasing any of them before the manœuvres had ended; the divisions were raised on the troop training grounds, while the Reich Labour Service was mobilised to man the positions in the west. Every imaginable but incon-spicuous makeshift had to be exploited: hastily improvised ammuni-tion and supply columns were camouflaged as being connected with the manœuvres, and the railway movements as being linked with the Reich Party Rally. In retrospect one can only admire the Army's achievement in laying all this on: under Halder, the General Staff achieved the seemingly impossible without exciting the least suspicion or allowing anybody to detect what really lay behind these 'manœuvre' preparations. For sheer ingenuity they could not be beaten; Hitler himself suggested many of the ideas and he was kept constantly up to date by the Commander-in-Chief of the Army about how things were going.

In August Halder took the opportunity of a voyage on the [Führer's yacht] *Grille* on the occasion of a review of the fleet to brief the Führer and myself from a map on his actual operational plan. The Führer asked numerous questions but did not express any particular opinion; he asked for a map to be prepared showing all the dispositions and how our forces were to be deployed, and for a brief memorandum on the probable sequence of events. He was particularly interested in those points of the enemy's frontier fortifications where it was planned to break through, as he had made a careful study of their value and their weaknesses. There were a number of differences of opinion on this score, particularly over the use of medium artillery, of which we had only a modest quantity, and over the armoured forces and the airborne operations. The briefing conference ended without either a decisive yes or a clear no from him: he [Hitler] wanted to chew it all over again at his leisure. Halder was as wise to him as ever and at once turned over to him the map and all his notes, with a request that a decision should be reached shortly as the orders would have to be issued to the various Armies.

Upon his return to Berlin, the Führer gave me his views and asked me to pass them on to Brauchitsch. After a certain amount of to-ing and fro-ing with me, he announced that while by and large he was in agreement with the plan, he was forced on principle to object to the plan for employing the armoured groups, which was all wrong, and which he wanted to see changed to provide for them to link up and lunge towards Prague from the south-west, up through Pilsen. Halder told me he refused to make such an alteration, because our very weakness in medium artillery would oblige us to fragment our armoured forces to ensure that our infantry could break through the crucial points. I was unable to argue with Halder's logic, but could perforce only comply with my instructions from Hitler; I advised Brauchitsch to talk it over with the Führer himself, but he refrained from doing so.

The Führer, moreover, had again migrated to Berchtesgaden during the second half of August, It was at this time that [Mr. Neville] Chamberlain made his first historic visit to the Führer at the Berghof, and I and our Foreign Secretary [von Ribbentrop] were both summoned to attend. For the British Prime Minister to pay a visit seemed to me at the time to be a most unusual event. The old gentleman had actually flown over from London to Munich;

apparently it was the first time he had ever flown anywhere. The so-called 'German problems' and the maintenance of peace were of course high on the agenda. As always during political functions I was merely the representative of the Armed Forces summoned for the guest's reception and departure, and I took no part in the talks; my presence seemed very superfluous to me, however interesting it was for me to get to know Europe's leading statesmen—or at least to see them and exchange a few conventional words in conversation with them. I left the Berghof soon after Chamberlain; it was apparent that Hitler had not been satisfied by the result.

During the first half of September, the annual Reich Party Rally took place, only this time it served simultaneously to camouflage our troops' concentration in the areas of the 'manœuvres' which had themselves been so planned that at one time the general trend of the manœuvres would seem to be towards the Czech frontier, while at another time it would be in the opposite direction.

Shortly before, I and Major von Lossberg had delivered to the Führer in his home in Munich the exact timetable of events for the *Green* contingency [operations against Czechoslovakia]; the timetable laid down in detail for the Army and Air Force all the steps to be taken, the troop movements and the orders to be issued, etc., starting with the day of the attack, D-day, and working backwards.

This timetable was governed by two characteristic considerations:

1. At what point did it become impossible to camouflage our troop movements any longer?
2. How late could the issue of an order halting troop movements be left?

This calendar of deadlines would serve as a guide to Hitler as he guided his diplomatic measures in harmony with the unrolling skein of the military master plan.

I showed him how the timetable would work (it had been formulated by Jodl in close collaboration with the fighting services). According to the plan, Hitler had only to fix the date for D-day and the whole plan would tick smoothly over like clockwork; it would be possible each day to see what was due to happen and when.

Hitler was delighted with this 'programme' and dismissed us both from his presence without further ado. That was the first time I ever saw the inside of his modest flat. After a brief meal in a nearby restaurant, Lossberg and I drove back that same afternoon along the autobahn to Berlin; it had been an exacting day.

At the [Nuremberg] Party Rally, which I had been required to attend this year as well, Hitler inquired of me whether the General Staff had amended its operational plan in accordance with his wishes. I telephoned Halder and he said they had not: they had not been able to amend it in time, as the orders had had to go out. I asked Hitler for permission to fly to Berlin to speak with Brauchitsch personally; I made the excuse that for security reasons it would be imprudent to use the telephone. I determined on no account to return to Nuremberg without having achieved my purpose. I spoke alone with Brauchitsch and he saw the position in which we both now found ourselves; he promised to speak at once with Halder along these lines. But when I called on him two hours later to pick up his final decision for my flight back to Nuremberg, he rejected any prospect of making any alterations; that was quite impossible, and I would have to tell Hitler that.

I already knew better of the Führer than that, and I knew he would not be satisfied with that answer; and that was how things turned out. Brauchitsch and Halder were directed to present themselves to him in Nuremberg next day. The talks between them began in the '*Deutscher Hof*' hotel just before midnight and lasted several hours: Hitler's idea was to bring these recalcitrants round by calmly and patiently lecturing them in detail on the use of modern battle cavalry (in other words armoured formations); I had already suggested a perfectly viable compromise solution to them. I deplored the waste of so much time, particularly at night, on this as I could predict that in the end all their opposition and all their unjustified obstinacy were bound to collapse in defeat, with a consequent fresh loss of prestige for both of them. By three o'clock it was too late: Hitler lost his patience and ordered them categorically to unite the armoured formations as he had required and use them as a combined force in the break-through attack through Pilsen. Coldly and sullenly he dismissed the gentlemen from his presence.

As we were quenching our thirsts in the vestibule after losing this battle, Halder asked me in a voice quivering with indignation: 'What's he really after?' I was so irritated that I retorted: 'If you really haven't found out yet, then you have my sympathy.'

Only now did Brauchitsch intervene to make amends. The new orders were at once drawn up and Hitler's demands were fully met. As Halder was writing out the orders, I could only ask Brauchitsch: 'Why do you fight with him, when you know that the battle is lost before it's begun? Nobody thinks there is going to be any war over this, so the whole thing wasn't worth all that bitter rearguard action. You are throwing down your trumps in quite futile gestures and in the end you only have to give in just the same; and then when it really is a matter of life and death your opposition will lack the necessary authority to be effective.'

I have described this episode in detail only because it illustrates in one characteristic example (a controversy that was not even of the first order) the symptoms of the conditions under which we had to work with Hitler. If he once got an idea into his head, no man on earth could ever shake him out of it; he always had his way, whether it was approved or disapproved by his advisers.

During the second half of September [in fact, on 22nd to 23rd September, 1938] Chamberlain paid a second visit to us, this time at Godesberg on the Rhine. Brauchitsch had provided me with Stülpnagel as an observer in case military measures were called for, so at least I had somebody to talk to during the political discussions, which went on for hours on end and from which we soldiers were always excluded. Late that afternoon there was a dangerous element of tension in consequence of a telegram from Prague reporting the mobilisation of the Czech Army. While I telephoned Jodl and arranged for him to clarify the position with our military attaché in Prague, Hitler dictated a letter to the British Prime Minister to the effect that he was adopting complete freedom of action and was prepared if necessary to safeguard German interests by force of arms, should the current talks be vitiated by the Czech mobilisation. Fortunately, the reports coming in to that effect were refuted both by Jodl and by Chamberlain himself, with the result that the talks were resumed next day and ended, if not with a final solution, at least with the creation of a suitable basis for avoiding war. After dusk that evening we flew back to Berlin making a detour round the thunderstorms raging all over the country; it was an incomparable spectacle to see the electric discharges from some ten thousand feet up, with the lightning streaking out both level with and below our plane.

On the next day I drove out to a deer rutting as the guest of Director Luenitsch [General Manager] of *A.E.G.*, the General Electric Company, and on the second day at J., near Berlin, I brought down the strongest deer of my life; to me it seemed a good omen for the imminent solution of the Czech question.

As is well known, it was Mussolini's intervention that finally brought about the Munich talks between the four statesmen in the

Führer's building at Königlicher Platz at the end of September. The only statesman I did not already know at the reception was M. Daladier to whom the French Ambassador François-Poncet introduced me while we all partook of a small standing buffet. I was left out of the talks, although Göring did take part in them. The result [i.e. the seceding to Germany of the Sudetenland] is well known, but I do not believe it is generally known that it was Daladier who finally removed the British Prime Minister's obdurate resistance over the Sudeten question by saying: '*We won't tolerate war over this, the Czechs will just have to give way. We will simply have to force them to accept the cession.*' Schmundt took all that down as they went along.

At the ambassadors' conference where the territories to be transferred were decided upon, our military High Command *was* represented because even though the ethnic and language frontiers were to be the guiding factors, the new strategic frontier and the amputation of the Czech frontier fortifications played quite a considerable military rôle: these were the instructions I gave, and through the medium of my observer they served as a term of reference for our Foreign Office representatives. The exceedingly valuable services performed by François-Poncet in ensuring the acceptance of the German demands, and the humorous threats he uttered to the others —'Now then, hurry up! The Old Man (Hitler) is already on his way to Berlin'—are all history now. The fact was that France had no intention of going to war over Germany's eastern problems; Hitler's recognition of this and his unshakeable faith in France's supineness—he had repeatedly reassured them he would never go to war with them over Alsace-Lorraine—were disastrous for the outcome of his diplomacy in the Polish problem, for after Munich England began to think quite differently and forced the reluctant French to join her camp.

I am convinced that the swift progress we had made since the summer of 1938 with the construction of our western fortifications, and the scale of the manpower and material effort we had devoted to them, both had a major hand in influencing the French in their reappraisal of the treaty of alliance they had guaranteed Czechoslovakia*. The western fortifications could hardly remain concealed from the French, and indeed they were not intended to; they obviously gained enormously in effect as their defensive value was demonstrated during the autumn of 1938: only a very few divisions

* In Keitel's original manuscript there follow further details on the construction the West Wall; these have been omitted by the Editor.

were required to man these fortifications, reinforced by some three hundred thousand men of the Reich Labour Service and improvised reserve units, and they were equipped only with grossly inadequate weapons and armaments. The whole thing was only one vast bluff. By means of bonuses, day- and night-shifts and a magnificent effort from the men, maximum output was obtained. Each week Todt had to report how many complete bunkers had been poured, and the result was that by 1st October, 1938, the required number of almost five thousand fortification sites—admittedly only finished in the rough—was attained.

As early as May I had accompanied the Führer on a tour of inspection of the construction sites, which at that time had still been a purely Army engineering project. The construction programme was under the overall command of the headquarters of the Second Army Group in Kassel. At my own suggestion, General Adam, one of Blomberg's protégés and previously Commandant of the Military Academy in Berlin, had been appointed successor to Ritter von Leeb as Commander-in-Chief of the Second Army Group on 1st April, 1938. I had thought at the time that such a competent and gifted general—before Beck he had been Chief of the General Staff—should not be tied to the Military Academy, and had placed him at Brauchitsch's disposal.

Adam welcomed the Führer in his capacity as 'Commander-in-Chief West' and made an introductory speech on the prospects of defending the western front in view of the troops the War Office had allocated to him and of the current progress that had been made with the construction of the fortifications. According to what Adam himself afterwards told me, his comments were in line with the view currently held by Beck, the then Chief of the General Staff; he admitted the express intention of forcefully exposing the vulnerability of the whole system and the impossibility of offering an effective resistance west of the Rhine for more than a few days. The main objective in all this was to dissuade Hitler at any cost from his plans for an attack on Czechoslovakia, which were already anticipated and probably not entirely unknown.

General Adam, who had been earmarked as Commander-in-Chief for the western front, gladly seized the opportunity to hint that he wanted a considerable reinforcement of his undoubtedly inadequate forces; what commander-in-chief, indeed, would not, as one can never have too many troops? But he also took it upon himself to paint his predicament in really drastic terms and, moreover, in his own peculiar language which was never exactly diplomatic.

The result was a new outburst from Hitler, who rejected the complaints out of hand; it was a highly embarrassing situation, which was hardly alleviated when Hitler broke off General Adam's speech with an abrupt 'Thank you' and dismissed him from his presence. I was obliged to stand there and listen to him ranting at me that this general had been a bad disappointment to him, and he would have to go; he had no use for generals like these who had no faith in their mission from the very outset. My protests that that was not what Adam had meant, that he had only wanted to thrash out as many of his problems as possible, and that he was one of our most competent generals, were of no avail; Brauchitsch had the same lecture from him, and this outstanding soldier was pensioned off.

We drove along the frontier in a few long hops. At several places Hitler ordered defence works to be moved right up to the political frontier, for example at Aix-la-Chapelle, Saarbrücken, and so on. Hitler intervened personally everywhere, declaring that the General Staff's ideas were wrong and misconceived.

At the end of August [in fact from 27th to 29th August, 1938] I accompanied Hitler on a second tour of the West Wall, now in a very advanced state of completion. General von Witzleben accompanied us, receiving numerous detailed instructions for further improvements, which were immediately passed on to Todt as orders. The Army was now responsible only for the tactical survey and allocation of the sites and for the design of the battle installations. The tour served a simultaneous second purpose: as a propaganda deterrent to France.

Very soon after Munich it became clear to me that while Hitler was perfectly happy with the political victory he had scored over Britain, he had had to forgo the strategic solution of the Czechoslovakian problem, for he had originally resolved to oblige Czechoslovakia to join the orbit of the Greater German Reich in close military alliance either by treaty obligations or, if this should prove impossible, by force of arms.

As it became increasingly evident that there was no prospect of winning over Czechoslovakia by peaceful means, as a result of the firm backing she was now enjoying from the European powers, a plan began to take shape late in October 1938 to eliminate the country as an enemy state by force of arms at the very first opportunity; she was already greatly weakened by the loss of her frontier fortifications. Accordingly, towards the end of October, preliminary directives were issued for the maintenance of military readiness for

73

the time when all the political requirements would—one way or the other—obtain, by exploitation of the widely-publicised independence struggle of Slovakia.

So the final elimination of the Czech question had only really been shelved, when General Jodl left the High Command at the end of October to take up his active appointment as an artillery unit commander in Vienna. Had I had any idea that there was a war in the offing, I would never have let him go like that. After the calamity with General von Viebahn in March and April, I decided to go without a replacement for Jodl as chief of the operations staff and had his work transferred to Colonel Warlimont, head of the national defence department, in close conjunction with myself.

The Czech frontier fortifications [in the area which had been seceded to us] aroused great interest not only among us soldiers, but naturally in Hitler as well; they had been constructed on the model of the French Maginot line under the supervision of French construction engineers. We were greatly surprised by the strength of the larger blockhouses and gun emplacements; a number of firing trials took place in the Führer's presence, with the fortifications being bombarded by our own standard artillery pieces. Most surprising was the penetrating power displayed by the 88-millimetre anti-aircraft guns, which were able to smash right through the normal bunkers at a point-blank range of two thousand yards, a function—it should be said—which the Führer had required of them in advance; so he had been right to order their use in this way.*

Early in November 1938, after the High Command had been instructed to draw up General Staff studies on the re-occupation of Danzig and Memel in case circumstances should conspire to favour the execution of such a plan, I had to lay on a tour of inspection of the eastern fortifications. He [Hitler] told me that he desired to form a picture of the strength of our fortifications against Poland: nobody could tell, he explained, whether the Danzig affair—and the return of Danzig to the Reich was his unshakeable objective—might not blow up into a conflict with Poland itself. I asked Brauchitsch to arrange for such a tour of inspection, and said that it would be quite out of the question for him to refrain from taking part himself, as he had on the two previous tours in the west; his method of withdrawing into the background whenever it was a matter of sidestepping outside interference or of avoiding becoming embroiled in unseemly disputes, had long dawned upon me and I did not like it,

---

* In Keitel's original manuscript there follow further details on the construction of the West Wall; these have been omitted by the Editor.

because then they could fight it all out with me afterwards and accuse me of not having represented the Army's interests actively enough.

My forebodings were more than justified: courageously though the engineer General Foerster defended the progress made largely under his command on the major fortification works at the bend in the Oder and Warta rivers, Hitler could not find a kind word to say about any of them: these enormous projects were 'useless mantraps', with no firepower and only one or two pathetic little machine-gun turrets, and so on. The final outcome was the dismissal of General Foerster from his command; it took a lot of trouble and a personal request from me to the Führer, to have him appointed commanding general of the Sixth Army Corps in Münster.

Even so, the East Wall preoccupied Hitler so much during that winter that some time later he inspected the Oder front from Breslau down to Frankfurt-on-Oder, only this time without me. The embankment fortifications were the cause of the upset this time because they were clearly visible to the enemy from some way off. But in this instance, too, Hitler was subsequently proved right during our French campaign, for it took only one direct hit from our 88-millimetre artillery to smash each of the French concrete blockhouses visible on the opposite bank of the river.

In any event, despite all the vexations they caused the War Office, the intensified work on the eastern fortifications and East Prussia's special rôle (which I will not go into here) did give all of us the soothing feeling that we no longer had to reckon with the possibility of a war with Poland in the immediate future, always assuming, of course, that we were not directly attacked. The latter contingency was naturally not ruled out even by Hitler, as there was always the possibility that the Poles might come to Czechoslovakia's aid.

It was in this way that in the spring of 1939 the OKW's new 'Directive for Deployment and Battle' came into existence; in fact, it was really planned only for *defensive* purposes should Poland, aided and abetted by the Western Powers, decide to act against us, whether as the result of or in connection with the Danzig problem.

For the sake of historical accuracy I must reiterate that this directive was of a purely *defensive* nature. I believe that Brauchitsch has already borne this out in the witness box.

With my appointment as chief of the OKW I ceased to be a free man: any liberty to dispose of my time as I pleased and to order my family affairs as I wished had to give way to my permanent dependence on Hitler and the unpredictable claims he made on my time. How often I have had unexpectedly to interrupt even my brief weekend leaves at Helmscherode or hunting expeditions in Pomerania to report to him, more often because of some petty whim of his than for any real reason. Readily though leave and even vitally necessary journeys from the Führer's headquarters to Berlin were granted me, the passes were just as ruthlessly rescinded and I was recalled again. Whether I was myself partially to blame because of my strongly developed sense of duty, or whether it was because Hitler's adjutants' office hesitated to put a brake on these demands, I do not know; unfortunately, I never found out what was in the air until I arrived. Usually it was something that had happened which only I could sort out, and as a rule it was nothing particularly delectable.

When could I ever devote a few leisure hours to my wife or children? For me there was peace no longer, even though there was still no war to tie me to headquarters. My wife has borne it all in the most admirable fashion. What kind of husband and father could I be to her and our children, coming home edgy and irritable as I now invariably did? Now that we no longer had to count every penny, and now that we could get theatre tickets every week and afford other luxuries too, I had no time for these things. I was tied to my desk nearly every evening, plodding through the mountains of work that had accumulated during the day. I used to get home dead tired and drop straight off to sleep.

On top of all this, I felt responsible now not only for Helmscherode and my married sister at Wehrkirch, but for the Blomberg children too: they had nobody apart from me to turn to, now that their father was abroad.

At first Blomberg wrote to me regularly, often with numerous requests all of which I was happy to see to. Some weeks after his departure, I received a telegram from him in Italy: 'Send my son Axel out to me at once with passport and foreign currency for travel expenses, to discuss vital matters with me.'

I called the son in to see me—he was an Air Force lieutenant—and sent him out to his father. On his return eight days later, he brought me a letter his father had written after lengthy discussions with him. In this letter, he asked me to break it to Hitler that he now wanted to separate from his wife, although he would only put this plan into effect if the Führer would take him into his favour again and reinstate him. I asked the Führer to read the letter for himself; as

I had expected, he rejected the condition out of hand, pointing out that at the time he had enjoined him to have the marriage annulled at once. Blomberg had turned that down saying it was an impossible demand to make of him, said Hitler, so each had gone his own way and the clock could not now be put back. Carefully though I broke this to Blomberg, he has always thought I contrived Hitler's refusal out of sheer selfishness on my part in order not to forfeit my position as Chief of the High Command. I learned all this from Axel Blomberg only later. My own reassurances to the contrary were not believed, and through no fault of my own a growing strain was placed on our hitherto friendly relations.

The marriage of our children [Karl-Heinz Keitel and Dorothea von Blomberg] took place in May. I had to stand in for both fathers, and after the church wedding I gave a wedding banquet in the main hall of the War Ministry building, while the eve-of-wedding party itself was held in our home, a very private affair.

Hans-Georg had passed his school-leaving examination with flying colours in the Easter term of 1938, but his teachers assessed his character and conduct more highly than his knowledge of ancient languages, which were his one great weakness. When he decided to leave home to become a soldier, my wife took it very hard; my wife was now alone most of the day, as both our daughters had their own careers. Nona did work at home in the evenings, but Erika liked going to parties, theatres and the cinema, and she had a very large circle of friends.

Diverse and interesting though all the official functions were for my wife and myself, they were after all only in the line of duty, and they cost us many an evening that we would have spent quite differently had we been free to choose; but all that was now inevitably bound up with my office. We formed close friendships neither with the families of the high state officials nor with those of the Party leaders, let alone with the diplomatic corps. Either one went out to some outside function, or one had to entertain official guests oneself, and that was as far as it went. My wife was reputed to be an expert in keeping her mouth shut and in self-effacement; they said I was as 'slippery as an eel', and they soon gave up any endeavour to communicate or converse with me. For the diplomatic corps I was tedious and sphinx-like, quite the opposite of my predecessor Reichenau who had liked to play first violin in that particular orchestra.

By February 1939 the machinations of the Czechs were beginning to intensify: the press published increasingly frequent reports of

77

border incidents and of excesses committed against the German minorities in Bohemia and Moravia. Official Notes were sent to Prague, and our ambassador [Friedrich Eisenlohr] was recalled to Berlin as well as our military attaché, Colonel Toussaint.

The Führer repeatedly announced that he had put up with as much as he could stand and did not intend to stand impotently by much longer. I gathered that the so-called 'cleaning up' of rump Czechoslovakia was drawing near. Although when I asked the Führer he would neither admit his ultimate intentions nor give me any kind of date, I took the necessary steps to see that the War Office was assured of being able to unleash a swift and sudden invasion should the need arise. In my presence, the Führer called in Brauchitsch, talked about the increasingly intolerable position of the German minorities in Czechoslovakia and announced that he had resolved upon military intervention, which he termed 'a pacification operation'; it would certainly not require any military conscription over and above that provided for in the orders drawn up in the autumn of 1938. As we soldiers—and even I—learned nothing further of the diplomatic overtures between Prague and Berlin than we were told by our military attaché, we were obliged to fall back upon conjecture; we were banking on the same kind of diplomatic surprises as we had witnessed several times before.

I put my own money on 'the Ides of March': apart from 1937 it had always been the date since 1933 that Adolf Hitler had chosen to act on. Was it always coincidence, or was it superstition? I am inclined to believe the latter, for Hitler himself often referred to it.

Sure enough, on 12th March [1939], the advance orders went out to the army and air force to stand by for a possible invasion of Czechoslovakia at six o'clock on the morning of 15th March; no forces were to approach within six miles of the frontier before then. None of us soldiers learned what circumstances were to be invoked for the unleashing of such an attack.

When I reported to the Führer at the Reich Chancellery at mid-day on 14th March to collect his instructions for the armed forces, whose readiness next day had been assured in accordance with his orders, he mentioned just briefly to me that President Hacha had the day before announced his intention of coming for discussions on the crisis, and he was expecting him to arrive in Berlin that evening. I asked for his permission to warn the War Office at once that in these circumstances the invasion was to be postponed for the time being. Hitler firmly rejected my suggestion and explained to me that come what may he was still planning to march into Czechoslovakia

78

next day—whatever the outcome of the talks with the Czech president might be. Nevertheless I was instructed to place myself at his disposal at nine o'clock that evening at the Reich Chancellery, so that I could issue to the War Office and Air Force High Command his executive orders for the invasion to begin.

I arrived at the Reich Chancellery shortly before nine o'clock; Hitler had just risen from the dinner table and his guests were assembling in the drawing room to see the film '*Ein hoffnungsloser Fall*' (A Hopeless Case). Hitler invited me to sit next to him, as Hacha was not due to arrive until ten o'clock. Considering the circumstances, I felt properly out of place in this milieu; within eight or ten hours the first shots would be being exchanged, and I was gravely disturbed.

At ten o'clock [Foreign Secretary] Ribbentrop announced Hacha's arrival at Bellevue Castle; the Führer replied that he was going to let the old gentleman rest and recover for two hours; he would send for him at midnight. That was equally incomprehensible to me; why was he doing that? Was this premeditated, political diplomacy?

Hacha of course could not have known that no sooner had dusk fallen that evening, 14th March, than the '*Adolf Hitler*' SS-body-guard troops had already invaded the Moravian Ostrau strip to safeguard the modern steel mill at Witkowitz against seizure by the Poles; we still had no reports on how this operation had gone.

At midnight Hacha arrived, accompanied by his Foreign Secretary [Chvalkovsky] and the Czech Minister in Berlin [Mastny]; they were received by Hitler and a large company in the Führer's study at the new Reich Chancellery building. Göring was there as well. After an introductory dialogue, during which Hacha delivered himself of a long-winded description of his career in the Austrian civil service—a situation which in my mental turmoil I again failed to comprehend—Hitler interrupted him to say that in view of the lateness of the hour he was obliged to come round to the political questions which were the reasons for Hacha's presence. We were asked to withdraw. Twice I was obliged briefly to interrupt the discussions between the statesmen (I believe that apart from them only Ribbentrop was present, with Hewel to take the minutes). The first occasion was when I had to hand in a brief note I had written to the effect that Witkowitz had been occupied by the Bodyguard troops without a struggle; Hitler read it and nodded his satisfaction. The second time was to deliver a warning about the lateness of the hour; the Army was asking for a final decision on whether they were to march or not. I was dismissed abruptly with the reply that it was still only two o'clock and the order would be issued before four.

Some time later Göring and I were called back in again. The gentlemen were standing round the table and Hitler was telling Hacha that it was up to him to decide what he intended to do; Keitel would confirm that our troops were already on the march and would be crossing the frontier at six o'clock, and he—Hacha—alone had it in his power to decide whether blood would be shed or his country be peacefully occupied. Hacha begged for a respite, as he had to telephone his government in Prague, and could he be given a telephone line to them? Would Hitler see that the troop movements were halted at once? Hitler refused: I would confirm, he said, that that was now impossible as our troops were already approaching the frontier. Before I could open my mouth, Göring intervened to announce that his Air Force would be appearing over Prague at dawn, and he could not change that now; it was up to Hacha whether there would be any bombing or not. Under this great pressure, Hacha explained that he wanted to avoid bloodshed at any cost and turned to me to ask how he could contact his country's garrisons and frontier troops and warn them of the German invasion, so that he could forbid them to open fire.

I offered to draft a telegram to that effect addressed to all his commanders and garrison headquarters at once, for him to send to Prague. When I had finished it, Göring took it out of my hands and accompanied Hacha to a telephone where he was given a line to Prague. I went to the Führer and asked him to issue the War Office with an immediate executive order for the invasion, which should contain a clear instruction not to open fire, in similar vein to the instructions issued to the Czech army; if nevertheless there were signs of resistance, immediate attempts were to be made to negotiate, and force of arms was to be used only as a last resort.

This order was passed to the Army at three o'clock, which left three clear hours for its complete distribution. It was a great weight off the minds of us soldiers; Brauchitsch and I admitted to each other how relieved we were at this outcome. In the interval, Hacha had dictated his instructions through to Prague and I saw him afterwards, very exhausted, in the ante-room of the Führer's study, with Doctor Morell fussing over him. I felt enormously sorry for the old man and I walked over to him and reassured him that I was convinced there would be no shooting at all on the German side, as orders to that effect had now been issued, and I had no doubts that the Czech army would comply with the cease-fire and their orders not

80

to offer resistance. In the meantime the two Foreign Secretaries had drafted a protocol of the agreement, the signing of which followed at a further gathering in Hitler's study.

After the War Office—I think it was Brauchitsch himself—had confirmed to me that all the orders had been issued, I reported to Hitler and asked if I might retire; I would report to him next morning in good time to accompany him to his special train. I had ordered Lieutenant-Colonel Zeitzler of the OKW operations staff to accompany me on the journey to the Czech frontier; there were no further dispositions for me to make as the overall direction of the occupation was solely the responsibility of the War Office, whose reports to the Führer Zeitzler had to collect and summarise for me from time to time.

From the frontier onwards we drove in a long convoy of motor cars along the broad road to Prague; very shortly we came across the marching columns of our army. It was cold and wintry, there were snow drifts and black ice, and the mobile columns with their lorries and guns had to overcome the most formidable obstacles to their progress, particularly whenever our convoy wanted to overtake them.

We reached the outskirts of Prague as dusk was falling, simultaneously with the first troop units, and escorted by a mobile company we drove down the Hradshin to where we were to be billeted. A cold supper was bought for us in the town as we had brought nothing with us: cold Prague ham, bread rolls, butter, cheese, fruit and Pilsner beer; it is the only time I ever saw Hitler drinking a tiny glass of beer. It tasted wonderful to us.

I had to share an overnight room with my adjutant, but I was compensated next morning by the fabulous view over the city of Prague, which I still remembered from my honeymoon. The German Air Force's propaganda fly-past over Prague—scheduled for 16th March—had to be abandoned because of fog. Towards midday Hitler received the Czech government to accept their declaration of loyalty; at their head was President Hacha, who had reached his presidential palace by special train from Berlin only some hours after us, to learn upon his arrival that the Führer had already installed himself in another wing of the official residence.

Apart from the various official receptions and the State ceremony for the declaration of the Protectorate on the 16th, at which I was called upon to represent the armed forces, Hitler had no time for me, except when he received the brief reports our War Office sent in. I

81

felt very superfluous most of the day; everybody was talking politics and I was kept out of that on principle.

On 17th March we drove with a military escort through Brünn to Vienna. We stopped over at Brünn to have a look at the strangely beautiful old Town Hall there, which made a particularly vivid impression on me with its ancient conference chamber lit up by candles. In addition to the crowds of curious sightseers, several thousand native Germans had poured into the market square and they were making a tremendous din. To their enthusiastic acclaim the Führer inspected a German guard of honour which had been drawn up on the square.

Our motor journey ended that evening in Vienna, after proceeding right across Czechoslovakia; in Vienna the ovations of March 1938 in front of the Imperial Hotel were repeated all over again. Down in the vestibule I met Freiherr von Neurath who had been called upon by the Führer to accept the office of 'Protector of Bohemia and Moravia'; I learned of this from Neurath himself and I gained the impression that he found the prospect rather unedifying.

A delegation had arrived in Vienna from the new government of the independent Slovak state, consisting of President Tiso, Minister of the Interior Durczansky, and Tuka who was both Foreign Secretary and War Minister combined. The Führer had decided that von Ribbentrop should draw up a Security Zone Treaty with them and that I was to work out the military clauses basic to it. Ribbentrop and I met the Slovak party late that evening—it was already approaching midnight—in the offices attached to the Gauleiter's residence in Vienna. In accordance with my instructions from Hitler, I outlined the purpose and import of the 'security zone' which was to be occupied by German troops, just as Hitler had personally sketched it for me on the map: it took in a frontier strip about twelve to fifteen miles wide running in Slovak territory along the Czech border on both sides of the Vaag valley, and included a large troop training ground and a modern underground weapons factory operated by the former Czecho-Slovak state.

It was not easy for me to justify our armed forces' insistence on sovereign military rights and on stationing army and air force contingents there, in the eyes of these gentlemen (who probably recognised the significance of this frontier strip for their own national defence), nor was it easy to persuade them that all this was being done for Slovakia's own protection. Nevertheless, I must have been able to meet the objections the Slovaks raised during their lengthy and often critical questioning to their satisfaction, for even though

82

they were not wholly convinced, I did obtain their approval. I attribute this in the first instance to old Tuka, who idolised the Führer and helped to obviate the mistrust of the other two ministers. While Ribbentrop began to draft the treaty with the Slovaks, I drove back to the hotel to report my success to Hitler; I told him that the gentlemen would greatly appreciate an opportunity of being received by Hitler himself; at first he flatly refused, saying that it was already long past midnight and he was tired besides. But as I had promised Tiso and Tuka that I would arrange the audience for them, I insisted that he should see the Slovaks for ten minutes at least, and he finally agreed. Ribbentrop of course took his own time in coming, with the result that the audience finally took place at two o'clock in the morning; it ended a quarter of an hour later, after the Führer had smoothed over some of their last misgivings. The security zone was promised to us and that same night the agreement was signed by von Ribbentrop and the gentlemen.*

The Führer's Birthday [on 20th April] 1939 was celebrated as usual with a major military parade after the usual morning reception for the senior military commanders. The parade lasted for over three hours, a magnificent spectacle in which all three branches of the armed forces and the Waffen-SS as well were represented. At Hitler's express request, our newest medium artillery, heavy tank guns, ultra-modern anti-aircraft guns, air force searchlight units and the like were paraded while fighter and bomber-squadrons roared overhead along the East-West axis [Brandenburg Chaussée] from the direction of the Brandenburg Gate. President Hacha, who was accompanied by Reich Protector von Neurath, was the Führer's most honoured guest, and he was accorded all the honours due to a Head of State; the diplomatic corps was mustered to a man.†

My hopes that, now that the Czech problem had finally been solved, the armed forces would be granted the respite until 1943 they had so solemnly and so often been promised for their fundamental organisational overhaul were doomed to disappointment. An army is not a weapon for improvisation: the raising of an officer- and NCO-corps and its education and internal consolidation are the only foundations upon which any army like the one we had in 1914 can be built. Hitler's belief that National Socialist teaching could be

* In Keitel's original manuscript there follow details of the return journey to Berlin, via Breslau; these have been omitted by the Editor.

† In Keitel's original manuscript there follow further family details and matters concerning the affairs of his estate at Helmscherode, especially on the restoration of the estate chapel; the latter is interesting as an instance of the field-marshal's continued firm religious convictions and protestant faith, despite Hitler's hostile attitude to the two great Christian faiths. The passage has been omitted by the Editor.

used to make up for a basic lack of ability—in other words of military acumen—has proved illusory. Nobody would deny that it is possible to perform miracles with fanatical enthusiasm; but just as in 1914 the student regiments were senselessly bled to death at Langemarck, the élite troops of the SS have paid the greatest price in human life since 1943, and to the least avail. What they really needed was a perfectly rounded officer corps; but that had been sacrificed by then, with no hope of its ever being replaced.

As early as April 1939 I became with increased frequency the target for comments by Hitler to the effect that the Polish problem was imperatively demanding a solution: what a tragedy it was, he said, that the sly old Marshal Pilsudski—with whom he had been able to sign a non-aggression pact—had died so prematurely; but the same might happen to him, Hitler, at any time. That was why he would have to try as soon as possible to resolve this intolerable position for Germany's future whereby east Prussia was geographically cut off from the rest of the Reich; he could not postpone this job until later, or bequeath it to his successor. You could now see, Hitler added, how dependent reasonable policies were on one man's existence: for Poland's present rulers were anything but inclined to follow the path the Marshal had laid down, as had become abundantly clear during the talks with the Polish Foreign Secretary, [Colonel] Beck. Beck, said Hitler, was pinning his hopes on England's assistance, although there was not the least doubt that as Britain had no economic interest in these purely domestic German affairs, she had no vital political interest either. Britain would take back her outstretched hand from Poland once she saw our resolve to remove this aftermath of the *Diktat* of Versailles, a condition which would be quite intolerable in the long run. He did not want a war with Poland over Danzig or the Corridor, but he who desired peace must prepare for war: that was the basis of all successful diplomacy.

While the mills of diplomacy began to grind in Warsaw, in London and in Paris, the Führer grew emboldened in his resolve to create a *fait accompli* one day over Danzig: surely, that neither could nor would give the major powers any cause to intervene on Poland's behalf, thereby permitting her to assail us by force of arms? Even so it was obviously our duty to prepare for such a contingency, namely that Poland would attack us on that pretext.

Accordingly, during May 1939, the Führer's directive—preparation for the *White* contingency—emerged, coupled with demands from Hitler to be ready by 1st September at the latest to go over to a war footing for a counter-attack on Poland should she prove

84

intransigent, and to elaborate a plan of action for our army and air force. As in the case of Czechoslovakia, the order meant we had to avoid any kind of mobilisation whatsoever, nor could we use the regulations drawn up for mobilisation, or count on the state of alert resulting from the application of the mobilisation plan. This in turn meant that everything had to be based on the army's peace-time strength, and on the possibilities afforded within this framework.

After the Führer had addressed his instructions to his commanders-in-chief, first of all verbally and in person, and then more formally by the basic directive referred to, he retired as was his wont to the seclusion of his residence at the Berghof. Naturally that hampered my work at the High Command quite considerably, for everything had to be sent up to me either by courier or via his military adjutants, if I were not to travel down to Berchtesgaden myself, something I usually endeavoured to accomplish in one day by plane.

In contrast to this, the Reich Chancellery had a permanent home at Berchtesgaden under Reichsminister Doctor Lammers, and the Party Chancellery a permanent residence in Munich; Göring also had a dwelling at the Berghof, and the Foreign Secretary an official residence at Fuschl, near Salzburg, which had been assigned to him by Hitler. Only the OKW, the High Command, lacked such a facility for its work at the time, although from the summer of 1940 onwards I was able to arrange for it to have some space partly in the Reich Chancellery quarters and partly in the barracks at Berchtesgaden. The result was an enforced physical detachment of the OKW from the real governmental nerve-centres and a lack of personal contact with the people who mattered, two circumstances which merely provided further encouragement to Hitler in his desire to make all his decisions himself and to sabotage any kind of community of effort.

I accordingly learned as good as nothing of our negotiations with either Poland or London, and of their bearing on the Danzig Corridor question, except when Hitler himself took the initiative during my conference visits to him, or I brought it home to him how deeply worried the Army and I were about the possibility of an armed conflict with Poland when our army's re-equipment programme was still at such an unsatisfactory stage. Again and again Hitler reassured me that he had no desire whatsoever for war with Poland—he would never let things go as far as that, even if France's intervention in the spirit of her eastern commitments really was likely to occur. He had made to France the most far-reaching offers, he said, and even publicly disavowed his interest in Alsace-Lorraine; that was probably

85

a guarantee which no other statesman than he could ever have justified to the German people; only he had the authority and the right to make such an offer.

Indeed, he even went so far as to entreat me not to tell the War Office of how his mind was working, as he feared they would then cease to apply themselves to planning for the Polish contingency with the gravity and intensity which were such a vital element of his diplomatic charade, as the 'concealed' war preparations being made in Germany could not be kept wholly secret from or unobserved by the Poles. I believed I knew the War Office's mentality and the General Staff's conscientiousness better than he, and I did not consider myself bound by his entreaties.

I believed Hitler, and I was taken in by his powers of verbal persuasion; I assumed that there would be a political solution, though not without the application of threats of military sanctions.

The summer of 1939 passed with feverish activity in the Army General Staff. The construction of the West Wall proceeded at an accelerated rate; in addition to construction firms and the Todt Organisation, virtually the whole Reich Labour Service and several Army divisions were employed on it, the latter two concentrating on earth-works, barbed-wire entanglements and the final fitting out of the rough concrete fortifications for the defence of Germany.

As was only natural, Hitler's final tour of inspection in August 1939—on which I accompanied him—was made as much for propaganda purposes as for inspecting actual construction progress, about which he had anyway had himself kept continuously informed with maps on which the bunkers that had been completed, were still under construction, or were being planned, had been marked in. He had studied these maps so thoroughly that during our tour of inspection he knew exactly what was still outstanding and where to find each of the fortifications in the terrain. Often one could only marvel at his memory and powers of imagination.

I had deemed it my duty during the course of that summer to leave Hitler in no doubt that both the General Staff and his leading generals shared the gravest anxiety about the possibility that a war might break out; not only were their memories of war as such all too forbidding, but they considered the army totally unprepared for war, and they regarded the danger of war on two fronts as a particularly ominous spectre which would inevitably seal our fates should it ever emerge. I thought it important for him to know this, although

I was aware that this would only intensify his mistrust for his generals still further.

It was for this reason that early in August 1939 he conceived the idea of addressing his ideas to the various army chiefs of staff by themselves, in other words without their Commanders-in-Chief, at the Berghof. From the shadows I was probably in the best position to study its effect and I realised that he had failed to achieve his object: for while General von Wietersheim [chief of staff of the Second Army Group] was the only one to find his tongue enough to show by his questions how little he agreed with what Hitler had outlined, this in itself probably crystallised in Hitler's mind the suspicion that he was confronted with an iron phalanx of men who inwardly refused to be swayed by any speech they thought was just a propaganda speech. Hitler never spoke to me about his impression of this meeting, but he certainly would have done had he been at all satisfied with it.

It was a bitter disappointment for him, and his disillusionment turned into a pronounced distaste for the General Staff and for its 'caste' arrogance.

All the more remarkable was his Berghof speech delivered on 22nd August to the generals of the eastern armies ranged against Poland, a speech delivered with the finest sense of psychological timing and application. Hitler was an extraordinarily gifted orator, with a masterly capability of moulding his words and phrases to suit his audience. I would even go so far as to say that he had learned his lesson from the ill-conceived meeting with the chiefs of staff, and had realised that trying to set them at odds with their commanders-in-chief had been a psychological error. Other versions of this particular speech have been subjectively distorted, as the minute taken by Admiral Boehm, who must be regarded as absolutely impartial, clearly shows.

On 24th August, Hitler arrived in Berlin and on the 26th the invasion of Poland was due to begin. The events in the Reich Chancellery during the days prior to 3rd September are of such world-wide and lasting historical importance that it will be better for me to leave their logical analysis and exact interpretation to professional historians; I myself can contribute but little from my own experience, and unfortunately I dispose over no notes or memoranda upon which to base my own recollections.

Towards noon on 25th August, I was summoned for the first time to the Reich Chancellery to see the Führer. Hitler had just received from [the Italian] ambassador Attolico a personal letter from Mussolini, a few paragraphs of which the Führer proceeded to read out to me. It was the Duce's reply to a highly confidential letter written by Hitler from the Berghof a few days before, in which he had told him about the planned clash with Poland and about his determination to resolve the undecided issue of the Danzig Corridor by military action should Poland—or England on Poland's behalf— refuse to give way.

Hitler had for various reasons named a day several days later [i.e. than had actually been planned] for his operations against Poland; as he told me himself, he was counting on the contents of his letter being immediately forwarded to London by his so 'reliable' Foreign Office, and this, he imagined, would make it plain that he really was serious in his intentions, without on the other hand divulging the true timetable of his military operations, so that even if the Poles were forewarned the planned element of tactical surprise would not be lost to the attackers. Finally, by bringing forward the announcement of the date, Hitler hoped to rush the British into precipitate intervention to prevent the outbreak of war. This he certainly expected them to do, and for this he was banking on Mussolini's support.

Mussolini's reaction was Hitler's first disillusionment in this gamble; the latter had counted upon Italy's support as a matter of course, and even upon aid of a military nature; Italy had after all signed without reservation a military aid pact [the 'Pact of Steel'], and Hitler had expected from Mussolini the same brand of *Nibelungen*-loyalty as he had himself to no personal advantage displayed towards Italy at the time of the Abyssinian campaign. Mussolini's letter was a rude shock to Hitler: for the Duce wrote that unfortunately he would not be able to stand by his agreement as the King of Italy was refusing to sign the mobilisation order, and as this was the Monarch's sole prerogative, he was powerless to act. Nor was that all: Italy was claimed to be unready for war, she lacked arms, equipment and ammunition. Even if he, Mussolini, did control her industrial armament capacity, there was a great shortage of raw materials: copper, manganese, steel, rubber and so forth. If he were to be granted tangible aid by Germany in these fields, he would naturally consider reviewing Italy's position in the event of a shooting war.

After this refusal from Italy, Hitler had me telephoned at once to find out whether there was any possibility of our parting with the required materials: he had asked Attolico to check back with Rome what quantities of these scarce commodities were needed and told him that he had directed me to find out how far we would be able to meet Italy's requirements.

Only now did the real reason for Hitler's disillusion at Mussolini's 'treachery' come to light. In effect he said: 'There's absolutely no doubt that London has realised by now that Italy won't go along with us. Now Britain's attitude towards us will stiffen—now they will back up Poland to the hilt. The diplomatic result of my letter is exactly the opposite of what I had planned.' Hitler's irritation was painfully obvious to me, although outwardly he put on a great show of composure. He added that London would clearly take its Polish treaty off the shelf and ratify it now that there was no prospect of support for us from the Italian side.

I drove back to the War Ministry to have a word with General Thomas about whether we could possibly part with the kind of raw materials demanded by Italy, over and above her current quotas, and in what quantities.

Early that afternoon [25th August] I was summoned to the Reich Chancellery again, only this time urgently. Hitler was even more agitated than he had been that morning; he told me that a wire had reached him from the Reich Press Chief [Doctor Otto Dietrich] according to which the Anglo-Polish Treaty was to be ratified that very day; there was still no confirmation from the Foreign Office, he said, but experience showed that diplomats moved more ponderously than telegraphic agencies. He believed the telegram on hand to be substantially true and asked whether the army's troop movements could be stopped, as he wanted to win time for further negotiations, even though he could no longer count upon Italy's support.

At my instance, Schmundt fetched the time-table on which the various measures and the stages of our military preparations had been marked in for each day up to D-day. On 23rd August, D-day had been fixed as the 26th; in other words we would not be up to the Polish frontier until one day after the authorisation of troop movements, which had been so planned that with one night's march hostilities could begin early on the 26th. The Führer ordered me to issue an immediate preliminary order: 'D-day postponed. Further orders follow.' Then he sent for Brauchitsch and Halder at once.

In half an hour Brauchitsch was there. Halder had to come over from Zossen, the War Office command post, as soon as he had issued the first orders for everything to stop. In my presence, a lengthy conference took place with these War Office representatives about the consequences of the hold-up, the possibility of revealing the troop movements that had been undertaken to date, and so forth. Hitler proposed to make up his mind about D-day on the 26th, as soon as he had obtained an overall view of the situation.

On the forenoon of the 26th I was once again suddenly ordered to report urgently to the Reich Chancellery. It was a hive of activity. The Führer was standing with von Ribbentrop in the conservatory, while Attolico was waiting for an audience with the Führer in the drawing room. The arrival of Henderson [the British ambassador] was expected at any moment.

Highly agitated, the Führer told me: 'Ribbentrop has just brought me a telegram from our embassy in London: "Treaty with Poland signed last night." Didn't I tell you yesterday that this is all Italy's fault? As soon as they saw the news from Rome about Italy's attitude to the Polish dispute, Britain ratified the Treaty! All troop movements are to be stopped at once! I need time to negotiate. Send for Brauchitsch and Halder, then come straight to the drawing room for the conference with Attolico. He has had a reply from Rome.'

As soon as I had issued my instructions and joined the talks with Attolico, Hitler showed me what Italy was demanding from us by way of raw materials. The demands were so exorbitant that there could be no question of our making such deliveries. The Führer indicated to Attolico that he thought there must have been some slip of the pen, or perhaps faulty hearing on somebody's part: the figures seemed improbably high. He concluded by asking Attolico to check once again, as the quantities had surely been wrongly taken down. Attolico at once hastened to assure him—as I heard for myself— that the figures were absolutely correct. I was thereupon personally charged to find out from the Chief of the Italian Armed Forces through the medium of General von Rintelen, our military attaché, what the maximum requirements of the Italian High Command were.

Hitler and I shared the impression that Attolico's demands had been deliberately inflated to ensure that we were powerless to meet them from our own resources, and the Italians would then be able to back out of their obligations, justifying their shortcomings by our failure to meet their demands. What General von Rintelen learned subsequently confirmed our suspicions, for he was told the same quantities as had been demanded by Attolico; we had no hope of meeting them. The Duce had chiselled out of us the liberty of action he wanted.

In agreement with the Commander-in-Chief of the Army and the Chief of the General Staff, D-day was now finally postponed to

31st August, in other words by five days; this was after both of them had reassured Hitler that our troop movements to date had not necessarily revealed our hand. Final orders were to be issued at five o'clock on the afternoon of 30th August at the latest, to guarantee transmission of the order to attack on the 31st. Before I left the Reich Chancellery, still on 25th August, hard on the heels of the Commander-in-Chief of the Army, I learned that Ambassador [Sir Nevile] Henderson had arrived for a talk with Hitler. At the time I did not learn what the outcome was.

Although I was at the Reich Chancellery on each of the days that followed, I spoke with Hitler only three times, as he was in almost continuous conference. The first occasion was in the conservatory, I believe it was on the 29th, when he read out to me his ultimate demands, tabulated in a seven-point memorandum which he had probably just dictated. The most fundamental parts were:

1. the return of Danzig to the Reich;
2. an extra-territorial rail and motor road across the Corridor, giving access to east Prussia;
3. the cession to Germany of those territories of the former German Reich with 75 per cent ethnic German population (I think that is how it ran); and
4. under international supervision, a plebiscite in the Polish Corridor to decide upon its return to the Reich.

He asked me what I thought of them and I replied: 'I find them very moderate.' He added that he intended to convey them to London as the final basis upon which he was prepared to negotiate with Poland.

The second occasion was when I called on Hitler on 30th August. He said he had no time for me as he was just dictating a letter to Daladier in reply to a letter from him appealing to Hitler as an old soldier to do everything in his power to avoid war: I ought to have a look at Daladier's letter some time, he said, as apart from the humanitarian considerations it was very much a portent of how they were thinking in France; they certainly had no intention of going to war over the Corridor.

My third encounter with him was on the afternoon of the 30th, together with Brauchitsch and Halder (?). On this occasion D-day was postponed yet again, by twenty-four hours, to 1st September; in other words the army's invasion, planned for the 31st, was again held up. Hitler explained that he was waiting for the arrival of a Polish government plenipotentiary from Warsaw, or at least for the granting to Lipski, the Polish Minister in Berlin, of governmental authority to conduct binding negotiations on his government's behalf. He had, he said, to wait until then, but he added that on no account would he countenance a further postponement beyond 1st September, unless of course his ultimate demands had been accepted in Warsaw.

I must say that we had all gained the impression by then that he no longer believed in that possibility himself, even though our hopes up to then of avoiding war had fastened largely upon the secret German-Soviet pact of 23rd August, by which in the event of a war with Poland, Stalin had agreed to the partition of Poland and hence to Russian military intervention, with a demarcation line being drawn between the German and Russian spheres of influence. We were sure that confronted with this possibility Poland would never let things go so far as war; and at that time we still firmly believed in Hitler's desire to avoid war.

In spite of all this, I had as a precaution (it was probably not until 23rd August, after Hitler's address to his generals at the Berghof) telegraphed General Jodl in Vienna and ordered him to report to Berlin. According to his mobilisation papers he had been earmarked for the office of chief of the High Command (OKW) operations staff for the period from 1st October 1938 to 30th September 1939, so that in an emergency he would be on hand. Jodl reached Berlin on 26th or 27th August. Naturally he was completely in the dark and had first to be briefed by Colonel Warlimont and myself on the events during his year's absence. As late as July or early August he had received confirmation in a letter from me that his request to take over command of the newly formed 2nd mountain division as its commanding officer on 1st October, 1939 at Reichenhall had been granted—a sure proof incidentally of how little I thought then that war might be around the corner.

Jodl was first presented to the Führer by me in Hitler's special train, in which we all accompanied him to the eastern front on the night of 2nd September.

On 1st September, our army had launched its planned assault on the eastern front: as dawn broke, our air force had executed the first bombing attacks on railway junctions, troop-mobilisation centres and especially on airfields in Poland. There had been no formal declaration of war; against all our advice, Hitler had decided against it.

During the day a number of brief military reports was passed to the Führer by the army and air force, but he was otherwise so pre-occupied with the diplomatic steps being undertaken by the various interested ambassadors and emissaries, from the early hours of the morning until far into the night, that I hardly saw him and then only for a few minutes at a time. At the time I was ignorant of the far-reaching political manœuvres during this and the next few days. I heard about them only during Hitler's Reichstag speech at the end of September, and learned of them in detail only here at Nuremberg.

The War Office had already left Berlin on the night of 31st August to take up its headquarters on the eastern front.

As far as the political interventions are known to me today, the attempts to reach an armistice and resolve the dispute by diplomatic means lasted until 3rd September, with Mussolini, Chamberlain, Daladier and the American President leaving no stone unturned during those first three September days to persuade Hitler to stifle this incipient world war at birth. They made no impression on Hitler. He left unanswered England's Ultimatum issued at midday on the 1st and France's of the same evening—to the effect that he should call off the attack even now after hostilities had commenced; in consequence, war had been declared by Britain and France in the West on 3rd September. But even at that late date, the intervention and mediation attempted by Mussolini and Roosevelt could still have prevented any prolongation of the war, although I am not aware whether or what kind of guarantees or hopes they extended to Hitler of meeting his Polish demands, should he accept the proposed cease-fire in Poland.

The fact is that Hitler never let any of us soldiers know (either at the time or later) under what conditions he would still have felt able to call off the attack and prevent its escalation into a full-scale war involving the Western Powers as well. We were fobbed off with the assertion that the ultimatum and declaration of war by Britain and France [on 3rd September] had been unjustifiable meddling in our eastern affairs, which were issues for Germany and Poland to thrash out between themselves, and of no economic or like consequence for either Britain or France, as none of their European interests was being compromised in any way. We soldiers would see, he told us, how groundless were our fears for the western front: of course Britain had had to make some clear and unambiguous gesture in the spirit of her newly signed Treaty with Poland, but she was in no position to intervene with force either at sea or—and indeed far less—on land; and France was hardly likely to be dragged into a war for which she too was quite unprepared just because of Britain's obligations to Poland. The whole thing was a rattling of sabres for the benefit of the rest of the world, certainly nothing worth taking too seriously.

He had no intention of being taken in by methods such as these. That was the tenor of Hitler's daily incantations both to the War Office and to us, during our journeys to the front.

Despite our grave doubts, it did seem almost as though even now Hitler's intuition was to prove right again, for the daily reports from the west brought only news of minor skirmishing with outlying French units in the zone between the Maginot Line and our West Wall; they were suffering bloody reverses at the hands of our weak defending garrisons. In no place had heavy fighting broken out.

All that really could be regarded only as sabre rattling, aimed primarily at tying down our forces in the west and at establishing armed reconnaissance of our reflexes and of the strength of our West Wall. Looked at purely from the military point of view, this procrastination by the French army was wholly inexplicable unless —as was hardly probable—they had quite considerably over-estimated the strength of our forces in the west; the only alternative was, as Hitler had said, that they just were not ready for war. Certainly it was a rejection of every accepted tenet of military strategy for them just to look on while the Polish army was slaughtered, instead of exploiting to the full the favourable situation which offered itself to the French Army command all the time that our main forces were tied down in the attack on Poland. This was the strategic dilemma confronting us soldiers: was Hitler to be proved right again after all? Would the Western Powers really fail to pursue the war once Poland had been destroyed?

Hitler seldom intervened in the Commander-in-Chief's conduct of the battle: in fact, I can recall only two occasions, the first being when he demanded the rapid reinforcement of our northern flank (which had attacked from East Prussia) by means of transferring to East Prussia tank units to stand by to stiffen and extend the eastern flank far enough to encircle Warsaw from the east of the River Vistula; the second occasion was when he intervened in Blaskowitz's [Eighth] Army operations, to which he had taken the strongest possible exception. Otherwise he limited himself rigorously to ex-pressions of opinion and exchanges of views with the Commander-in-Chief and to giving verbal encouragement; he never intervened to issue orders to them himself. This was far more frequent with the Air Force, to which he often issued personal instructions in the interests of ground operations; almost every evening he was on the telephone to Göring.

I handed over to Jodl the duty of reporting on military develop-ments at conferences in the headquarters coach; he was aided by three liaison officers, one for each of the three branches of the armed forces. The latter three had, in fact, been seconded to Hitler as Intelligence officers for their respective Commanders-in-Chief, but there was no room for additional personnel in the Führer's train.

I will mention only those few of my visits to the front as are particularly imprinted upon my memory: firstly, there was one to the Army commander von Kluge [Commander-in-Chief of the Fourth Army] whom we visited on 3rd September: a war conference, meal and inspection of the Tuchel Heath battlefield, which offered us an impressive picture of the Polish casualties. Second was a visit we made setting out from the headquarters of the Second Army Corps: the Führer visited the front with General Strauss to see his troops crossing the Vistula at Culm and the ensuing battle. Thirdly, we visited General Busch (Eighth Army Corps) for the crossing of the San and a parade by large sections of the troops, including wounded men back from the front, in honour of the completion of the army bridge shortly before.

The fourth occasion was a visit to my friend General von Briesen (30th Infantry Division) who had been in the middle of the weakly defended flank of Blaskowitz's Army and had with just his one division beaten back a mass break-out attempt by a cut-off Polish Army, in a bitter struggle against enormous odds. Only the Führer's authority had sufficed to get us through to this headquarters position, well within range of the enemy's guns. In a schoolroom, von Briesen —whose left fore-arm had been shot away in the battle—outlined to him the developing fight his division had put up during the hard and bloody days of the battle. Asked about his injury, he confessed he had led his last reserve battalion into action himself. As we made our way back from the command post, which was inaccessible except on foot, Hitler said to me: 'That is a real Prussian general of the Royal school. You can't have enough soldiers like him. He's a man after my own heart. Before today is over I want him to be the first divisional commander to get the Knight's Cross. He has saved Blaskowitz's army by his gallantry and drive.'

My fifth recollection is of flying to an airfield and of proceeding thence across an army bridge over the Vistula, north of Warsaw, to the command post of the Second Army Corps' artillery commander. From a vantage point in a church steeple north-east of Praga—a suburb of Warsaw on the Vistula's east bank—the latter was calling down artillery fire on the outer fortifications of Warsaw. It was here that news reached Hitler that Colonel-General von

Fritsch had died in action that morning at an infantry commander's headquarters, during an advance by the 12th Artillery Regiment.

I also remember a visit to the western side of the Warsaw encirclement action, and observing the effect of our artillery bombardment of the city's suburbs from a tower of Warsaw Sports and Racing Stadium. Three attempts to force Warsaw to capitulate had preceded this last visit to the front, with the result that now the artillery barrage and air bombardment of the city had begun as warned.*

On 20th September we transferred the Führer's small headquarters to Zoppot. Starting out from there, we paid a visit to the Westerplatte peninsula near the port of Danzig and to the port and city of Gdynia, as well as to the adjoining high ground, where there were still signs of the violent fighting in which the Pomeranian frontier-guard division had been involved. Those were the troops that the then Major von Briesen had trained and inspired in the 'loyal Pomeranian' spirit during his years of service in the eastern frontier forces. The officer casualties suffered by the Pomeranian nobility in this yeomanry division had been particularly heavy.†

The state funeral of the late Colonel-General von Fritsch took place in Berlin at the Heroes' Memorial Hall on 25th September. It was bad flying weather, so the Führer was obliged to abandon his plan to take part in the ceremony. Despite this I took off with Funk [my pilot] heading at first for Stettin, as the airfield there was not fogbound like that at Berlin. For more than an hour we waited there for visibility at Berlin to improve, but it did not. Finally, as it was getting late, we took off anyhow in the hope that it would have cleared enough for us to land by the time we arrived. It was a most unpleasant flight, but Funk managed to bring us down safely at the military airfield at Staaken, outside Berlin. I arrived at the funeral only just in time to lay a wreath on the coffin on the Führer's behalf, and Brauchitsch and I followed the coffin in the endless funeral procession comprising both the services, the State and the diplomatic Corps, until it was finally laid to rest at the military cemetery.

Colonel-General von Fritsch had accompanied the 12th Artillery Regiment into the Polish camaign as a supernumerary. The Führer had hesitated a long time about whether to give him command of an Army Group or of the autonomous East Prussian Army, as

---

* In Keitel's original manuscript there follow details about his youngest son, Hans-Georg, fighting as an N.C.O. in an artillery regiment outside Warsaw; these have been omitted by the Editor.

† In Keitel's original manuscript there follow details of Zoppot and of Hitler's visit to Danzig; these have been omitted by the Editor.

Brauchitsch had urged him to and as I had actively advocated. In the end the Führer had decided against it, explaining that in that event he would have to reinstate Blomberg as well, and that was something he could never bring himself to do. The reason probably was that, at the time, he had held out to Blomberg some prospect of being reinstated should war break out; as he now had no desire to keep that promise, he had had equally to eschew giving Fritsch a high-level post, as that would have been an open insult to Blomberg. Those are my own views, but they are based on remarks that Hitler made at the time to Schmundt, his adjutant.

The widespread rumour that Fritsch was so embittered that he had deliberately sought death in action is quite false, according to what the officer who reported Fritsch's fatal injury to the Führer (in my presence) saw with his own eyes: a stray bullet had struck the Colonel-General while he was conversing with his Staff Officers, and within only a few minutes he had bled to death.

The war in Poland ended with a big military parade through the streets of the partially destroyed Warsaw, to which the Führer and I flew with our lieutenants from Berlin.

At the airfield a big banquet was laid out in the Führer's honour, before we took off back to Berlin. As soon as Hitler caught sight of the well-stocked horseshoe table set up in one of the hangars, he turned abruptly on his heel, told Brauchitsch that he never ate with his troops except standing at a field kitchen, stalked back to our aircraft, and instructed the pilot to take off at once. While I did find that the Commander-in-Chief of the Army had been rather tactless in laying on the banquet, he had certainly acted with good intentions. During the flight the Führer's anger subsided and he several times began to say something about that banquet, as he now seemed to be reproaching himself for his behaviour.

When I told all this to Brauchitsch in the course of the next few days, he confided to me that the banquet had been a great success— even without Hitler.

No sooner had Warsaw fallen than the first divisions began to roll towards the western front, although up to then the situation had been no worse than just a few localised outbreaks of fighting flaring up here and there in the approaches to the West Wall. The first troops were directed to the northern flank in the area near and to the north of Aix-la-Chapelle (Aachen) because the Führer thought that our miserable frontier forces confronting Holland and Belgium were far too weak, and that this was as good as inciting the

French to skirt round to the north of the West Wall and lunge straight into the defenceless Ruhr region. But at that time our opponents in the west were probably still chary of violating Belgium's neutrality, because the latter's king had apparently refused to permit French troops to cross his territory, as we learned later via Rome, thanks to the family ties linking the two Royal houses.

The Soviet Union's demeanour throughout our Polish campaign was of especial interest and particularly edifying. After we had launched our attack, Hitler had, of course, arranged for Stalin's immediate intervention in the campaign to be requested through diplomatic channels; we had a vested interest in this, because we particularly wanted the quickest possible conclusion of the campaign—we wanted a lightning war—in view of our western frontiers' vulnerability. Stalin, on the other hand, intended to reap his reward in the division of Poland with as little [Russian] bloodshed as possible, and he informed the Führer that he could not be ready to attack before three weeks at the earliest, as his forces were neither prepared nor mobilised. From the very outset, the High Command had ensured that our military attaché in Moscow [General Köstring] was kept in the picture, and further attempts were made through diplomatic channels to persuade them to change their attitude, but there was no further news from Moscow: just that they could not get ready to intervene any faster.

But, just as we were crossing the River San in the south and Warsaw was within our operational grasp, the Red Army—despite their alleged 'total unreadiness'—was suddenly marching into Poland, overrunning the last of the Polish troops as they fell back and taking them into captivity, while they deflected a large part of the others into Roumania. There were no brushes between our forces and those of the Red Army; the Soviet troops halted a respectful distance away from the demarcation line and only the most urgent military intelligence was exchanged.*

The Army's troop trains had been rolling westwards at the maximum carrying capacity of the railway system ever since the fall of Warsaw, with the troops often marching considerable distances to the railheads. Nothing seemed less probable to the War

---

* In Keitel's original manuscript there follow here further details on the lack of contact with the Russians and a suspicion that the Russians took more prisoners in Poland than did the Germans; to which he added a polemic about the Soviet murder of Polish officer P.o.W.s at Katyn. Keitel put the number at 10,000 but, in fact, it was about 4,000 (see Hans Thieme's essay *Katyn—ein Geheimnis*, published in *Vierteljahresheft für Zeitgeschichte* [Munich], No. 4, 1955, p. 409 et seq.). The whole passage has been omitted by the Editor.

Office than the likelihood of an autumn or winter campaign on the western front; while I was still at the Strand Hotel at Zoppot, on about 22nd September, I was shown an order the Army General Staff had issued ordering the partial demobilisation of the army. At the time I telephoned General Halder and said that his order was quite impossible, as the Führer had not yet authorised it; the order was withheld, or rather reworded to the effect that the lessons we had learned during the Polish campaign necessitated fresh dispositions for a possible war in the west.

The strength of the War Office opposition to Hitler's idea of putting the Army on a war footing in the west as early as October 1939 was soon demonstrated by various incidents. The War Office, together with the vast majority of the Army's senior generals, including von Reichenau, had not only military but political reasons for its stand, and I shared them to the full.

Quite apart from their daunting recollections of the First World War, and the strength of the formidable Maginot line against which there were then virtually no weapons of destruction, they considered that the Army was as yet not capable of launching any fresh assault after its eastern campaign, without a pause to recover, to regroup and remobilise, to finish its training and to complete its re-equipping. Particular doubts were expressed about winter warfare, with the fog and rain, the short days and the long nights, which made mobile warfare virtually impossible. In addition, the fact that the French had not exploited either the good weather or the weakness of our western defences earlier could only lead us to conclude that they did not really want to fight, and that any attack we might launch would only foul up the prospects of peace talks—probably making them impossible. It was clear to us that the Maginot line would oblige us to press our attack through northern France, Luxembourg and Belgium and possibly even through Holland, with all the consequences we had suffered in the 1914–1918 war.

Hitler, on the other hand, thought that the strategic disadvantage in each day wasted outweighed the opprobrium of infringing another country's neutrality, which was just as much an obstacle to the enemy as to us, but to whose implications the enemy was likely to be more susceptible than the average German soldier. For Hitler, the significant issue was the time that the enemy would gain for rearming and strengthening his forces, especially now that the British Expeditionary Force had arrived; he afterwards put the increase in size of the latter during the seven months we lost up to May 1940 at five-fold, an increase from four to twenty divisions;

in this context, he added, each British division had to be counted as equivalent to three or four French ones as far as fighting value was concerned. But the most decisive factor weighing in Hitler's mind was his anxiety for the Ruhr industrial region of the Rhineland and Westphalia, the heart of German rearmament: the loss of the Ruhr would be synonymous with the loss of the war; he believed that the strong and mobile Anglo-French army in northern France might at any time attempt a sudden thrust through Belgium to break into the Ruhr, and in all likelihood it would be detected too late to be effectively countered.

In October 1939 these two points of view stood diametrically opposed to each other. At the time I was inclined to share the War Office's point of view; the result was the first serious crisis of confidence between Hitler and myself. Whether he had somehow found out that I had been over to Zossen for a long discussion with Brauchitsch and Halder I don't know. In any event when I publicly told him what I thought, as I was bound to do, Hitler violently accused me of obstructing him and conspiring with his generals against his plans; he demanded of me that I accept and identify myself with his opinions and represent them without reservation to the War Office. When I tried to intervene to point out that I for one had certainly kept Brauchitsch adequately informed on his [Hitler's] well-known assessment of the situation and of his intentions, he began to insult me and repeated the very offensive accusation that I was fostering an opposition group against him among his generals.

I was extremely upset and talked the whole thing over with Schmundt. He tried to soothe me, and told me that at midday General von Reichenau had been for lunch with the Führer and had had a long private interview with Hitler afterwards. Hitler had afterwards very angrily told Schmundt that much to his rage Reichenau had given voice to the same fundamental objections as the War Office. So that was probably the reason for his aggressive mood towards me that evening—it all happened on the same day.

I asked Schmundt to tell the Führer that in view of his lack of confidence in me I wished to be posted elsewhere, as it was impossible for me to continue working under those conditions. How diligently Schmundt performed this errand for me I don't know; I did not enter the Reich Chancellery myself, but merely waited in case I was called in for an interview. But when nothing had happened even by next day, I wrote a handwritten letter to Hitler and, referring to the lack of confidence in me which he had voiced, asked to be posted elsewhere, and if possible to the front. I handed this letter to Schmundt to give to Hitler.

The result was an interview between Hitler and myself, in which he told me that he was rejecting my request and he would prefer not to have such requests made to him in future: it was his prerogative to tell me when he had no further need of my services, and until then I had to do as I was told in the office to which he had appointed me. My letter, he suggested, was the result of over-sensitivity on my part; he had not told me that he no longer had any confidence in me. With that, he at once went on to other matters, outlining his own assessment of the situation, with an angry outburst about Reichenau, who, he said, would do better to bother less about diplomacy and more about the quickest way of getting his armoured group ready for battle again: all he was doing was just writing it off as unserviceable as the result of wear and tear on the engines, tank-tracks and so forth.

Finally I was ordered to tell Brauchitsch to call on him. At the same time Hitler told me that he had already had a lengthy discussion with Brauchitsch in my absence, in which the latter had outlined the War Office's views. He concluded by saying that the War Office should not dabble in political and military questions, nor was that the General Staff's concern; it did not even have enough drive to pull the Army together again after the brief campaign in Poland: there was no problem in knocking the armoured formations back into good shape again, if only there was the will to do it.

I was ordered to be present at this new conference with Brauchitsch. He (Hitler) said he had very closely considered what his decision should be [on the campaign in the west] and during the next few days he would hand the Commanders-in-Chief a memorandum he had himself written on the problems of world war, with all his own views about it.

The conference with Brauchitsch took place in my presence—I believe it was on the next day. [It was on 5th November, 1939.] Von Brauchitsch and I silently listened to Hitler's very extensive discourse on the War Office's point of view as far as it was known. Brauchitsch followed him, giving two reasons why he could not agree:

1. During the Polish campaign the infantry had been shown to be over-cautious and insufficiently attack-minded; it also lacked training, it showed little command of the tactics of attack and its NCOs lacked proficiency.

2. Discipline had unfortunately become very lax and there were at present conditions reminiscent of those in 1917—there had been drunken orgies and bad behaviour in troop trains and on railway stations. He had been sent reports on all this by the stationmasters, and there was a series of affidavits on hand which had led to reprimands for bad breaches of discipline.

He concluded that the Army needed intensive training before there was any possibility of unleashing it on a rested and well-prepared enemy in the west.

After the Commander-in-Chief had finished speaking, the Führer jumped up in a rage and shouted that it was quite incomprehensible to him that just because of a little lack of discipline a Commander-in-Chief should condemn his own Army and run it down. None of his commanders had said anything to him about any lack of verve in the infantry when he had been at the front, but he had to listen to such criticisms now after the Army had won a unique victory in Poland. As Supreme Commander he, personally, would have to reject out of hand such charges against his Army. He concluded by demanding to see all the legal papers concerned so that he could read them for himself. Then he left the room, slamming the door behind him, leaving all of us just standing there. Brauchitsch and I separated at once without another word, each going our own ways. It was plain to me that this signalled the break with von Brauchitsch and that what little confidence there had been between them was finally shattered.

Every day I was asked for the legal papers he had demanded; I only ever saw one that Hitler threw onto my desk.

Afterwards I learned from Schmundt that von Brauchitsch had asked to be relieved of his office after this disturbing scene, that he had been called in alone to see Hitler, and that his request had been categorically refused him.

Some days earlier—it was probably in the first half of October—General Halder had been summoned to the Führer to brief him on the plan of campaign for the West; Jodl and I were also in attendance. While Hitler several times interrupted Halder's address with frequent questions, he kept his views to himself at the end, although he did ask Halder to turn the map with its entries over to him. After he had gone, Hitler turned to us and said something like: 'That is just the old Schlieffen plan, with a strong right flank along the Atlantic coast; you won't get away with an operation like that twice running. I have quite a different idea and I'll tell you (i.e. Jodl and myself) about it in a day or two and then I'll talk it over with the War Office myself.'

Because I have not much time left, I will not go in detail into the strategic questions arising from all this, as they will be dealt with by others anyway; I will only go so far as to make it quite plain that it was Hitler himself who saw the armoured break-through at Sédan, striking up to the Atlantic coast at Abbeville, as the solution; we would then swing round [northwards] into the rear of the motorised Anglo-French army, which would most probably be advancing across the Franco-Belgian frontier into Belgium, and cut them off.

I had some misgivings, as this stroke of genius could go awry if the French tank army did not do us the favour of automatically driving through Belgium towards our northern flank, but held back instead until they recognised Hitler's planned break-through operation. General Jodl, on the other hand, was as little inclined to share my fears as was Hitler himself.

It should be mentioned that one day some time later the Führer told me with some great pleasure that on this particular strategic issue he had had a long personal discussion with General von Manstein, who had been the only one of the Army's generals to have had the same plan in view, and this had greatly pleased him. Von Manstein had, at the time, been Chief of Staff to von Rundstedt's Army Group A, which was, in fact, to bring the planned operation to a triumphant and crushing conclusion.

The consequence of the stubborn resistance put up by the War Office was a change in the character of our dealings with Hitler: what had been accomplished hitherto by verbal directives and instructions was now performed by the issue of written orders. The OKW operations staff elaborated the Führer's instructions for him, acting as his military *bureau*; they were then issued to the Commander-in-Chief [of the Army] signed either by Hitler or by myself on his behalf. In this way the OKW operations staff now edged into the saddle. Previously the Führer had dealt verbally with his commanders-in-chief often to the total exclusion of the OKW— an arrangement upon which the Commander-in-Chief of the Army had laid the greatest value; but after their serious *contretemps* the latter appeared in person only when called for.

The date for the attack [on France] had provisionally been fixed as 25th October [1939], but Hitler doubted that it could be met; the fact was that he wanted to build up sufficient pressure to exploit to the full what little time there was for the preparation and concentration of his troops. In fact, even the necessary overhaul of the tank units was not complete by then: spare engines, gears and tank tracks were in particularly short supply. Besides, the weather was wholly unfavourable. The result was that we were obliged to put up with a series of delays, for on one thing Hitler was quite firm: he would launch his attack only when there was a forecast of several days of good flying weather, so that our Air Force could be exploited to maximum purpose.

The next dates in November came and went in the same way, and Hitler decided to wait for a lengthy period of clear, frosty weather during the winter instead. During the days that followed, Diesing, the Air Force Meteorologist, sweated blood for every one of the daily weather forecasts he had to make either before or after the main war conferences, painfully conscious of his responsibility should his forecast prove wrong. During January 1940 Hitler realised that there seemed little further prospect of any definite period of clear and frosty weather, and he resolved to postpone his attack on the western front—which had by now virtually frozen solid—until May.*

Discussions had been taking place since October 1939 with the Navy on the vital importance of Norway as a naval and air base for the further conduct of the war, should the British manage to get a foot-hold there: they would be in a position to dominate the Bay of Heligoland and the exit channels for our fleet and submarine forces as well as confronting our naval ports and the passage from the Baltic out into the Atlantic with a serious threat from their Air Force.

During December 1939, after contact had been established with the former Norwegian Defence Minister Quisling, a bold plan began to take shape for seizing the Norwegian ports from seaward. The OKW operations staff established a special *bureau* for this purpose, and staff studies were initiated with the German Navy's co-operation. In view of the great distance from Narvik—more than 1,250 miles— and of the vast superiority of the British fleet, the plan can only be called audacious; the Führer was well aware of this, as was Raeder, the Navy's Commander-in-Chief; Hitler accordingly intervened personally in the plan to a very great extent, while at the same time totally concealing his intentions from the Army and the Air Force. For the first time the OKW began to function as a working head-

* In Keitel's original manuscript there follows a lengthy description of the by now well-known history of the postponement of the date of attack and Hitler's reasons; this has been omitted by the Editor.

quarters for Hitler's overall command of the armed forces, as it took over the unified command of a theatre of combined operations by the Navy, Army and Air Force.

It proved an ideal example of how well a joint and centralised command could be concentrated in the hands of the OKW operations staff, to the total exclusion of the Army General Staff and the Air Force: it was clearly laid down that all actual war transactions, including troop transports and logistics, were the sole responsibility of the navy, while such Army and Air Force units as were landed there were directly controlled by the OKW. The real invasion operation was launched on 9th April [1940].*

Of course the winter of 1939–1940 was not only extremely arduous for myself and the OKW, but also highly fertile in internal crises. The daily war conferences and midday briefing sessions in the Reich Chancellery took place in Hitler's presence with almost monotonous regularity. Jodl and I each had a study and an office for our adjutants and secretariats next to the former Reich Cabinet Chamber; I never arrived from the War Ministry until about noon, and then I sometimes came back in the evening again for an hour; Jodl himself never really worked anywhere but in the Reich Chancellery, because of the absence of any study for him in the operations staff's quarters in Bendlerstrasse; thus he was always on hand for the Führer should he be required for anything. In this way his relationship with Hitler became more intimate, as did the latter's recognition of his ability, which was all very pleasing for me. I do not deny that I would have preferred to have been kept more thoroughly briefed all the time on everything that was happening but, as it was, my co-operation with Jodl was never once in the least impaired. Although nothing was more foreign to my nature than jealousy, nothing would have been less feasible than for me to have insisted on retaining control in my own hands: I was never permitted to make decisions; the Führer had reserved that right to himself even in seemingly trivial matters.

It was on the 19th and 20th April that I had my second serious *contretemps* with Hitler, because he was planning to detach the administration of occupied Norway from the military leaders—which, in my view, was the principal task of our commander-in-chief there—and transfer civil authority to Gauleiter Terboven.

I declared myself firmly opposed to this and walked out of the conference chamber when Hitler began to rebuke me in front

---

* In Keitel's original manuscript there follows a description of a number of high-lights of the Norwegian campaign; these have been omitted by the Editor.

of all the other participants. On 19th April Jodl wrote in his diary:

Renewed crisis; chief of OKW walks out of chamber. . . .

Although I endeavoured once again, as soon as I had a few calm moments alone with Hitler next day, to convince him of the impropriety of the appointment, I made no headway with him; Terboven became the 'Reich Commissioner for Norway'. The consequences are well known.

On 8th May, as all the expert opinion was that a period of fine weather seemed to be in the offing, the order to launch the attack [on the western front] was issued for the 10th. At six o'clock on the morning of 10th May, a courier was to hand the Queen of the Netherlands a personal note from the Reich government, explaining that developments had made it inevitable for German troops to cross Dutch territory; the Queen was invited to direct her army to permit the troops to march through unmolested to avoid any bloodshed; she herself was invited to remain in the country. Despite the most minute preparations for this Mission and a visa issued by the Dutch Embassy in Berlin, our Foreign Office courier was arrested on crossing the frontier on 9th May, and his secret letter was seized from him. The outcome was that The Hague was thus apprised of the imminent outbreak of war and had all the confirmation that might be needed—the courier's letter—in their hands. At the time Canaris steered suspicion towards Herr von Steengracht in the Foreign Office, but he [Canaris] approached me wringing his hands and entreating me to say nothing of this to the Führer or von Ribbentrop. Today it is clear to me that Canaris himself was the traitor.

We had been kept well briefed on the attitude of Belgium and Holland, who for some months had merely been posing as neutrals; we knew about Belgium because of the kinship of her Royal household with that of Italy, and about Holland thanks to our security service's cunningly-contrived capture of a member of the British secret service at Venlo. In actual fact both countries had forfeited any claim to neutrality by turning a blind eye on the Royal Air Force's flights over their sovereign territories.

Under conditions of maximum secrecy we left Berlin at noon on 9th May, departing from a small station at Grunewald and heading as long as the daylight lasted for Hamburg, where the Führer was supposed to arrive next day; as soon as dusk fell the train's direction was reversed, and we arrived at Euskirchen, not far from Aix-la-Chapelle (Aachen), at three o'clock that morning. While it was still dark, and beneath a beautiful canopy of stars we drove out by car to the command post at the Führer's new headquarters, *Felsennest*; this latter had been built by the Todt Organisation far from any village, a bunker installation blasted out of a wooded mountain-top.

In the Führer's bunker I had a windowless air-conditioned concrete cell next to his; Jodl's cell was next to mine, while the military adjutants were quartered on the far side of the Führer's room. Sound carries extraordinarily clearly in concrete rooms like these; I could even hear the Führer reading newspapers.

Our office quarters were five minutes' walk away down a forest track: they were wooden barracks with good windows, a small conference room, three adjoining rooms and an attractive bedroom for Jodl's General Staff officer (adjutant) who lived there all the time. [This was Major (G.S.) Waizenegger.] I was very envious of his airy room: he was much better off than we were in the bunker. The headquarters of the Commander-in-Chief of the Army was half an hour's drive away along the forest lanes, again in barracks clustered round a forester's house which was where the C.-in-C. himself lived. Both encampments were so well concealed and so remote that they were never detected by the enemy air force, nor were they ever compromised. One or two air attacks were executed on the railway station at Euskirchen, but they were not meant for us.

In the first communiqué issued by the High Command, at noon on 10th May, I was responsible for the sentence:

> In order to direct the overall operations of the armed forces, the Führer and Supreme Commander has moved to the front. . . .

I fought with him for probably half an hour to get him to consent to this disclosure; he explained that he preferred to remain anonymous in order not to lessen the glory of his generals. I did not relent, however, for I knew it had to be made known some time that he really was exercising the Supreme Command and that he was the warlord behind the operation. Finally he gave in to me.

The fact was that Hitler was familiar with every last detail of our tasks and operations, he knew the targets set for each day and the plans of attack, and he often exercised a close personal influence on them. Late in October [1939] every one of the Army-Group and Army commanders had been summoned individually for Hitler to brief him in detail on the final offensive and on the planned direction of the operation. With each one he had discussed all the details, sometimes asking awkward questions and showing himself to be remarkably well-informed on terrain, obstacles and the like, as the result of his penetrating study of the maps. His critical judgment and suggestions proved to the generals that he had immersed himself deeply in the problems inherent in executing his basic orders, and that he was no layman. Afterwards he was furious about the superficiality of his friend Reichenau, who made a public fool of himself, while on the other hand he particularly praised the detailed preparation and war-game practice that had gone into the planning of the most formidable task confronting von Kluge's [Fourth] Army, the breakthrough in the Ardennes.

His greatest interest was reserved for von Kleist's armoured group, largely because it was this group that was to put this planned breakthrough toward Abbeville into effect. Again and again he remarked how favourable the terrain was for a tank battle; their first and foremost task was to win that as quickly as possible, without any sidelong glances. The careful work that Zeitzler had put into the logistical build-up as the group's chief of staff met with great approval.

Most of all, he occupied himself with the task assigned to Busch's [Sixteenth] Army, and he personally went over with him every stage in the provision of a flanking cover to the south, to shield the armoured group's smooth breakthrough; and he particularly stressed how vital it was for the armoured thrust to succeed.

In this way Hitler had already brought to bear his own personal influence as Supreme Warlord without thereby detracting in any way from the magnificent work of the General Staff; it accordingly seemed important that he should admit to the German people that he was in command in the military sense as well, and that the responsibility was his. That was after all how things were.

During the whole of the campaign in the west, which lasted for forty-three days from 10th May to 22nd June [1940] Hitler flew out to visit his front-line commanders only four or five times. In that fine weather and in view of the enemy air activity there was no sense in flying over the actual theatre of operations in a transport aircraft. All the more frequent as a result were his meetings with the Commander-in-Chief of the Army for purely tactical and

THE INVASION OF FRANCE, 1940

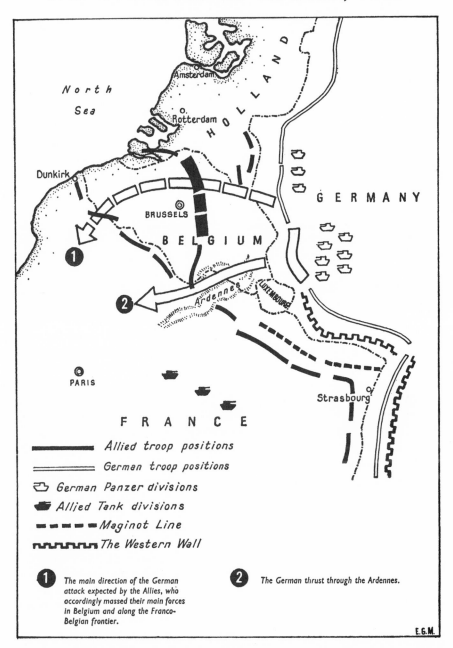

North Sea

Amsterdam

Rotterdam

HOLLAND

Dunkirk

BRUSSELS

BELGIUM

GERMANY

LUXEMBOURG

Ardennes

PARIS

Strasbourg

FRANCE

Allied troop positions

German troop positions

German Panzer divisions

Allied Tank divisions

Maginot Line

The Western Wall

1 The main direction of the German attack expected by the Allies, who accordingly massed their main forces in Belgium and along the Franco-Belgian frontier.

2 The German thrust through the Ardennes.

E.G.M.

strategic conferences; they passed peacefully and without open differences of opinion. Hitler had every reason to acknowledge the achievements of the Army's command, closely as it had adhered to his fundamental requirements, but he gave voice to his satisfaction regrettably seldom. The result was that I myself went out in my trusty Junkers 52 to pay increasingly frequent visits to the Army and Army-Group commanders, particularly during the first phase up to the middle of June, when there was not much air activity. We kept pretty low altitudes most of the time, so that enemy spotter planes and fighters were less of a danger to us.

That first morning in the *Felsennest* headquarters the atmosphere was electric with tension: among us there was nobody who was not exercised by the question of whether we had succeeded in taking the enemy tactically by surprise or not. Hitler himself was waiting feverishly for the first reports on special operations he had had mounted against the Belgians' strong modern block-fortifications at Eben-Emael, which was to be captured by a surprise combined airborne and ground-forces assault involving the use of gliders. Hitler had personally briefed and exercised the participating commanders and NCOs of the Air Force units and Engineer battalions involved in this operation; he had gone into the smallest imaginable detail and used a scale model for the purpose.

I venture to mention this only as an example of how the Führer liked to immerse himself in every detail of the practical execution of his ideas, so wide was the sweep of his unparalleled inventiveness. I was unable to avoid the effects of this again and again on every facet of my own office functions; for as a result, the senior commanders and those of us on his own staff were equally obliged to adopt this exceptionally minute *modus operandi*; there was no end to his questioning, intervening and sifting of facts, until with his fantastic imagination he was satisfied that the last loophole had been plugged. In view of this it can probably be seen why we often had conferences and briefings that lasted for hours on end with him: it was a natural consequence of his working ritual, which represented a marked divergence from our traditional military dogma in so far as we had been accustomed to leave it to lower echelons and commanders to interpret how the orders given to them were to be carried out. But now, whether I liked it or not, I had to learn to adapt myself to his system.

Hitler appeared every day at about noon in our small barracks, and again during the late afternoon, to be briefed on the situation. By now the duty of outlining the latest developments to him had been completely taken over by General Jodl. Apart from the western front, the OKW was still preoccupied with the problematic and highly exposed Norwegian theatre, which continued to give us cause for alarm until the end of May, when the British and French relinquished their hold there. Basically, I was out and about every other day, mostly in the area of von Rundstedt's Army Group, where he was directing the Führer's vital breakthrough operation, coupled with a wheel to the north. His Chief of Staff had in the meantime been replaced by General von Sodenstern, who was an old colleague of mine from my days in the Troop Office [the disguised General Staff] from 1926 to 1933, and bound to me by the ties of a close friendship. I was able to speak out openly to him on everything, including even the Führer's special wishes, without having to fear that he would go telling Halder, the Commander-in-Chief of the Army, about 'interference' by the Supreme Commander, which would only result in renewed ill-feeling towards me.

General von Rundstedt also wisely recognised the difficulties of my position at that time and listened with great understanding to the tactfully moderate 'hints' I gave him, hints that had, in fact, originated from Hitler himself. My visits to him, which took place every day during the crucial days of the actual breakthrough, always passed in the closest harmony. I received the latest battle maps very early on each morning, and took them back to Hitler . . .*

Italy's entry into the war was more of a burden to us in the OKW than a relief. The Führer was unsuccessful in his attempt to hold Mussolini back at least for a while; we had a very considerable vested interest in his doing so, as for us to support their planned penetration of the French fortifications along the Alpine front would sap the strength of our own Air Force, and did in fact entail our dividing and weakening our Air Force, at the time of the fighting around Paris, in favour of the Italians. Even then, despite our assistance and the weakness of the French Alpine front, the Italian offensive very rapidly ground to a halt. These Italian allies of ours, who had suddenly recalled their treaty obligations to us only because they thought that France had been beaten, were to prove our most ill-starred and emptiest blessing as the war progressed, for nothing did more to impede our collaboration and *entente* with

* In Keitel's original manuscript there follow here further details no longer of any interest, in which he describes visits to the front-line and the well-known course of the breakthrough in the Artois region; and an account of how his youngest son, Lieutenant Hans-Georg Keitel, was gravely wounded in an artillery regiment; these have been omitted by the Editor.

the French, even as early as the autumn of 1940, than our having to respect Italian aspirations and the Führer's belief that we were obliged to subscribe to them.

The signature of the Armistice with France, in the forest of Compiègne on 22nd June 1940, was the climax of my career as Chief of the OKW. The conditions to be imposed upon France had already been formulated at the OKW operations-staff level in advance of the collapse, and upon receipt of the French petition I had personally worked over them and drawn them up in what seemed to me to be the most appropriate form. In any case, we were at no pains to hurry ourselves, because the Führer wanted to see certain strategic objectives, like the reaching of the Swiss frontier, attained first of all.

As soon as the date and place for the armistice negotiations had been fixed, the Führer called for my draft and retired for a day to go over it and, in many instances, to rephrase it, so that I found that while the content of my draft had not been changed, its original formulation had. The preamble was Hitler's idea and flowed from his pen alone.

The ceremonial signing of the armistice, at the same historic location in the forest of Compiègne where the Germans had sued for peace in 1918, a spot upon which the passing Gods of War had left no trace, had a strong effect both on me and, probably, on the other participants as well. My emotions were mixed: I had a feeling that this was our hour of revenge for Versailles, and I was conscious of my pride in the conclusion of a unique and victorious campaign, and of a resolve to respect the feelings of those who had been honourably vanquished in battle.

After briefly and formally saluting the French delegation, which was led by the Alsatian General Huntziger, we climbed up into the railway coach which had been preserved there as a national memorial. The Führer sat at the centre of the table, while I sat down beside him with the actual surrender Instrument. The three Frenchmen sat facing us. The Führer opened the ceremony by inviting me to read out the preamble and the terms we were demanding. After that, the Führer left the coach with his five aides and departed from the scene, with the guard of honour presenting arms to him. General Jodl took a seat on one side of me and a staff officer of the military operations office on the other, with Minister Schmidt from the Foreign Office to act as our interpreter, which throughout the negotiations he did most admirably.

The French asked for an hour's respite to study our terms, and they withdrew into a nearby tent. They were in telephone contact with their Army High Command across the front lines, and the link functioned relatively well despite a number of interruptions caused by the fighting. During this interval I was able to raise with the Führer, who was waiting nearby, a number of points Huntziger had opened the talks with.

As was to be expected, the French tried valiantly to moderate our demands, and in order to win time for the telephonic transmission of the document's text—with which they had immediately begun—they claimed that they had to obtain Marshal Pétain's decision on a number of matters. I had of course taken the necessary steps to ensure that we could unobtrusively listen in to their telephone conversations.

The French exploited the talks to table further proposals, even after I had—with Hitler's and Göring's agreement—made certain concessions as far as the disarmament of the French Air Force was concerned. According to our own interception reports Pétain had demanded still easier terms which Huntziger in his reply had told him were quite out of the question, in view of my uncompromising attitude.

I therefore decided at five o'clock that evening to give Minister Schmidt [Chief Foreign Office Interpreter] an ultimatum to hand to the delegation, which had again withdrawn for consultations; the ultimatum would be timed to expire at six o'clock. When the French finally appeared again and began making fresh demands—probably inspired by Pétain—I announced that I was not prepared to entertain any further discussions and that I would be forced to break off the talks as inconclusive if by six o'clock I had not been informed of their readiness to sign the treaty in its present form. Upon hearing this the French withdrew again for final consultations; a few minutes after six o'clock they had completed their last telephone conversation, and Huntziger announced to me that he had been authorised to sign.

When the ceremony was over, I dismissed all the participants in the discussions and remained with General Huntziger alone in the saloon of the railway coach. In a few military phrases I informed him that I had complete understanding for his position and the difficult duty which he had had to perform. He had my sympathy as an officer of the defeated French Army and I expressed to him my own personal esteem; then I shook hands with him He rejoined that he would like to apologise for having failed at one time to maintain the required degree of reserve, but that my disclosure shortly before the document was signed that this would only come into effect at such time as the appropriate armistice had also been signed with Italy had deeply shocked him: the German armed forces had conquered France, but the Italians had never done so. He saluted shortly, and left the room.

That evening there was a brief celebration in the mess diningroom at the Führer's headquarters. A military tattoo was followed by the hymn *Nun danket alle Gott*—Now thank we all our God. I addressed a few words to the Führer as our victorious warlord, and at the end of my speech there was general acclaim for the Führer from all sides; he just held out his hand to me, and left the room. That day was the climax of my career as a soldier . . .*

While the mass of our armies in the west completed their broad sweep to the south, the King of the Belgians was surrendering in northern France and Belgium, and the British Army was embarking at Dunkirk. Of course, the disaster which could have been meted out to them had not occurred, although the signs of the rout visible all along the roads leading to Dunkirk offered the most devastating picture I have ever seen or even thought possible. Even if the mass of the British troops had succeeded in reaching their ships and saving their bare skins, it was only a wrong assessment of the enemy's movements and of the terrain that had prevented von Kleist's Tank Army from capturing Dunkirk by the short route from the west.

For purposes of historical accuracy, I would like here to deal briefly with my own knowledge of the circumstances of the decision [to halt before Dunkirk], because the versions given by the Army General Staff and its Commander-in-Chief have—as I heard even at the Trial—unjustly credited Hitler with the responsibility for making the wrong decision. I was present at the vital briefing conference with the War Office when a decision on this question was demanded from Hitler: the fact was that they did not have the guts to accept responsibility for it themselves if, as might happen, the operation failed. However little they were otherwise disposed to depend upon Hitler and accept his advice, in this particular case they unshouldered the burden of responsibility on to him.

Uppermost in everybody's mind at the time was how in 1914 the low-lying Flanders plains between Bruges, Nieuport-Dixmuiden and so on, had flooded, a circumstance which had checked the

---

* In Keitel's original manuscript there follow details from hearsay of a meeting between Hitler and Mussolini at the advanced second Führer's headquarters in the Belgian village of Bruly-de-Pesche, code-named *Wolfsschlucht*—Wolf's Ravine—where the Field-Marshal had his headquarters in the schoolroom of the evacuated village. These have been omitted by the Editor.

German northern flank and bogged it down. There are the same general features in the terrain to the south and south-west of Dunkirk, with an extensive low-lying plain, intersected by thousands of waterways, and all well below sea-level.

Kleist's Tank Army was standing by to the west of the low ground, ready to lunge through this zone along two or three roads, and this was the situation that was outlined to the Führer; his attention was drawn to the fact that the armoured units would have to keep to the roads in view of the innumerable trenches and canals lying across the land; in other words, in the event of any serious resistance or of the roadblocks which one might expect, there would be no opportunities for them to deploy and display their real fighting power. Had the enemy made such provisions—something which obviously nobody could predict for certain—the consequences might then under certain circumstances be lengthy fighting around the bottlenecks and, if the worst came to the worst, even a retreat and a detour round the impassable terrain, with an inevitable loss of time.

So they left the decision to Hitler, and he—who is above reproach of any lack of dash or daring—determined that it would be preferable not to attempt the raid, but to make the detour around the sure but narrow coastal strip instead. If the competent commanders-in-chief had really been sure of their stuff, they would never have checked back with him but just acted. There is now no doubt that the Führer's order was in the final synthesis wrong: for the Tank Army's diversion and attack made very heavy going of the narrow coastal strip and the British were able to hold Dunkirk and the port long enough for the greater part of their troops to embark, thanks largely to the gallant stand made by the French, who fought us to the finish there.

I saw Paris once only during the war, and that was after the signing of the Armistice with the French, when I was able to accompany the Führer on a tour of the main points of interest in the city. We took off at four o'clock in the morning, and landed at Le Bourget, arriving in the city itself in the early hours as Paris still slept. After looking out over the city from Montmartre, we visited the Arc de Triomphe and the other main points of interest—admittedly only those of architectural interest. The Führer dallied longest at the Opéra, with whose internal architecture he was more familiar than the French guide, and of which he knew and wanted to see details of whose existence the Frenchman did not even dream. Then, with enormous reverence he paid a visit to Napoleon's tomb.

As Paris gradually came to life around us, we left the city and flew back to our headquarters. That was the occasion on which I first became acquainted with the later Minister of Munitions, Professor Speer, who was accompanying the Führer in his capacity as an architect.

Some days later we left our one-time headquarters in France and transferred to the Black Forest, where Todt had built a second headquarters for us during the winter of 1939–1940.

During our stay there, military preparations for an invasion of Britain feverishly gathered momentum. It was the job of the Armed Forces High Command to co-ordinate the efforts of all three services for this combined operation. Nobody was in the dark about the risk we would be running; everybody was well aware that its success would demand a maximum effort by army, navy and air force, but everybody realised that the longer the invasion was postponed, the stronger the British defences would become.

Nobody feared the British Army since its collapse and its enormous material losses at Dunkirk; but the Royal Air Force and the vastly superior Royal Navy were factors which could not be ignored. The War Office was accordingly strongly in favour of risking the operation and made every possible effort to promote its execution: for the first time, Hitler found himself under considerable pressure from that quarter, a circumstance to which he was totally unaccustomed. The air force was also ready, and confident of its ability to provide an umbrella over the naval and landing operations, but they rightly insisted on a period of good weather as being a pre-condition for the success of the whole operation. Our Navy, on the other hand, the service on which would fall the onus of ferrying the ground forces, and fulfilling anti-aircraft and supply rôles, as well as providing a screen against the enemy's naval forces, rightly expressed grave fears not only of the great naval superiority of the enemy, but also of the Channel, whose navigability in changeable weather conditions provided at best an indeterminable element of danger. The latter factor was particularly important, as for our 'invasion fleet' we disposed only of small canal tugs and barges from the Rhine and the Franco-Belgian waterways; above a wind speed of two or three knots none of these craft would be manageable. Moreover, for us to concentrate them in sufficient force was also a considerable problem because, as a result of the destruction of the lock gates and bridges, large sections of the canal system were closed and in consequence those barges that were available to us could not be moved up to the loading and embarkation points. We also had to shield them from

116

enemy air reconnaissance; convert them for the easy loading and un-loading of artillery; and we had to equip them with anti-aircraft guns, and with engines to enable them to sail under their own power. It is remarkable when one considers how much was done along these lines in the short time available: the navy and army engineers vied with each other to produce the necessary craft and even the air force helped, mounting the 'Siebel project' [named after Colonel Siebel of the Air Force] for the rapid development of self-propelled craft for the invasion equipped with anti-aircraft guns. They also put up a consistent umbrella over the invasion ports to guard against prying eyes and controlled our own camouflage measures to prevent any carelessness.

The army worked out the tactical arrangements and the correct order of precedence in the invasion down to the smallest detail, and embarkation and disembarkation exercises rounded off the prepara-tions. But even though the army pressed ahead as fast as it could for the invasion, overcoming all the misgivings that were expressed about whether it would succeed, the preparations could not really be regarded as complete until the end of August. The navy had the greatest misgivings about it all: theirs was the responsibility for safeguarding the troop transports as the armada sailed, but they lacked the necessary seaworthy escort vessels for this, and if the weather were to turn out unfavourable the air force umbrella would also fold up. It seemed an enormous risk to be taking, particularly in view of the losses the navy had sustained in the Norwegian campaign.

So the responsibility for the final decision was left to Hitler alone. Plans were laid for the operation (*Sea Lion*) to be executed during the first half of September, which decades of Channel observation had shown to be the last fine-weather period before the autumn storms and mists closed in on Britain. Although the Führer appeared to be throwing himself into all the preparations with great en-thusiasm, and demanded the adoption of every conceivable im-provisation to speed the preparations, I could not help gaining the impression that when it came to the question of actually *executing* the operation, he was in the grip of doubts and inhibitions: he was wide awake to the enormous risk he would be running, and to the responsibility he was being called upon to shoulder. The multi-plicity of imponderables was too large, the necessary conditions for success were dependent on too many coincidences, for him to bank with any degree of certainty on the chance satisfaction of all the prerequisites. I also had the feeling that not only was Hitler appalled by the thought of the senseless loss of human life a *failure* would entail, but above all he was reluctant to countenance the inevitable loss of his last chance of settling the war with Britain by diplomatic means, something which I am convinced he was at that time still hoping to achieve.

It was all the easier for him to reach the decision he did, early in September, to authorise the launching of a strategic air offensive against Britain, whereby the Commander-in-Chief of the Air Force, Göring, hoped to destroy Britain's air force and armaments industry, especially as with the German air force's great numerical superiority these air battles, with the heavy losses they would inflict on the British, would inevitably be to the advantage of our planned invasion should it ever take place. But the massive German air offensive, although it was executed with exemplary skill by the German units involved, gradually slowed to a standstill as the illusory and comforting impression gained currency that the British fighter squadrons had been wiped out; and operation *Sea Lion* itself was never put into effect, because nobody ventured to predict a sufficiently long period of fine weather for it. The reduction of Britain in the autumn of 1940 became an illusion, and the last chance of bringing the war to a swift conclusion had been lost.

Hitler never told us soldiers whether he ever really entertained hopes of winding up the war with Britain after the collapse of France. I do know that attempts were made to extend such feelers, although when I asked Hitler outright about them he insisted he had not asked for any direct negotiations with Britain, other than the [peace] offer implicit in his Reichstag speech of 19th July. One day, no doubt, the British archives will show the world which of these versions is true.

We all flew back to Berlin from our headquarters in the Black Forest to be present at that memorable Reichstag session on 19th July. Never before and never again were the generals of the German armed forces represented in such strength on the rostrum. A seat had been allocated to me behind Raeder and Brauchitsch on the government benches, behind the Cabinet Ministers, while Göring took the chair as Reichstag president. The Führer was greeted with a tremendous roar of applause as he entered the chamber, just as he had been on arriving in Berlin and during his drive through the Brandenburg Gate.

The honours showered upon the armed forces at this Reichstag session were probably the strangest event of my life as a soldier.

The honours announced in the form of promotions and decorations for the senior commanders—especially those of the Army and Air Force—exceeded all expectations; Göring became a *Reichsmarschall*, and he was awarded the Grand Cross to his Iron Cross.

As far as I was concerned [Keitel was promoted to *Generalfeld-marschall*] I though it all too much of a good thing, because without wishing to injure the feelings of the other generals who were promoted to field-marshal, I was disturbed that the rank was no longer restricted only to front-line 'warriors'. I failed to see what justification there was for such an honour being bestowed upon myself as Chief of the OKW or upon the Secretary of State for Air [Colonel-General Erhard Milch]. I had not been a front-line general and had led no troops into action. I could not see why the Air Force generals were not promoted to *Luftmarschälle*—'air marshals'—instead. I would be lying if I denied that I was pleased by the honour, but I would also be lying if I denied that inwardly I was downright ashamed of myself, although the cheers from the whole House as Hitler announced my name, last of all, showed that they were in broad agreement with the award.

It was on this occasion that Hitler designated the then *Wehr-macht-Führungs-Amt*—armed forces operations office—'my own armed forces *operations staff*', a move that he had discussed with me shortly before the Reichstag session; and at the same time, he promoted its chief, Major-General Jodl, to full general, by-passing the rank of lieutenant-general.

Shortly after this Reichstag session Hitler moved his quarters to the Berghof; with Jodl and a few colleagues I followed soon after, moving into the Reich Chancellery's quarters at Berchtesgaden, and at the end of July I took ten days' leave to pay a visit to my hunting friends in Pomerania. For one last time I was able to throw off my harness for a few carefree days, to devote my time to hunting roe-buck, deer and wild boar, to stroll through my fields at Helmscherode and go to Hildesheim to purchase new farm implements and rubber-tyred farm carts for the estate; during those few days I was just a full-time farmer again—my lifelong dream—a farmer again for the last time in my life.

4

Prelude to the Attack on Russia
1940–1941

W HEN I returned to Berchtesgaden from my leave, on about 10th August, 1940, I still had no idea of Hitler's further plans; I knew only that there was no hope of ending the war with Britain, for the United States and all her unlimited resources stood behind her. Now that our plans for an invasion [of Britain] in the autumn of 1940 had had to be shelved until the spring of 1941 at the earliest, there remained only for us to look for some other way of forcing the British to sue for peace.

I was charged by the Führer to analyse the prospect of contributing to the Italian war against the British in North Africa, in a personal meeting with Marshal Badoglio, the Chief of the Italian General Staff; I was to offer him two German armoured divisions, in recognition of the serious position into which we knew Marshal Graziani their C.-in-C. in Tripolitania had got himself with the British on the Italian colony's frontier. Jodl and I stayed at Innsbruck for a day and a half for these discussions, which naturally took in other questions implicit in the Italian war effort, in particular her armaments problems, the intensification of the anti-aircraft defences round the munitions plants in northern Italy, assistance with fuel supplies and so forth.

Our talks ended with Badoglio rejecting our offer, claiming that tanks would be ineffective in the desert because of their lack of mobility in desert sand. The only concrete benefits we derived were the hams which Badoglio left for Jodl and myself in our hotel room as a food 'subsidy'. We returned to our Berchtesgaden headquarters without having accomplished our mission. Our only achievement was an agreement that we should send a team of tank experts to North Africa under Colonel Freiherr von Funck.

Prelude to the Attack on Russia

An additional measure in our campaign against Britain had been arranged between the Führer and Mussolini—the despatch of German Air Force units to southern Italy to subdue the Mediterranean convoy traffic to the British naval and air base in Malta, and thereby help to protect Italy's sea communications with Tripoli, which were already under attack from the British. All this could unfortunately not be put in hand without reducing German front-line [air] strength tied down in the Battle of Britain; but Mussolini had talked the Führer round by promising to despatch Italian submarines to engage the British in the Battle of the Atlantic. But this offer was of as little value to us as the Italian Air Force had been: the latter's operations against Britain from northern France had altogether miscarried. The Führer however had deduced that he could not reject these offers without offending Mussolini, especially as we were at the time planning to send German U-boats to the Mediterranean as well.

Finally the Führer was planning—while keeping the whole thing absolutely secret from Italy—to seize Gibraltar, with the acquiescence of Spain, of course. The diplomatic feelers and military investigations for that were still outstanding, but work was to begin on them very shortly.

What most disturbed me at this time, however, were the Führer's thoughts on a possible war with the Soviet Union, upon which theme he expanded in more detail in a private talk with Jodl and myself on the very first day of my return from leave. As Jodl told me as we drove home, it was a continuation of discussions which he had first brought up with Jodl as early as the end of July; as I found out for myself, investigations were already in hand to see how far the transfer of several divisions from France could be accelerated: the Commander-in-Chief of the Army had been ordered by Hitler himself to concentrate a number of divisions in Poland, and to estimate the time it would take to move troops up to offset the considerable concentrations of Russian forces in the Baltic provinces and in Bessarabia, a circumstance which filled the Führer with strong forebodings about Soviet intentions.

I immediately raised the objection that we had forty to fifty divisions tied down in Norway, France and Italy; and as they could not be released from those countries, they would not be available for any war in the east; but without them we should be far too weak. Hitler replied at once that that was no reason to fail to take action designed to avert an imminent danger; he had already ordered Brauchitsch, he said, to double the number of armoured divisions.

Finally he added that he had not created this powerful mobile army only to have it rot for the rest of the war: the war would not come to an end of its own accord, and he was not going to be able to use his army against Britain in the spring of 1941 after all, as an invasion would not be practicable then. As he immediately resumed his discussion with Jodl, I did not speak again, but resolved to find out from Jodl afterwards what had already been mooted while I was away and what appeared to have been already put in hand.

Next day I requested a brief interview with the Führer, intending to ask him to his face what reasons he had for his ominous interpretation of Russia's intentions. His reply, in brief, was that he had never lost sight of the inevitability of a clash between the world's two most diametrically opposed ideologies, that he did not believe it could be evaded, and that that being the case it was better for him to shoulder this grave burden now, in addition to the others, than for him to bequeath it to his successor. Besides, he believed there were indications that Russia was already girding herself for war with us, and she had certainly far overreached the agreements we had made on the Baltic provinces and Bessarabia while our hands had been tied in the west. In any case, he said, he only wanted to take precautions against being taken by surprise, and he would not reach any decisions until he had recognised how justified his distrust of them was. When I again objected that our forces were already fully extended in the other theatres of war, he rejoined that he intended to speak to Brauchitsch about expanding our forces and releasing some of those from France. On that note our interview ended, as he was called away to a briefing conference.

The whole thing bothered me so much that I decided to write a personal memorandum on the problem, without calling upon the operations staff, and without any detailed statistics to back me up. That was how my memorandum of the second half of August 1940 came about, without even Jodl's knowing about it. As a result of the [Nuremburg] Trial, the story of my visit to the Foreign Secretary, von Ribbentrop, at Fuschl has become well known: I wished to win him over to dissuading the Führer from the idea at any cost, before Hitler had the chance to tackle him on the subject. In this I was successful: during a very private discussion à deux, Ribbentrop swore to support me from the political side. Each of us promised the other to say nothing of our talk to Hitler, lest we be accused of conspiring against him.

After a war conference some days later, I showed my handwritten memorandum to the Führer; he promised to discuss it with me once he had had time to peruse it. For several days I waited in vain, then I reminded him about it; I was summoned to see him by myself that afternoon. What I then had with Hitler was not so much a discussion as a one-sided lecture on my memorandum's basic strategy; it had not convinced him in the least. My reference to our previous year's pact with Russia was just as misleading: Stalin had as little intention of abiding by it as he had himself, once the situation had changed and a new set of circumstances obtained. In any case, Stalin's only motives in signing the pact had been firstly to guarantee his share in the carve-up of Poland and secondly to spur us on to launch our attack in the west, in the belief that we would get bogged down there and bleed to death. Stalin had planned to exploit this period of grace and our own heavy casualties as a means of subduing us all the more easily afterwards.

I was very upset by this savage criticism and by the tone of voice in which he had delivered it, and I suggested that it would be better for him to replace me as Chief of the OKW with somebody whose strategic judgment was of greater value to him than my own; I felt that in this respect I was not suited for my position, I added, and I requested to be sent to a front-line command. Hitler harshly rejected this: did he then have no right to inform me if in his view my judgment was wrong? He really would have to forbid his generals to go into a huff and ask to resign every time somebody lectured them, and in any case *he* had no chance of resigning his office either. He wanted it understood once and for all that it was nobody's right but his to relieve a person of his office if he saw fit, and until then that person would just have to put up with the job; during the previous autumn, he said, he had had to tell Brauchitsch the same as well. We had both risen to our feet; I walked out of the room without a word. He held on to the memorandum I had written; no doubt it vanished into his safe and probably it was burnt. The draft I wrote might be among the papers of the OKW operations staff, as Jodl and Warlimont claim to have read it.

Here I will skirt round the further developments in our relations with the Soviet Union, Molotov's visit to us early in November, and how Hitler decided that a Russian campaign was now definitely to be prepared. The actual sequence of events during January 1941, with Hitler's thorough briefing by the Chief of the Army General Staff on the stage reached both by our own and the enemy's war preparations has been dealt with in such detail during the Trial—and to some extent in my own affidavits for defence counsel—that I need dwell upon them no longer here. But it cannot be stressed too much that, however much we continued to reinforce our eastern frontiers and the demarcation line between us and the Russians, we always lay both quantitatively and qualitatively far behind the Russians' own troop concentrations. The Soviet Union was methodically preparing for an attack on us; and their preparations along the whole front line were exposed by our own attack on 22nd June 1941.

It was inevitable that as a result of our difference of opinion over war with Russia my general relations with Hitler again deteriorated, and I often detected from his asides when we were dealing with questions bearing on the eastern front that the differences between us had not been satisfactorily resolved.

Admittedly, once our preventive attack* had been launched, I was forced to concede that he had been right after all in his assessment of the imminence of a Russian invasion of our country, but—perhaps because of my recollection of the Red Army's autumn manoeuvres in 1931 when I had visited the Soviet Union as their guest—my view of Russia's capacity to make war was different from Hitler's.

He always assumed that Russia's real armaments industry was still in embryo and nothing like fully expanded; he stressed moreover that Stalin had purged the élite among his military commanders in 1937, so there was a shortage of able brains to back him up.

He was obsessed with the idea that the clash was bound to come sooner or later and that it was wrong for him to sit back and wait until the others were ready and could jump on us. Statements from Russian staff officers captured by us confirmed Hitler's judgment on this score too; only in his assessment of the capacity of the Soviet armament industry—even without the Donets basin— was Hitler misled: the Russian tank forces had a quantitative lead over us which we never could and never did catch up.

I must, however, categorically deny that—apart from some general-staff-type studies made by the OKW's operations staff and the Army General Staff—any preparations were made for a war with Russia before December 1940, except that orders were issued for the railway system and railheads in what used to be Polish territory to be improved to enable them to carry our troops more rapidly to the eastern frontiers of the Reich.

It was probably in connection with his eastern ambitions—and eastern anxieties as well—that Hitler decided in September to meet

---

* Keitel used the phrase *Präventiv-Angriff* to underline his view, but the Editor of this book would be more inclined to accept the view of one of the leading experts in this field, Dr. H.-A. Jacobsen, that the German attack on Russia was an unprovoked aggression.

Pétain and Franco. We had, since the armistice, maintained active contact with the Pétain regime which was settled in the town of Vichy in the unoccupied half of France; among other things, Pétain had expressed a desire to transfer his seat of government to Paris. The Führer had postponed a decision on this for the time being, probably with the intention of seeing what his encounter with Pétain would bring forth.

Early in October I travelled to France with the Führer in his special train. His meeting with Pétain and Laval took place at Montoire railway station, to the south of Paris. I received the elderly Marshal in front of the station building, and saluted him standing at one end of the guard of honour drawn up for him, as he left his closed car. He wore the uniform of a general; he saluted me, and walked past the guard of honour without looking at the soldiers, while Ribbentrop and Laval followed on his heels. Silently we walked through the station building to the Führer's saloon railway coach drawn up just across the platform from the barrier.

As the Führer saw Pétain emerging from the ticket hall, he left the train and came out to meet him; he shook his hand and personally guided him back into his coach. I did not take any part in their conference—I never did in political matters—but after their talk and an almost too affectionate farewell from the Führer to the Marshal, I led the latter back out of the station, and retracing our steps past the guard of honour presenting arms, we walked over to his motor car. Before the Marshal climbed in, he thanked me briefly for the way I had dealt with General Huntziger's armistice delegation. Then, without offering me his hand, he climbed into his car and drove off.

Of the course of their talks I can relate only what I learned from Hitler myself: the Marshal had behaved very properly but with the greatest reserve. Pétain had inquired what form France's future relations with Germany would take and what were, by and large, to be imposed as peace conditions. Hitler, on the other hand, had tried to learn from Pétain the extent to which France would be prepared to accept the cession of certain territories to Italy, if Germany was to guarantee France her colonial empire, with the exception of Tunis. It was obvious that the results of the talks were very meagre: the decisive questions remained unresolved.

We continued our journey to the Spanish border, passing through Bordeaux to the frontier station at Hendaye; Franco arrived there soon after with his Foreign Secretary and lieutenants. In addition to myself, Brauchitsch was also there with an Army guard of honour to receive our guests with the usual formalities. Naturally, we soldiers took no part in the very lengthy discussions in the Führer's coach. Instead of dinner both sides took a break for consultations, and after the Spanish defender of the Alcazar [General Moscardo], who was on Franco's staff, had run out of stories with which to regale us we were all getting bored to tears. I spoke briefly with the Führer: he was very dissatisfied with the Spaniards' attitude and was all for breaking off the talks there and then. He was very irritated with Franco, and particularly annoyed about the rôle played by Suñer, his Foreign Secretary; Suñer, claimed Hitler, had Franco in his pocket. In any event, the final result was very poor.

On our return journey there was a further private interview between Hitler and Laval, probably a continuation of their first discussion a few days earlier. I always understood that the French statesmen were fighting for a clarification of our demands for reparations from their country, and that they were baffled by our additional insistence on representing the demands of Italy, a country to which they insisted they owed nothing.

The news reached us on our return journey through France that Mussolini was planning to attack Greece by force of arms, because the Greeks had rejected his demands for them to cede certain territories to Albania. Count Ciano, his Foreign Secretary, was the instigator of the whole dispute. Both of these Italian statesmen had been lulled by the belief—in which they had been reassured by the governor of Albania—that it would only take a little sabre-rattling for the Greeks to give way without further ado.

The Führer described this '*encore*' by our Ally as downright madness, and at once decided to go down through München for a meeting with Mussolini. As I had a number of urgent matters to attend to, I left the Führer's train and flew back to Berlin, so as not to miss the Führer's train when it left München on the following evening. The train was already slowly pulling out as I jumped aboard at the last moment.

The meeting took place next morning in Florence. Mussolini greeted the Führer with the memorable words, 'Führer, we are on the march!' It was too late to stave off the disaster. Obviously Mussolini had learned of Hitler's intention to restrain him from his project, during the diplomatic preliminaries with our Ambassador, and that was why he had acted so quickly—to confront us with a *fait accompli*.

For several hours the four-cornered discussions dragged on in Florence, between the two leaders and their Foreign Secretaries. I dispelled my boredom by talking with our military attaché and the Italian General Gandin (chief of the operations division of their General Staff), the only one of the Italians to speak German. At noon lunch was served in private to Hitler and the Duce, and I was invited to join them; the conversation was free and informal. Just before the meal, a military despatch arrived from Albania, bringing details of the first victories in the campaign, which had begun early that morning. Mussolini read out the despatch to Hitler and myself, in German of course: German was always the working language for our talks with Mussolini.

We left for home immediately after lunch. I had meanwhile ordered our military attaché there to send us daily telegrams on the war in the Albanian-Greek theatre; I had sworn him to tell only the unvarnished truth. Hitler did not really lose his temper until we were in the train; then he began to fulminate about this new 'adventure' as he was already terming it. He had sternly warned the Duce of the folly of taking it all so lightly: and it *was* a folly, he said, to invade at this time of year, and with only two or three divisions, advancing into the mountains bordering Greece where the weather alone would very shortly call a halt to the whole operation. In his view, as he had told Mussolini, the only possible outcome was a military catastrophe; but Mussolini had promised to send more divisions into Albania should these weak forces be inadequate to smash the attack through. By Mussolini's own account, however, it would take several weeks for even one extra division to disembark in Albania's [two] primitive harbours. If he had wanted so much to pick a fight with poor little Greece, Hitler continued, why on earth had he not attacked Malta or Crete: that would still have made some sense in the context of our war with Britain in the Mediterranean, especially in view of the unenviable position of the Italians fighting in North Africa. The only positive result had been that the Duce had now asked for a German armoured division to be sent to North Africa after all, after our General von Funck had satisfied him that Marshal Graziani was pressing very urgently for one, and that it *would* be possible to make some use of it after all.

I very much fear that Hitler probably did not in fact speak to Mussolini as bluntly as he afterwards described to me, for he hesitated—as I subsequently discovered several times—to say anything likely to injure this military dilettante's vanity. Only later did I realise that Mussolini exploited the Führer whenever he could, but that their friendship was a very one-sided one—Hitler regarding the Duce very much as a golden boy.

Within a very few weeks everything had happened just as Hitler had predicted: the feeble Italian offensive, launched without sufficient reserves, had not only become hopelessly bogged down in the heavy going but ended up in a parlous situation as a combined result of a counter-offensive by the Greeks and the foul weather. That was when the requests for aid began to come, as the poor dockyard facilities in Albania were causing a bad enough bottleneck in the supply organisation for the Italian fighting units, let alone enabling the Italians to make provision for the injection of reserves into the fight. Hitler was willing to send a mountain division, but there was no hope of sending it either by sea or across Yugoslavia; we lent a hand with our last Mediterranean-based German troopships and with Air Force transport squadrons. Had the advent of winter not equally mitigated the Greek counter-offensive and blunted its impact, the sorry end of the adventure would have come six weeks later.

In recognition of this and inspired by the feeling that he ought not to leave his Ally to find his own way out of the predicament—an honourable instinct which Mussolini, had the tables been turned, would have felt able to ignore at any time—Hitler evolved the plan of sending an army across Hungary and Bulgaria into Greece in the following spring, in the hope that at least in Albania Italy would be able to hold out until then. It would of course have been more propitious to approach Yugoslavia about the possibility of moving up German troops for the 'rescue' of Mussolini by means of the shortest overland route [i.e. across Yugoslavia]; but the Führer categorically refused even to contemplate this military proposal: in no circumstances did he want to jeopardise Yugoslavia's position as a neutral, which was equally in Italy's own interests.

It would require a whole volume if I were to describe the military history of the preparation and execution of the Balkan campaign in the spring of 1941. The political opposition to our plans displayed by Hungary, Bulgaria and Roumania was inspired by several motives: Hungary's attitude was ostensibly pro-British, but in view of Germany's assistance in securing in the Vienna Award a considerable alteration of Hungary's frontiers with Roumania—to the latter's disadvantage—Hungary's Imperial Administrator [Admiral Nikolaus von Horthy] was obliged to show his gratitude in some way. Roumania had adopted a Germanophile foreign policy after her King had been exiled and General Antonescu had assumed office as Head of State; at Antonescu's own request we had kept a strong military mission and a staff of technical advisers in Roumania since

1940; like Hitler he was both Head of State and Supreme Commander of the Armed Forces. Our relations with King Boris of Bulgaria were always most cordial: he was an admirer of Hitler and proud of his service in the German Army during the 1914–1918 war.

As far as the purely military measures themselves were concerned, I conducted the initial talks with the Hungarian War Minister [General von Bartha] and with Antonescu and the Bulgarian War Minister [Lieutenant-General Daskaloff]; later on the respective military attachés in these countries acted as intermediaries and—as in Italy—were given the powers of Generals of the German armed forces, with all the enlarged duties and prerogatives that flowed from them; the only exception was in the case of Roumania where—in addition to the military attaché—the head of the military mission, General Hansen, acted as general in command.

My personal relations with Administrator Horthy and King Boris of Bulgaria were particularly good and, one might almost claim, affectionate; there were several instances of this, and it undoubtedly eased many of my difficulties. I never enjoyed an intimate association with Antonescu: he was a capable soldier, dedicated to his mission in life, openhearted and forthright, but uncommunicative and often blunt: it was obvious that he was having a difficult time politically with the Iron Guard and militarily by reason of the corrupt and rotten body of the State—the Civil Service and the Army. He showed an iron determination for ruthless reform but it is open to doubt whether, particularly in the political sphere, he was meeting with any success. He sought the Führer's counsel, but did not heed it; as a result he stood by himself as a politician trying to buttress his position with a worthless Army. He was incorruptible and a fine soldier, but he lacked the time to carry his reforms through.

Preparations for a war with Greece—a campaign which as the Führer repeatedly told us he deeply regretted—preoccupied the War Office and the OKW operations staff all winter.

At the end of October we left Berchtesgaden and I finally had a united OKW in Berlin again. Even so, the War Ministry building was so cramped with the now expanded operations staff that I resolved to transfer my office to Krampnitz, near Potsdam, where there was adequate office space for us in the Cavalry and Armoured Troops' School. In order to be able to live with his wife once more, General Jodl had moved his quarters into the little command post built some years before by Blomberg at Dahlem. During the day, he used to work either at home or in the rooms placed at our disposal next to the old Cabinet Chamber in the Reich Chancellery building.

It was in any case high time for me to be reunited under one roof with all my Command's departments and sections, as the work and my own personal influence on it had been markedly wanting as a result of my absence since May; admittedly I had schooled the heads of the various departments over a period of years, but during my absence they had been obliged to rely almost entirely on correspondence or telephone communication with me. It should not be overlooked that my purely operational rôle, in concert with the Führer and with Jodl, was a very minor part of my duties; and that even if my Ministerial functions did assume a rather lesser importance during the military campaigns, sometimes falling into complete abeyance, they nevertheless did still exist and the backlog of work had to be caught up with. Many matters used to arise which could not be dealt with without my active consent. Although I never regarded it as particularly burdensome, the job gave me no respite: I took no leave at weekends or on public holidays the whole year round; I sat at my desk from early morning until far into the night. I sought recreation in my numerous flights and in my journeys in the Führer's special train—so long as he made no demands upon me—and in the various missions on which the Führer sent me to Italy, Hungary, Roumania, Bulgaria and so on: when I was under way, nobody could reach me by telephone (although my wireless car did receive signals during the journeys). Often I took some of my heavier work with me, because I could devote my undivided attention to it, which was impossible in my office with the innumerable conferences and inevitable interruptions there.

Early in November 1940 the Russian Foreign Secretary Molotov arrived in Berlin at the Führer's request to discuss the political situation. I was present as the Führer received the Russian guests at the Reich Chancellery; the reception ceremony was followed by a banquet in the Führer's chambers, with myself seated next to Molotov's aide, M. Decanosov [the Soviet ambassador] but unable to converse with him as there was no interpreter near at hand. Subsequently the Foreign Secretary held a banquet in his hotel, where I was again seated next to M. Decanosov; this time with the help of an interpreter I was able to speak with him on a number of general subjects: I told him of my visit to Moscow and of the manoeuvres I had seen in 1931, and I asked him a question or two about the recollections I had of my visit then, so there was a degree of laboured conversation between us.

I heard nothing of the diplomatic discussions themselves, except once when I was summoned to be present as the Russians came to take their leave of the Führer after what was the last and obviously the most important conference: of course, I asked Hitler what their outcome had been, and he replied that they had been unsatisfactory; even so, he was not going to decide yet to prepare for war, as he wanted first of all to wait for Stalin's reaction in Moscow. Nevertheless it was at once clear to me that we were heading for war with Russia, and I am not at all sure that during the talks Hitler himself had left no stone unturned to prevent it, even though to have done so would probably have necessitated giving up his representation of the interests of Roumania, Bulgaria and the Baltic states. But it is apparent that here too Hitler was again absolutely justified, for within one or two years, as soon as Stalin was ready to attack us, the Russians would certainly have stepped up their demands; Stalin was by 1940 already strong enough to realise his aims in Bulgaria, and in the Dardanelles and Finnish questions; but our finishing France off in only six weeks had thrown his whole programme out of joint and now he wanted to play for time. I would not venture to set up such a hypothesis, had our preventive war on Russia in 1941 not shown the advanced stage they had reached with their preparations to attack us.

Of course one can only muse on what might have been, had things only worked out differently: even if it was too much to ask of our good fortune that Italy should have stayed out of the war altogether as a benevolent neutral, just consider the difference if Hitler had been able to prevent their irresponsible attack on Greece. What would we not have saved by way of aid to Italy for her senseless Balkan war? In all probability there would not have been any uprising in Yugoslavia in an attempt to force her entry into the war on the side of the enemies of the Axis, just to oblige Britain and the Soviet Union. How differently things would then have looked in Russia in 1941: we would have been in a far stronger position, and above all we should not have lost those two months. Just imagine: we would not just have frozen to a standstill in the snow and ice, with temperatures of minus forty-five degrees just twenty miles outside Moscow, a city hopelessly encircled from the north, west and south, at the end of that November; we should have had two clear months before that infernal cold weather closed in—and there was nothing like it in the winters that followed anyway!

How true was the saying that a permanent alliance can never be forged with the powers of fate! The most daunting imponderables await the statesman and warlord who takes risks; and that was what happened in my view when Yugoslavia's participation in the Tripartite [Axis] Pact was ratified in Vienna. Otherwise there would have been only one other solution open to us, to have sued for peace with Britain at *any* price, and to have relinquished all the fruits of our victories to date. Would that have been acceptable to Britain? After the loss of her French ally, she had once again put out the strongest feelers towards Moscow. In view of her traditional policy of opposition to whichever force in central Europe was most powerful, I will never believe that Britain would ever have let us out of the trap in which she and her American ally now had us and confident as she rightly was of Moscow's intentions.

Hitler's final decision to prepare for war with the Soviet Union came early in December 1940; preparations were to be such that at any time onwards from the middle of March 1941 he could issue the final orders for the programme of troop movements to our eastern frontier, which was consonant with launching the actual attack early in May. The main prerequisite was that the railways had to be able to operate all their available routes at maximum capacity and free of breakdowns. Even if these orders did seem to leave the final decision open until the middle of March, I was now in no doubt whatsoever that only some quite unforeseen circumstance could possibly alter his decision to attack.

Over Christmas, I was my own master for ten whole days, a circumstance I had not enjoyed for several months. Just as the year before the Führer had travelled to the western front to inspect the West Wall, this year he visited the channel coast and our Atlantic Wall, in order to be among his troops this Christmas too, spending his mornings on the inspection of war installations, battery-emplacements and other features of the Atlantic Wall.

So this year too I was able to spend Christmas and the New Year of 1940–1941 with my family. It was not only the last time I would ever spend Christmas at home; it was to be the last time my proud little flock of children would ever come together under my own roof. . . .*

From the beginning of December 1940 we had energetically thrown ourselves into the planning of a combined land and air attack on the Rock of Gibraltar, from the Spanish hinterland. The Spaniards, and especially the Spanish General Vigon—a close friend of Field-Marshal von Richthofen (of the Air Force) and of Admiral Canaris

---

* In Keitel's original manuscript there follows a lengthy passage on his family and children; this has been deleted by the Editor.

—and a general who enjoyed both Franco's confidence and the actual authority of a field-marshal, had not only given us permission to carry out a tactical reconnaissance of the Rock from the Spanish side of the frontier, but had in fact accorded us the greatest assistance in doing so. The plan of attack was elaborated with all the frills and in close detail by a general of our mountain warfare troops and outlined to Hitler in my presence early in December.

The necessary troops for the operation were already standing by in France; the German Air Force had prepared advanced air bases in southern France; the critical point was to persuade neutral Spain —nervous as she rightly was of Britain—to turn a blind eye on the movement across Spanish territory of German troops of about Army Corps strength, together with their heavy artillery and anti-aircraft batteries, preliminary to the attack. On my own suggestion, Admiral Canaris was despatched to see his friend Vigon early in December, to negotiate Franco's agreement for the execution of the operation; General Franco had up to then turned a blind eye on the various General Staff and Intelligence preliminaries. We naturally agreed that once we had succeeded in seizing Gibraltar we would return the Rock to Spain just as soon as the war no longer required us to bar the Straits of Gibraltar to British naval traffic, a military responsibility which we would naturally take care of ourselves.

Some days later Canaris returned to report to the Führer, who had personally entrusted him with and briefed him for the mission: Franco had refused to co-operate, pointing out that such a grave breach of neutrality might result in Britain's declaring war on Spain. The Führer listened calmly and then announced that in that case he would drop the idea, as he was not attracted by the alternative of transporting his troops through Spain by force, with Franco then suitably publicising his wrath about it. He feared that that might lead to a new theatre of operations, because Britain might then with equal justification land troops in Spain, perhaps through Lisbon, just as in the case of Norway.

Whether Canaris was the right man for that mission, I would now be inclined to question, in view of the treachery he now seems to have condoned for several years. I now assume that he did not make a serious effort to win Spain over for the operation, but in fact advised his Spanish friends against it. I myself am in no doubt whatsoever that we would have succeeded in seizing Gibraltar, had Spain so allowed, in view of the vulnerability of the fortress from the landward side, and that in consequence the Mediterranean would have been barred to the British: it would be worthwhile to devote special consideration elsewhere to the consequences thereof for the rest of the war in the Mediterranean. It was Hitler who had recognised the difference it would make not only to Britain's lines of communication with the near and far East, but above all to the ailing Italy.

After the Gibraltar operation had been written off, all thoughts reverted to the eastern question again. I think it was probably in the second half of January 1941 that Halder, the Chief of General Staff, outlined to the Führer in the presence of Jodl and myself the Army's operational plan for the attack on Russia, describing in close detail the Intelligence so far gathered on the enemy, on the series of border incidents reported along the demarcation line and on the planned railway troop movements preliminary to the invasion. On the latter score the Führer was particularly interested in arrangements for moving up in the last wave of troop concentrations the armoured units being brought up from the garrisons in central Germany where they had wintered and re-equipped, and where new units had been raised for them. For me, Halder's address was startling in as much as it gave me a first insight into the extent of Russia's war preparations and a disturbing picture of the steadily increasing concentration of Russian divisions on the other side of the frontier, as the reconnaissance efforts of our frontier guards had established beyond all possibility of error. At that stage it was still not possible to determine whether the Russians were actually girding themselves for an attack, or whether they were themselves only massing to ward one off; but the German invasion was soon to tear that veil of doubt aside.

At the end of March 1941, Hitler addressed the first all-service conference of senior commanders earmarked for the eastern front at the Reich Chancellery building in Berlin. I had managed to arrange for all the OKW's departmental heads to hear the Führer's address as well. I recognised at once that he intended to lay down a programme of action for us: in the small Cabinet chamber, rows of chairs and a speaker's lectern had been set up, just as though it were a public lecture. Hitler addressed us very gravely, in a well-organised and elaborately prepared speech.

Starting with the military and political situation of the Reich, and with the intentions of the Western Powers—Britain and America —he elaborated on his thesis that war with the Soviet Union had become inevitable, and that to sit back and wait for it would only worsen our prospects of victory. At the time he openly admitted that any hesitation would tilt the balance of strength against us: our enemies disposed over unlimited resources, which they had not even begun to strain, while we were not in the position to add to our manpower and material resources much more. Thus he had reached the decision that Russia must be forestalled and anticipated at the earliest possible moment; the danger, latent yet palpable, that she represented for us would have to be eliminated.

Then followed a weighty exposition on the inevitability of such a conflict between two diametrically opposed ideologies: he knew that it was bound to come sooner or later and he preferred to take it upon himself now than to turn a blind eye on this threat to Europe and bequeath this inescapable problem to his successor. He did not want to postpone its solution until later. For nobody who succeeded him would exercise sufficient authority in Germany to accept responsibility for unleashing the preventive war which alone would suffice to halt the Bolshevik steamroller in its tracks, before Europe had succumbed to it. There was nobody in Germany who knew the face of Communism and its destructive powers better than he from his fight to save Germany from its clutches.

After a lengthy harangue on the experience he had gained and the conclusions he had drawn, he finished with a declaration that war was a fight for survival and demanded that they dispense with all their outdated and traditional ideas about chivalry and the generally accepted rules of warfare: the Bolsheviks had long since dispensed with them. The communist leaders had given clear proof of this by their behaviour in the Baltic states, Finland and Bessarabia, as well as by their arbitrary refusal either to recognise the Hague Rules on Land Warfare or to consider themselves bound by the Geneva conventions on the treatment of prisoners of war. He followed this up by insisting that [Soviet] political commissars should not be regarded as soldiers, or treated as prisoners of war: they were to be shot down in the course of battle or executed out of hand. They would be the hardcore of any attempt at putting up a fanatical resistance; the commissars, said Hitler, were the backbone of the communist ideology, Stalin's safeguard against his own people and against his own troops; they had unlimited power over life and death. Eliminating them would spare German lives in battle and in the rearward areas.

His further statements on the liability to courts martial of German troops suspected of excesses against the civilian population, whether or not suppressing armed resistance, were inspired by the same motives, although the re-institution of such courts martial was to be left to the discretion of each commander as soon as he regarded his territory as pacified. Finally, Hitler announced that he was forbidding the transport of Russian prisoners of war into Reich territory, as in his view they represented a danger to the labour force, not only because of their ideology, of which he had already liberated the German industrial labour scene once, but because of the danger of sabotage. The impression he had made with his speech upon his audience was not lost to him, although nobody openly raised his voice in protest; he rounded off this unforgettable address with the memorable words: 'I do not expect my generals to understand me; but I shall expect them to obey my orders.'

It was now that in line with Hitler's statements the 'special regulations' for the administration of the former Soviet territories were drawn up, as a supplement to the basic directive for the preparation of the war in the east [the *Barbarossa* contingency]. In addition to the warrants of Göring and the Commander-in-Chief of the Army as bearers of the executive authority, it contained the clause I had so stubbornly contested relating to the authority of the S.S.-Reichsführer [Heinrich Himmler] as Chief of Police in the rearward operational areas. In view of our experiences in Poland and Himmler's not unknown megalomania I read into this a serious danger that he would only abuse the power Hitler had accorded to him for the maintenance of peace and order behind the front lines. My opposition was to no avail and, despite several protests and support from Jodl throughout, I was overruled.

It was not for some days that I was able to discuss our opinions of Hitler's speech with Brauchitsch. He was quite frank: deep down inside themselves, his generals wanted no part of this kind of war. He asked whether any written orders were likely to follow along those lines. I assured him that without clear directions from Hitler I would certainly neither prepare nor ask for such orders in writing; I not only considered written orders to that effect superfluous, but indeed highly dangerous. I said that I for one would be doing all I could to avoid having them. In any case, everybody had heard with their own ears what he had said; that would suffice. I was firmly opposed to putting anything down on paper on so questionable a matter.

Unfortunately, Brauchitsch was probably unconvinced by me, for in May the War Office circulated *draft* orders for Hitler's approval, prior to their issue to the Army's troops on the eastern front. That was how the notorious 'Commissar Order'—which is certainly known to all the commanders, but appears not to have survived in a verbatim text*—and the order on 'Liability for Court Martial in Soviet territories' came into being.

The former was apparently issued by the War Office after Hitler had approved its terms. The latter was issued by the High Command's legal department after it had rephrased the War Office draft; it bears my own signature, as being on behalf of the Führer. Both these orders were accepted as prime exhibits against me at the Nuremberg Trial, especially as they had been issued six weeks before our attack and there was thus never any possibility of justifying them in retrospect by circumstances obtaining during the Russian campaign. As their sole author—Hitler—was dead, I alone was called to answer for them by that Tribunal.

In the middle of March we began to move troops eastwards in preparation for the attack; D-day had been set for 12th May [1941] although no actual implementation order had been issued. This was the way Hitler worked; he would keep the final date for storming the frontier as open as possible until the very last moment, for one never knew what unforeseen circumstance might crop up in the final weeks or even the very last hours, demanding the greatest freedom of action.

At the same time, we were engaged with the crossing of the Danube and Field-Marshal List's march on Bulgaria; the latter's army made only slow progress in the winter weather, the roads being as bad as they were. At the same time we were also occupied with the diplomatic negotiations for Yugoslavia's participation in the Tripartite [Axis] Pact. At the same time, a new disaster was threatening the Italian troops in Albania. And all the time, Hitler was demanding the strengthening of our Army occupying Norway and the provision of 200 more coastal gun batteries of every calibre. I could extend this catalogue still further, if time was not pressing for me now. It will suffice for me to stress the extent to which our military organisation—even during this interlude between our victory over France and our attack on the Soviet Union—was preoccupied with all kinds of investigations to ensure that nothing that might just lead to a reverse had been overlooked. Day and night, even when it appeared that nothing much was happening, the High Command was consumed by intense activity. It was Hitler who kept us at it with his restless spirit and the fantastic imagination with which he not only thought out everything for himself but which

---

* It has in fact survived.

constrained him to provide the most elaborate safeguards should the improbable materialise.

At the end of March I accompanied Hitler to Vienna, where the new Four Power Pact with Yugoslavia was signed in Castle Belvedere, with all the customary pomp and circumstance . . .* When I was summoned to attend the Führer later that afternoon, he expressed his deep satisfaction and relief that there was no prospect of unexpected surprises in the Balkan theatre. He read to me a letter he had just dictated for Mussolini, containing several proposals, and particularly a demand for some degree of order to be introduced into his maritime communications with North Africa. To this end, he had suggested that some elderly destroyers and cruisers should be disarmed and stripped, and converted into fast transport ships less vulnerable to enemy submarine attack. Hitler invited me to tell him whether I had any objections about his having made such radical suggestions to the Duce; I shook my head firmly. If anybody was to tell Mussolini anything, then he, Hitler, was the man to do it; it had to be brought home somehow to Mussolini that things could not be allowed to go on like that, especially if Germany's troops were also dependent on seaborne supplies. That night we returned to Berlin in our special train.

Two days later, the Zvetkovic regime was overthrown in Belgrade, together with the Regent, Prince Paul, an admirer of the Führer's and a supporter of their foreign policy hitherto; the Four Power Pact had (ostensibly) caused an officers' revolt. I had already been called to see the Führer in the Reich Chancellery building and I reached it at the same time as Jodl. The Führer appeared in our conference chamber and showed us the telegram, bursting out spontaneously that he had no intention of standing for that: now he would smash Yugoslavia for once and for all; never mind what the new government might tell him, he had been disgracefully betrayed, and a declaration of loyalty now would only be a feint, a ploy to win time. He had sent for Ribbentrop and the Commander-in-Chief of the Army (Brauchitsch) as well, and as soon as they were all there he would give them his orders: there was only one way, and that was an immediate, concentric attack both from the north and, with List's army, from Bulgaria in the east; the Hungarian Minister Sztojay was to be sent for at once and told that Hungary would have to assist; she would get back her precious Banat

---

* In Keitel's original manuscript there follows here a historically unimportant description of social events in Vienna during the signing of the Pact; this has been omitted by the Editor.

territory in reward; we would all see how old Horthy would be behind us breathing fire and brimstone for that prize.

I interjected that our eastern front deadline could not be postponed, as troop movements were already proceeding according to our planned maximum railway-capacity programme and we could not reduce that programme to any further extent; Field-Marshal List's army was too weak to pit against Yugoslavia, and we could not rely on the Hungarians. That, rejoined Hitler, was the very reason why he had called in Brauchitsch and Halder; some solution would have to be found. Now he intended to make a clean sweep in the Balkans—it was time people got to know him better. Serbia had always been a State prone to *Putsche*, so he was going to clean her up; and so he stormed on—he was, one might say, properly under way.

After everybody had turned up, the Commander-in-Chief of the Army, the Foreign Secretary, and so on, Hitler announced the situation to us in his now familiar manner, and outlined his intentions. As always, it was just a stream of orders: an attack on Yugoslavia as early as possible; List's army was to encircle her to the right and, invading from the east, march on Belgrade from the south-east with a strong northern flank, while German and Hungarian units captured Belgrade from the north across the Danube and a new army comprising the rearward units of the troops massing to attack Russia made a lunge from Austria. Appropriate proposals by the War Office and Air Force High Command were to be tabled without delay. He himself would undertake the necessary negotiations with the Hungarians, he would send their Minister Sztojay off to Budapest that very day. Jodl's interjection that the new Yugoslav government should be confronted with an ultimatum with a fixed time limit was categorically rejected by the Führer. Hitler did not let the Foreign Secretary even get so far as opening his mouth. Brauchitsch was authorised to moderate the tempo of our troop movements, in order not to interfere so much with public transport. There was no further discussion; Hitler walked out of the chamber accompanied by the Foreign Secretary for an interview with the Hungarian Minister in Berlin who was already waiting below. After a brief exchange of views between Halder and Jodl there remained only one thing for all of us, and that was: 'Back to work!'

When one bears in mind that all our previous plans for the attack on Russia, the campaign in Greece and aid for Italy were just dropped for the time being and new dispositions, troop movements, redistributions, the agreements with Hungary about the operations, the transit of German troops and the organisation of the whole supply system had to be improvised from scratch, and despite all this the invasion of Yugoslavia—coupled with an air strike on Belgrade—followed only nine days later, the achievement of the operations staffs of the High Command, the War Office, and the Air Force can only be termed an outstanding performance, of which admittedly the lion's share was borne by the Army General Staff. Nobody knew this better than the Führer, but he gave no voice to his gratitude. I would have liked him to have given credit where it was due; the General Staff had deserved their share of praise, instead of the recriminations for which they were so often the butt.

Imperial Administrator Horthy was more than dubious about Hungary's ability to participate: he was reluctant to mobilise in the middle of the season for spring cultivation, as he could not deprive his peasants of their horses and manpower. The Führer was very put out by this answer. But the General Staff conferences did eventually result in at least a partial mobilisation in Hungary, with the Hungarian government raising a small army to sally forth into the 'Banat' to collect their little morsel for themselves (although they gave the German troops the honour of going in ahead while they themselves wrought their revenge in the rear). The Führer wrote Horthy a letter to explain that while the Hungarian troops were to fit into the overall scheme of operations, he himself was commanding them, but he would so co-ordinate them in advance with Horthy as Supreme Commander of the Hungarian forces that the latter's sovereign authority was not usurped. So the last reefs barring the way to a coalition war had been successfully and formally cleared, while still taking the old man's vanity into account. Hitler's political dexterity even enabled him to wean Croatia out of the united enemy front and to inspire her to sabotage the Yugoslav mobilisation decree.

As we had no permanent Führer's headquarters prepared and were unable to build one in the very few days available, the Führer's special train was brought into use as a cramped headquarters; it was shunted onto a single-track spur near a small hostelry, which latter offered the OKW operations staff modest accommodation and working space, while only Jodl and I lived with our lieutenants in the Führer's headquarters train; the command coach served us as a permanent office. Our signals communications functioned beyond reproach, another achievement of the signals officers permanently attached to the Führer's headquarters and of the Chiefs of Military

Signals, Generals Fellgiebel and Thiele, who really were technically superb and who often succeeded in performing the impossible. I truly never had cause for complaint in this respect.*

From the Führer's headquarters train we guided first the Yugoslav and then the Greek campaigns to their victorious conclusions; both countries had surrendered within rather less than five weeks. The following events have particularly remained in my memory: I recall Horthy's visit to us in the cramped confines of our special train; the visit passed off in the closest harmony, because the Führer had turned on his charm at full power and knew how to flatter the old gentleman—a talent to which the latter was very susceptible; Horthy moreover was not unnaturally in a charmed world, seeing one of his lifelong dreams come true: the clock was being turned back and the Banat—one of the most beautiful and fertile provinces of the former kingdom—was returning to his regency. I was not able to sample this new atmosphere myself until lunch in the narrow dining-car, where I sat next to Horthy at the common dining-table; he dominated the table talk with his beaming countenance and innumerable anecdotes on his experiences as a naval officer and as a farmer, horse-breeder and racing-stable owner. I led his conversation round to hunting anecdotes, although I knew that hunting was a theme anything but dear to the Führer's heart: he always said that hunting was nothing but cowardly murder, as the deer, the most beautiful of Nature's creatures, was unable to defend itself; the poacher, on the other hand, he lauded as one of his heroes and the very best type of soldier; he would dearly like to form an élite battalion of poachers, he said.†

After the surrender of Yugoslavia had been accepted [on 17th April, 1941] by Field-Marshal List on the Führer's behalf and in accordance with the OKW's directives, Hitler brought his personal influence to bear on the armistice with Greece, while still looking to Italy's interests and Mussolini's inordinate vanity, by dispatching General Jodl to take charge. The Führer was basically minded to give the Greeks an honourable settlement in recognition of their brave struggle and of their blamelessness for this war: after all the Italians had started it. He ordered the release and repatriation of all their prisoners of war immediately they had been disarmed; the poor countryside was to be preserved and the country's production was

---

* Keitel is referring to the fate of these two officers, after the bomb plot of 20th July, 1944: the Chief of Military Signals, General Fellgiebel, and his deputy, Lieutenant-General Thiele, were both executed for taking part in the conspiracy.

† In Keitel's original manuscript there follows here a description of the Führer's birthday of 20.4.1941; this has been omitted by the Editor.

not to be touched except where it might be used to aid the British, who had landed in Greece in March. If there still had to be fighting on Greek soil then it was with one aim only: to mop up every last Englishman in Greece and to drive them out of every island they had seized. After we had won the battle of Mount Olympus, defeated the British at Thermopylae and driven them out of Athens, we chased their scattered remnants into the Ismuth of Corinth and drove them out of every corner of the country, bar a handful of Aegean islands and the main British base on Crete. The quarrel over the troops' victorious entry into Athens was a chapter to itself: Hitler wanted to do without a special parade, to avoid injuring Greek national pride. Mussolini, alas, insisted on a glorious entry into the city for his Italian troops (who first of all had to be rushed up to the city as they had dawdled several days' march behind the German troops who had expelled the British forces). The Führer yielded to the Italian demand and together the German and Italian troops marched into Athens. From the Greeks this miserable spectacle, laid on by our gallant Ally whom they had honourably beaten, must have produced some hollow laughter.

On account of his preoccupation with the supply lines of our troops fighting in North Africa—gradually expanding to the strength of an armoured division under Rommel's command—the Führer began looking for ways to shield his lines of communication across the Mediterranean from attack by British naval forces and to afford them added safeguards. While Rommel had arrested the immediate danger threatening Tripoli by his bold and rapid action, the idea of seizing either Crete or Malta from the British, weakened as they were by their setbacks in Greece, began to germinate in Hitler's brain; the project could come to fruition only by means of an airborne landing, combined with or followed up by a military assault from the sea, in which latter aspect the help the Italians might be able to provide seemed likely to be more than problematic. Quite possibly Hitler wanted to demonstrate to Mussolini what a real Mediterranean campaign looked like. Of the two possible objectives, I declared myself in favour of an operation against Malta, which both Jodl and I agreed to be the British base of greater strategic importance and danger to us. But the final choice was left to the Air Force, and Göring decided the assault should be on Crete, undoubtedly thinking it was the easier of the two alternatives. Hitler agreed.*

* Keitel's original manuscript contains further details on this decision-making, but they have been omitted by the Editor as being of little consequence.

Prelude to the Attack on Russia

In the meantime, the Führer had decided that the new D-day for the invasion of Russia was to be about the middle of June. This involved the rapid release of the Army units engaged on mopping-up operations in the Balkans, and their re-injection into the troops massing behind our frontier with Russia. The consequence was a less than adequate pacification of the Yugoslav region, in which, in no time at all and incited by Stalin's open appeals and enthusiastic support, partisan warfare broke out. Unfortunately, the few remaining troops were unable to strangle this guerilla warfare at birth, and as time went on a situation arose which actually demanded the reinforcement of our security forces there, as the arrogant Italians who were supposed to have relieved us of this burden deserted all along the line, and put new backbone into Tito's partisan army, which helped itself to their weapons.

Britain and Russia did all that was necessary to foment new seats of unrest and tie down our German troops there, while the new Croat State, filled with misgivings over its 'Protector' Italy, was only hampered in its attempts to restore internal order by Italy's jealousy towards us. The Führer looked passively on at this tragedy, without making the least attempt to demonstrate his sympathy for the Croat people in the face of the intrigues which Mussolini was obviously inspiring. He let his Ally play his hand as he saw fit to keep him sweet, perhaps because other affairs seemed of greater moment to him then, or alternatively because he was prevented from acting by pledges he had given.

We returned to Berlin from Berchtesgaden at about the beginning of June 1941. At last the whole High Command was once more combined under my leadership, if only for a few weeks again. As I had been unable to be in two places at once, I had been obliged to accord the OKW, with the exception of its operations staff, a high degree of autonomy in many Berlin affairs, although communication by courier and telephone had, of course, provided a permanent link with me even in my absence. Perhaps I had erred in not accustoming Hitler to the necessity of accepting that the gravamen of my work lay in Berlin; but quite apart from that, he never left me to my own devices; he had me recalled if ever I was away more than two days at a time. It was impossible to separate the military operations staff (the command side) from the Führer's remaining staff (the War Ministry side) within the High Command; some sort of connecting link was necessary, and nobody could replace me as that. If I had had the time once I had assumed office to elaborate some other organisational structure more suited to the

143

requirements of war, there might have been some way out. Up to 1941 my periods of absence from Berlin were still tolerably brief; it was not until the permanent absence enforced by the war in the east began that I was faced with a problem which I was no longer able to resolve. In 1944 I had planned to solve it by making Warlimont my Chief of Staff and permanent representative in Berlin; but as a result of his illness for several months after the assassination attempt of 20th July, 1944, we never got round to it.

In the middle of June 1941 and for the last time before our attack on Russia, the Führer assembled all his senior frontline commanders and representatives of the various service High Commands, to hear him outline their tasks and to listen to a final speech in which he forcefully pressed his points of view on the imminent 'war of ideologies'. Drawing attention to the massive resistance being offered to our pacification operations in the Balkans, he said this was the lesson to be learned from treating the civilian populace too leniently; the treatment had only been interpreted as weakness and this uprising was the logical outcome. He had made a study of the methods the old Danube monarchy had always had to employ to establish the authority of the State over its subjects; and we could expect far more trouble from the Soviet citizens, who would have been incited to acts of violence and terrorism by the . . .* For this reason, he said, the mailed fist would ultimately be the kindest way: one could only smash terror with counter-terror, not with military tribunal procedures. It was not with lawbooks that he himself had smashed the German Communist Party's terrorist tactics, but with the brute force of his SA [Brownshirts'] movement.

It was now that I began to perceive what I described for my defence counsel in a memorandum over Christmas 1945: Hitler had become obsessed with the idea that his mission was to destroy Communism before it destroyed us. He considered there was no prospect in relying on permanent non-aggression pacts with Russian Communism; he had recognised that if he failed to smash the iron ring which Stalin—in conjunction with the Western Powers—would be able to forge about us at any time if he so saw fit, it would lead to Germany's economic collapse. He disdained suing the Western Powers for peace at any price, and staked everything on the one card: war! He knew that if the cards should turn against him, the world would be up in arms against us. He knew, too, what a war on two fronts would mean. But he shouldered the burden because

* In Keitel's text the last word is illegible, but may be presumed to read 'Commissars'.

he had wrongly assessed the reserves of Bolshevism and of the Stalin State, and it was thus that he brought about the ruin of himself and the Third Reich he had created.

Even so, during the summer of 1941 it almost seemed as though the eastern Colossus would succumb to the mighty blows inflicted by the German Army, for the first and probably the best Soviet front-line army had, in fact, been all but wiped out by that autumn, and they had suffered enormous losses in manpower and material: thousands of heavy guns and armoured vehicles littered the battlefields of the first encirclement actions and the prisoners numbered many more than a million. One wonders what army in the world could have withstood such annihilating blows, had the vast expanse of Russia, her manpower reserves and the Russian winter not come to its assistance?

As early as the end of July Hitler was already believing not only that the Red Army in the field had been beaten, but that the nucleus of their defences had been so gravely afflicted that it would be impossible for them to recover their enormous material losses before the country was overwhelmed by total defeat. For this reason—and this is of high historic interest—he was by the end of July or early August already ordering considerable sections of the Army munitions industry (apart from tank construction) to be switched over to accelerating munitions production for the Navy (submarines) and the Air Force (aircraft and anti-aircraft batteries) in anticipation of an intensification of the war with Britain, while on the Eastern Front the Army was to keep the defeated enemy in check using the weapons on hand, but with twice the armoured strike capacity.

It was not until the night of 21st to 22nd June, 1941, that the Führer's train, with a number of his closest staff including Jodl, myself and our adjutants, reached the Führer's new headquarters at a forest camp near Rastenburg. The War Office's operational headquarters had been accommodated in a very large forest encampment some thirteen miles away, while Göring, the Commander-in-Chief of the German Air Force, had had his headquarters train shunted into another encampment in the Johannesburg forest nearby; the result was that the various High Commands were now able at a moment's notice to engage in personal exchanges of thoughts, while within the space of an hour (or considerably less using their light Storch aeroplanes) they could all be assembled at the Führer's behest.

The OKW operations staff was in a special camp detached at a distance of a thousand yards from the Führer's headquarters proper, Security Zone I. I have often flown over the site at various altitudes, but despite my precise knowledge of its location I was never able to spot it from the air, except perhaps by virtue of the lane leading through the forest and a single-track railway spur which had been closed to public traffic. About two or three miles away a landing-ground had been laid out and the Führer's aircraft, courier units and the aircraft of the OKW itself were parked around it. I wish I knew how many flights I made from there between 1941 and 1944. I only ever heard of one fatal aircraft accident on that airfield, when [Munitions] Minister Dr. Todt was killed in a Heinkel 111 which crashed on take-off in February 1942.

Each midday a war conference was held in the Führer's presence, to discuss the morning telegrams from the various High Commands, which, in the case of the War Office, were in turn based on each evening's terminal despatches from the Army Corps. Only the Commanders-in-Chief in Finland, Norway and North Africa reported directly to the OKW, with copies for information to the War Office.

It was the custom for Colonel-General Jodl to outline the war situation including the Army aspect except when the Commander-in-Chief of the Army and the Chief of the Army General Staff were themselves participating; on these occasions General Halder dealt with the Army's situation. After 19th December 1941, when the Führer himself assumed the position of Commander-in-Chief of the Army [see page 164] the Chief of General Staff had to brief him each day on the Eastern Front and personally collect the Führer's orders; as the situation grew more tense, he [Halder] was obliged to appear at the evening war conferences towards midnight as well, at which Colonel-General Jodl otherwise outlined the situation to a small circle of officers by himself. Any instructions the Führer might issue on these occasions were afterwards despatched that same night by the OKW operations staff to the quarters concerned, by teleprinter, after their gist had already been conveyed by telephone.

These briefing conferences performed the secondary function of enabling the Führer to issue a stream of orders relating not only to the problems of strategy, but to any field with even the most tenuous bearing upon the military conduct of the war. As Hitler could never keep to the point on these occasions, but repeatedly diverged on still further problems as they were introduced by other parties, the midday war conferences lasted an average of three hours and the evening ones never less than one hour, although the strategic and tactical questions should not as a rule have consumed more than a fraction of that time. As a result I, who had already had to brief myself on the morning or evening war situation by reading the operations staff's summaries or by attending Jodl's evening briefings, could never afford to absent myself from these time-wasting conferences held by the Führer, as at any moment all kinds of questions, directives and measures were being invoked by Hitler, matters not even remotely concerned with strategy or diplomacy, but which had to be taken in hand, and for which he turned to me as his military Chief of Staff, however little they might come within the competence of the High Command.

All this could only be attributed to this autocrat's disorderly thinking processes and *modus operandi*; but in this way I found myself dragged into almost every sphere of activity of the State and Party machinery, without once having taken the initiative myself, hard-pressed as I was with my own proper duties. God knows, I had my work cut out trying to ward off all the work which was obviously nothing to do with my office; I and my adjutant could list innumerable cases where visitors, correspondents and telephone-callers have all made some demand or other upon my time, adding the stereotype justification: 'The Führer has referred me to you for this!' Or: 'When I outlined this to the Führer, he declared that the same ought to go for the Armed Forces too.' Or: 'You are to announce the following to the Armed Forces's' and so on. Or: 'To whom in the OKW should I address this particular matter?' and all the other standard formulae they used.

For all these outsiders, whether OKW or War Office, the 'Armed Forces' meant one man: Keitel. It is so symptomatic that the head of the High Command's legal department Dr. Lehmann, had to explain to my Defence Counsel that I allowed my name to be invoked by every imaginable quarter in matters which were no concern in the least of mine.

What was I to do? When Hitler personally gave me such instructions during his war conferences, was I to answer in the hearing of twenty-five people 'My Führer, that is nothing to do with me . . . tell your Secretary what it is you want.' Would it have been possible for those people who had been conferring with Hitler on their projects, and had been told by him to talk them over first with me, to have replied, 'We won't do that . . . Keitel will only throw us out on our ear?' Things just were not as simple as all that; it was not my bonhomie or my stupidity that was to blame, the whole system was wrong.

Could I have foreseen all that when this abortion of an office— Chief of the High Command—came into being? Did they give me time after the 4th February, 1938, to modify the weaknesses in the organisational structure which was only really designed to combine Hitler's power and executive authority with a military expert as his secretary?

In the Royal Prussian tradition, a real field-marshal was too good for that, and the office would have been too humble for promotion to field-marshal. Since my last and happiest military service as a divisional commander I have become a 'chair-borne' general; in the First World War I was the senior divisional general-staff officer for almost two years, and proud to share with my commanders the responsibility—as we saw it in those days—for our brave soldiers. In the Second World War I ended up a field-marshal, unable to issue an order to anybody outside the actual structure of the OKW, apart from my driver and my batman! And now, to be called to account for all those orders that were issued against my advice and against my conscience: what a bitter pill it is to swallow, but at least it will be an honourable one if in so doing I can shoulder responsibility for the whole OKW.

Hitler's intention was to bring home to his immediate entourage the significance of the Armed Forces, by having them represented by a field-marshal. General Schmundt, on the other hand, told me after my promotion that the Führer had desired to show me his gratitude in this way for bringing about the armistice with France. Be that as it may! My traditional background gives me cause to regret that the rank of field-marshal ceased to be restricted solely to generals who had shown particular mettle in the face of the enemy.

Soon after our first victorious battles, however, the same old quarrels began to break out between Hitler and the War Office. Hitler's strategy called for a variation of that propounded by the War Office: while the latter had advocated that Army-Group Centre should punch its way through with the aim of taking Moscow and capturing the Valdai heights to the north, thereby severing communications between Leningrad and the capital, Hitler wanted to hold back along a general line running from Odessa to Lake Peipus through Orel and Smolensk; having done that he would draw off some of the strength from Army Group Centre (by far the most formidable and heavily armoured of the Army Groups) and

148

BARBAROSSA—THE GERMAN INVASION
OF RUSSIA, 1941

Tallin/ Reval
Baltic Sea
●LENINGRAD

Scale of Miles
0 250

L.Peipus
Valdai Heights
Riga
Memel
Velikie Luki
Kalinin
Konigsberg
①
② Smolensk
●MOSCOW
Minsk
Bialystok
Brest-Litowsk
Bryansk Orel
Kovel
Kursk Voronezh
Lvov
Zhitomir Kiev
③
Kharkov
Rostov
R U M A N I A
Odessa
Bucharest
Black Sea
Krasnodar
Maikop
Sevastopol

① Army Group North (von Leeb)
② „ „ Centre (von Bock)
③ „ „ South (von Runstedt)

U.S.S.R. Western frontier June 22nd.1941 ‑‑‑‑‑
Front line on July 9th. 1941 ‑‑‑‑‑
„ „ „ August 20th. 1941 ▬▬▬▬
„ „ „ December 5th. 1941 ▬▬▬▬

E.G.M.

use a reinforced Army Group South to deprive the enemy of the whole Donets basin, and of the Maikop and Krassnodar oil fields; then he would seize Leningrad using a similarly reinforced Army Group North and link up with Finland. The latter two Army Groups would not have been strong enough to perform these tasks without reinforcement.

Hitler visualised these targets on the flanks as being of great economic value in the case of the Donets basin, and political and naval value in the case of Finland and the Baltic: from the point of view of military strategy he was not so much concerned with the city of Leningrad as such, or with its world status as a city of a million inhabitants, as with the naval base at Kronstadt and its elimination as a key naval base; it presented a considerable threat to our communications and submarine training in the Baltic. The War Office, on the other hand, believed that in their proposal lay the key to a rapid termination of the war. The Führer remained unconvinced.

He decided to fly out to the headquarters of Army Group Centre (at Borisov) having summoned the commanders of two Tank Armies, Hoth and Guderian, to meet him there. I accompanied Hitler, and took part in the ensuing conference between the Commander-in-Chief of Army Group Centre, von Bock, and the two tank generals, each of whom he [Hitler] wanted to siphon off to the neighbouring Army Groups as the first of the reinforcements. He came up against a blank wall of refusal, the two tank generals even going so far as to announce that their units were so battle-weary that they would need two or three weeks to regroup and to overhaul their tanks before they would be fully operational again.

Obviously we had no means of checking these claims; the two generals remained unco-operative—despite the award to them of the Oak Leaves to their Knight's Crosses—and refused to admit any possibility of alternative employment for their units, at any rate on such remote sections of the front. Von Bock naturally had no desire to lose them and trumpeted the same story. All three of them were aware of the War Office's plan of attack and saw it as their panacea; any weakening of Army Group Centre would jeopardise this plan, a plan which had electrified them all.

Although the Führer could see right through their ploy—no great feat for anybody—he hesitated to command the War Office to override their pleas and release the two tank generals as he had wanted, even though the period they were demanding for recuperation would delay his planned operation by some four weeks. The

War Office, Army Group Centre and the tank commanders had managed to put up a united front to their Führer. He was convinced that they did not *want* to do it and had just claimed that they were not *able* to; that was what he himself told me at the time.

Inwardly he was once again very annoyed at the War Office as a result of all this, but he managed to swallow his bitterness. There was a compromise, which, of course, shipwrecked Hitler's great strategic master plan, at any rate in so far as Leningrad to the north was concerned. Hitler for his part vetoed the attack on the Valdai heights as a typical example of the General Staff's obsolete 'high-ground' tactics. Hitler's full fury did not really manifest itself, however, until Army Group Centre executed a small-scale operation to secure the necessary freedom of movement it needed on its southern flank for the attack on Moscow, and Guderian's armoured group miraculously 'recuperated' enough for the operation within a remarkably short span of time.

This time Hitler himself intervened with the result that, to the east of Kiev, Army Group South opened its most devastating battle with the Russians. How often I had to hear him ranting on about the insubordinate, arbitrary generals who had thrown his whole master plan out of joint. In the interval so much time had been wasted on this not altogether unsatisfactory victory to the east of Kiev that in view of the approaching late autumn with its attendant bad going and mud, Hitler himself had had to drop this entire strategic master plan, because the regrouping alone had taken up so much of our costly time.

For this reason he authorised Army Group Centre's double encirclement action at Vyasma and Bryansk, the prerequisite for the plan—still not abandoned by the War Office—to invest Moscow before winter closed in. The fate of the latter operation, and the developing catastrophe in the snow and ice of the cruellest winter experienced by central Russia since the beginning of the 19th century, are adequately known. It would, however, be an interesting military study for somebody to analyse what prospects Hitler's original plan would have enjoyed, and what the consequences would have been for our Russian campaign in 1941, especially if—as I was told by a Russian Staff Officer—they really had anticipated the War Office's intentions in the autumn of 1941 by concentrating all their major reinforcements, together with their Far East divisions and their Reserve Army, about Moscow for months beforehand. What would have been the consequence of that move for the Hitler plan? Would it not have greatly improved its chances of success? At present it is to me still an open question, but it has certainly given me food for thought: errors in grand strategy can never be redeemed in the same war. By that I am not claiming that the War Office plan was itself an error: the real mistake was to adopt a compromise, if the respite demanded by Army Group Centre before they could attack was not, in fact, a vital prerequisite to re-establishing the fighting quality of its troops. For the Führer's plan of attack would certainly have demanded immediate and gruelling route-marches; and one must never forget the generals' dogma: 'My army can attack, but it can't go on marching.'

During the summer of 1941 the civilian population's resistance to our occupation forces intensified perceptibly in every theatre of war, with sabotage incidents and attacks on German security troops and installations. While partisan warfare began to assume a more menacing aspect in the Balkans where it was openly encouraged by Britain and the Soviet Union, and obliged us to launch full-scale operations against partisan centres, acts of sabotage became horrifyingly frequent in France and even in Belgium. Widespread air drops of agents and of disguised sabotage-troops, bomb incidents, the dropping of guns, ammunition, radio transmitters and spies were the order of the day. There was no doubt that, in the west, Britain's hand was behind all this: she was trying to incite the population to harass the occupation forces, destroy industrial, public-utility, transport and power-supply installations, and to create general unrest and disturb the public order; she hoped to incite the population to passive resistance and even to provoke reprisals from us which, in turn, would manure the ground for the growth of a future resistance movement. While the French police initially co-operated very efficiently with us in the prosecution and elimination of saboteurs in France, very soon a palpable change came over them, often evidenced by their sympathies with the wrongdoers and even by a degree of high-level participation in the guerilla war against our security forces.

The call for reinforcements for our security forces and the police units became increasingly urgent in time, and the early attempts at improvising security measures by taking hostages and exacting reprisals on them eventually became the order of the day. As the Balkans were also crying out for troop reinforcements, and the security forces allocated to the daily expanding occupied territories of the Soviet Union were no longer able to cope either, the Führer insisted on the employment of Draconian reprisal measures and ruthless action to deter the terrorists before things got out of hand—before the resistance movements could succeed in siphoning off so much of our manpower that the thing outgrew the capabilities of the occupying authorities altogether.

The summer and autumn of 1941 accordingly saw the issue of the first orders designed to combat these new techniques of stab-in-the-back, sabotage- and commando-warfare, a kind of warfare launched at the behest of dark forces—the *'secret service'* [sic.]—by gangsters, spies and other skulking vermin, and later reinforced by idealists, all of whom are now jointly idolised as great and patriotic national 'heroes'.

These orders numbered among others the military commanders' 'hostage laws', the Führer's *Nacht und Nebel*—'Cover of Darkness'— decree, which I myself signed, and all the other variations on those brutal directives of 1942 designed to emulate the enemy in his most degenerate mode of warfare, which could, of course, only really be appreciated in all its ferocity and effect at my central office into which all these reports flowed. The purpose was to make it quite plain to all those German officers, who had been brought up in a make-believe world of 'chivalry' in war, that when they are faced with methods like these the only one to keep his head is the one who least shrinks from exacting the most ruthless reprisals in a situation where an 'illegal war of the shadows' has unscrupulously systematised crime to intimidate the occupying power and terrorise the country's populace at large. That these British secret service methods were so alien to us Germans, and to our mentality, went far to justify the existence of warnings like these to our men; but whether the proper way of bringing this home to them was by issuing the slogan, 'Terrorism can only be combatted with terrorism' is a point which seen in retrospect people may be right to dispute. All good Germans should learn to let the house catch fire around them before they start to sniff for smoke. . . .

Early in June 1941, on my return to Berlin, I found Hans-Georg at our home there. His thigh injury had fully healed, but from the many operations on them the muscles and sinews were agony for him to ride on. So I finally gave him permission to transfer from his Halberstadt regiment to the 29th mobile artillery regiment, which belonged to the 29th (mobile) division. This was just what he had always dreamed of, being in a motorised unit, with the modern battle cavalry. Beaming with happiness, he left home once again, as his new regiment was urgently calling for him; after he had taken leave of his mother and sisters, who dreamt as little as he did himself what lay ahead, I accompanied him to the front door and with heavy heart bade him farewell. I said: 'God be with you! Be brave, but don't be foolhardy or reckless unless you *have* to.' He probably did not understand, but he briefly embraced me and swung off happily down the lane with his case, his rifle and other kit. When I returned to the drawing room, my wife said: 'How grave and different you were with him! What is the matter then?' I had of course been unable to deceive the delicate perception of a mother. I avoided giving a direct answer, but muttered something about having warned him to be careful of his leg.

All the harder fell the blow when the news came as early as 18th July that he had died in a field hospital from a serious injury suffered during a Russian strafing attack on the day before. My wife was at Helmscherode with the rest of the family: who was to tell her that her favourite son, for whom she had so often fretted, had been laid to rest in foreign soil, outside Smolensk? I sent Professor Nissen [the family doctor] to Helmscherode, charged with this sad mission, because I had some fears for how my wife would take it with her delicate heart. That was when I first found out how strong the hearts of wives and mothers are.

The Führer's own sympathy was expressed in a personal letter to my wife; she was very grateful for it. As both my wife and I were against publishing any obituary notice, the Führer ordered the Press to publish one, explaining to us that the German people ought to learn that the sons of high-ranking generals were also laying down their lives on the field of battle.

With the commencement of the operations against Russia, the Führer had defined the operational command structure for the remaining theatres as making Finland, Norway, the west, North Africa and the Balkans immediately responsible to him, in other words to the High Command, in order to relieve the War Office of these burdens. During 1941 the only real hostilities were in Finland, North Africa and the Balkans; in the remaining so-called 'OKW-theatres' only guerilla warfare prevailed.

The Führer had made this ruling because apart from on the Atlantic coast these theatres were engaged in 'coalition' wars for the direction of which Hitler had for political reasons assumed both the command and the responsibility for collaboration with our allies: he wished to keep all the negotiations with their heads of state and their general staffs firmly in his own hands. At the same time, the ruling brought considerable relief to the War Office, even though the Army's organisation was still responsible for maintaining their fighting strength and for all equipment and quartermastering. In itself I considered the term 'OKW-theatre', which had crept into general usage, an unfortunate misnomer: it resulted in a wrong conception of the actual overall rôle of the High Command as the supreme court of command, superior to all three services in *every* theatre of war; this misconception was further amplified by the manner in which the Führer completely excluded his High Command from the direction of the offensive against the Soviet Union, apart from those matters involving Finland. The most unambiguous solution would have been to transfer the command of all three services in each individual theatre to an individual with a joint-service warrant giving him authority over army, navy and air force; each of these individuals would then be ultimately subject to High Command control. But that was something for which the Commanders-in-Chief and their staffs were not ready, and the C.-in-C.s of the navy and the air force refused to subordinate their local contingents to such an overall command.

Here only the Führer had the power—both tactically and in mediation—to intervene: neither Raeder nor Göring had any desire to grant the Commanders-in-Chief of the various war theatres (of whom almost all were army generals) authority over their contingents, as they feared they would forfeit their own immediate influence over them, even though they themselves were obliged to appoint local commanders to whom they could not refuse to delegate wide powers of independent action. I never got further with this tentative re-distribution of authority that I proposed than one or two modest beginnings, while the overall operational command of the war at sea and in the air was left intact for the Commanders-in-Chief of the navy and air force respectively.

The consequence was that in the Soviet Union the War Office—or, more accurately, Hitler and the War Office—was in command, to the total exclusion of the High Command. I am bound to make that point quite clear for the sake of historical accuracy, because the Soviet Union—at least at the Nuremberg Trial—seems to have assumed that the orders were actually initiated by the OKW.

Among our friendly allied states Roumania and Finland participated in the Russian campaign from the very outset; once it had begun, Italy, Hungary and Czechoslovakia each contributed a small contingent, an expeditionary force of about the strength of a weak

155

mobile Corps, and the Czechs with the equivalent of a light infantry division. Hitler made all the final arrangements with Antonescu in Münich; the latter had readily agreed to an increase in the numbers of advisers attached to our military mission [in Roumania] and had drawn the correct conclusions from it; I took part in the talks, together with the army commander foreseen for the German units, General Ritter von Schobert, and the chief of our military mission, General Hansen. For Antonescu the obvious objective was the recovery of Bessarabia, and this was reason enough for him to mobilise large parts of his army; the real purpose of our attack and its date were concealed from him.

In May 1941 I had had a meeting in Salzburg with the Finnish Chief of General Staff, General Heinrichs, and had reached basic agreement on lines laid down by Hitler on the subject of permission for German troops to mass under Lieutenant-General von Falkenhorst on Finnish territory; the agreement was afterwards put into operationally definitive terms by Jodl. Neither Jodl nor I suspected that our mission was only by way of confirmation of preliminary talks already held between Halder and Heinrichs at Zossen some months before.

General Heinrichs' manner was receptive towards us and he most readily agreed to lay all our requirements before Marshal Mannerheim as we wished. My personal impression, especially of General Heinrichs' character, was highly favourable, and I reported to the Führer that Finland was not going to miss this chance of settling old scores for Russia's attack on her in the winter of 1939–1940. The despatch of a general with plenipotentiary powers to the Marshal, independent of our military attaché, was at once agreed to and we never once had cause to regret the selection of General Erfurth for that post.

The Führer had strictly forbidden any kind of preliminary diplomatic discussions and even of staff level talks with Hungary and Czechoslovakia, although the War Office had stressed their importance in view of our current plans for the transit of troops through these countries and the admission of railway troop transports. Hitler refused to yield on this point, despite the risks it involved; he was afraid that the operation's security would be compromised, and was not satisfied that the advantages of arranging everything in advance outweighed the disadvantages. In the event, no great disadvantage arose, although I am unaware how far the Hungarian General Staff did permit us to make certain arrangements in advance.

Our invasion on 22nd June was in fact a tactical, though in no way a strategic, surprise for the Red Army.

On their own initiative, Hungary and Czechoslovakia raised an expeditionary force after hostilities had broken out—naturally keeping a firm eye on the frontier changes they were anticipating in their favour—and this they placed at the War Office's disposal. But as early as September 1941, the Hungarian Chief of General Staff [Szombathelyi] told me he wanted to pay a visit to the Führer's headquarters, as he desired to withdraw the Hungarian fast brigade (division)—against the War Office's wishes—even before we had crossed the river Dnepr: it was not equipped for a winter campaign, and it was required for the raising of new units in the coming year of the war. After a brief and conventional reception at the Führer's headquarters, the discussions were turned over to Halder and myself. I laid on a banquet for General Szombathelyi (also known as 'Knaus'—a typical Swabian) in my train, and during the afternoon took him over to the War Office's headquarters where he was shown a number of things.

I was so irritated by a number of more than offensive remarks he made about our command and operation of Hungary's one 'light division' that I bluntly told him, while adhering to protocol, to wean his troops first of all from their habit of plundering and looting everywhere they went and shipping their spoils back home. As soon as he saw that his arrogant manner had cut no ice with me, but had had the opposite of the desired effect, he suddenly became very amiable, oozing with flattery for our overall command of the army, and unable to express adequately how much he admired the Führer who had made such a deep and unexpected impression on him, mapping out as he had for him in broad sweeps the overall situation on a map of the eastern front. That evening he stayed as the guest of the War Office; he flew home next day having agreed with Halder on a compromise which foresaw a much later withdrawal of the Hungarian troops.

Early in 1942, I paid him a return visit on the Führer's instructions in Budapest. My mission was a difficult one, for this time I was to ask for the mobilisation of Hungary's peace-time army as well, and the despatch of at least half of it to take part in the planned summer operations. At that time, Hungary disposed over twenty-three brigades in the process of conversion into small divisions, including the mountain brigades and cavalry units, but excluding the occupation forces which had already been transferred or promised to the War Office for the rôle of security forces in the rearward areas. In addition to visits to the Imperial Administrator [Horthy], the War Minister [von Bartha], the Prime Minister [von Bardossy], and others, on two separate mornings very detailed negotiations took place with the Chief of General Staff and the War Minister.

On the first day we did not get much further than horse-trading over whether we could repay them with deliveries of a considerable quantity of armaments. Naturally I made concessions here, for without anti-tank guns, infantry weapons and similar modern hardware the Hungarian troops would be of no use to us in the face of Russians armed with modern weapons. But as Szombathelyi personally called for me that evening in his car to take me to a big banquet for the generals, he surprised me by asking how many of the 'light divisions' suggested by me that morning I was asking for. Making up my mind in a flash, I answered, 'Twelve!' He told me that he had been thinking of a similar number; he could promise me nine light infantry divisions and a still only weak armoured division, and said he was going to form a second armoured division for us if we sent him promptly the tanks which the Führer had personally pledged to the Imperial Administrator. Finally, there was also a cavalry division available, which Horthy would not release at any price for the time being. If I was to seek a pledge from the Imperial Administrator on these lines during my visit next day, he would back me up. The only opposition would then come from the War Minister and from Horthy himself, in whom their Prime Minister had inspired fears of Roumania's intentions and of Parliament itself. So we reached agreement in those few minutes before the car put us down outside the hotel. I myself was satisfied with the outcome, as a few well-equipped and well-trained divisions were more valuable to us than a large number of units of only meagre fighting power.

Although our three-way talks next morning still exposed a variety of critical points when it came to a discussion of details, with myself up against the two of them in a clash which at one point even had me threatening to break off the talks, an agreement was finally hammered out and committed to paper, especially covering the scale and timetable of the German munitions deliveries.

My audience with the Imperial Administrator passed more smoothly than I had expected, as the Chief of General Staff had obviously paved the way. The old gentleman was in a very good humour and his attitude to me was very obliging. Finally the German ambassador gave a banquet, at which a conversation I had *à deux* with Prime Minister Bardossy particularly impressed me: he told me that he fully realised that the ten divisions were to be used on the eastern front, as distinct from our planned reinforcement of the security forces patrolling occupied Russian territory, but he was gravely preoccupied by his inability to see how he was going to explain to the Hungarian people's parliament just why they were taking part in Germany's war. The people had just not been prepared for it; nobody, he said, was thinking of war, except perhaps against Roumania. I told him that in this struggle with Bolshevism, Europe had to exert itself to the utmost now, so how could they possibly be thinking in terms of settling old scores with Roumania at this time: it was beyond my comprehension! Our conversation ended on that note, as dinner was served. That afternoon, I flew back to the Führer's headquarters. Without doubt, Szombathelyi was the most far-sighted of all of them; he had exercised a very considerable influence on the Imperial Administrator. That, at any rate, was my impression.

After the Eleventh Army under General Ritter von Schobert, attacking from Roumania together with Roumanian troops, had in August 1941 linked up with Army Group South and after some hard fighting liberated Bessarabia from the enemy, the first meeting took place between Marshal Antonescu and the Führer at Field-Marshal von Rundstedt's Army Group South headquarters. After a war conference and a high-level discussion, the Führer personally awarded Antonescu the Knight's Cross in the presence of von Rundstedt and myself; it was obvious that the Roumanian marshal was deeply honoured by this. According to the Army Group's appraisal, his exceptionally energetic intervention and his personal influence on the Roumanian officers and troops had been exemplary; these qualities had, as his German aides had seen for themselves, characterised the military bearing of this head of state.

Naturally, Mussolini had no desire to lag behind Hungary and Roumania and had offered the Führer an Italian light (semi-mobile) Corps, in return for Rommel's armoured corps' being in Africa. The War Office was furious at this offer, which they valued anything but highly, as it was not a reasonable burden to place on our strained railway system that summer, for the Italians could be transported to the front only at the expense of indispensable war supplies.

While the Italians were on the way to the front, Mussolini arrived at the second Führer's headquarters site, located in Galicia, at the Führer's invitation. Both the headquarters trains had been shunted into a specially adapted railway tunnel. Early next morning we all flew out in several aircraft to Uman, to visit von Rundstedt; after a general war conference and a description by Rundstedt of the Battle of Uman, we drove out in motor vehicles to inspect an Italian division.

The impression given by the sheer expanse of black soil and by the—by German standards—immense size of the harvestlands of the Ukraine, was overwhelming. Often one saw in the gently undulating open and treeless landscape nothing for miles on end but the stooks of one enormous, endless wheatfield. One could sense the virginity of the soil, which by German standards is still only about one-third cultivable; and then again the vast expanses lying fallow, waiting for the autumn seeding.*

For the Führer and us German soldiers, the march-past and salute of the Italian troops was—despite their loyal '*Evviva Duce*'—a boundless disappointment: their officers were far too old and made a sorry sight, and could only have had a bad effect on the value of such dubious auxiliaries. How were half-soldiers like these supposed to stand up to the Russians, if they had collapsed even in face of the wretched peasant folk of Greece? The Führer had faith in Mussolini and in his revolution, but the Duce was not Italy, and Italians were Italians all the world over. These were our allies, the allies who had not only already cost us so dearly, who had not only abandoned us in our hour of need, but who were eventually to betray us too.

After the loss of my son, a further bitter blow fell with the death in action of my close friend von Wolff-Wusterwitz; he had been commanding a Pomeranian infantry regiment, and had been killed at the head of his proud troops when leading them into the attack.

After the latent tension existing between the Führer and von Brauchitsch had, outwardly at least, been considerably eased by Army Group Centre's crushing victory in the double-battle of Vyasma-Bryansk, the results of our first defeats began to cloud the scene.

It was Hitler's wont to find a scapegoat for every failure, and even more so if he could hardly fail to see that he himself was to blame for the failure's origins at least. When von Rundstedt in the south and von Leeb in the north were ultimately obliged to withdraw their spearheads which were attacking near Rostov-on-Don and Tikhvin, as Hitler himself had advocated, it could hardly be blamed upon either the War Office or the two Commanders-in-Chief concerned. Von Rundstedt protested most vigorously against the orders the

* In Keitel's original text there follow further remarks on the Ukraine as a 'granary' and on its exploitation by 'German skill and German sweat'; these have been omitted by the Editor.

War Office had been obliged to transmit to him forbidding him to withdraw his front to the river Mius line. Von Brauchitsch showed the drastically worded protest-telegram—which had been intended only for his eyes as Commander-in-Chief of the Army—to the Führer, for whom it had certainly not been intended. The Führer relieved von Rundstedt of his command, not because of this business, but because von Rundstedt (unaware that Hitler's hand was at the bottom of the War Office's orders to him) had threatened to resign if he was not believed capable of leadership.

The Führer went up in smoke over this, privately knowing full well that he himself had been behind it and feeling that von Rundstedt had turned against him. In a rage he ordered his instant dismissal, and called upon von Reichenau to command Army Group South. With Schmundt the Führer flew out to Mariupol to see Sepp Dietrich, commander of the SS '*Leibstandarte*' armoured division, to learn, as he said, the 'truth' about the situation from his trusted friend and to confirm his suspicions about the bad leadership of the army at high level. Hitler was disappointed: Sepp Dietrich stood up honourably and incorruptibly for his Army superior, and it was he who succeeded in eliminating the Führer's lack of confidence on this occasion. On the return flight he accordingly visited Army Group South to talk things over with von Rundstedt, and while he did not rescind the latter's 'permanent leave' he did assure him of his restored confidence in him.

Upon our return, Hitler declared his satisfaction to me about this, and his criticism of his old friend Reichenau, who had already taken over command of the Army Group and had begun to exploit the opportunities now presented to him of conversing with Hitler to comment offensively on the Commander-in-Chief of the Army and other senior commanders, was decidedly acid: Reichenau thought that the time was now ripe to exploit his new position to incite people against everybody he personally did not approve of. The result was quite the reverse, for otherwise Hitler would hardly have confirmed to me for a second time that my original verdict on Reichenau had been correct: he would *not* have made a good Commander-in-Chief for the Army. It was then that I knew for certain that if ever von Brauchitsch were to go, Hitler would never name Reichenau as his successor.

Early in December the drive for Tikhvin in the north, which the Führer had tactically launched against the War Office's advice, but which already contained in it the seeds of failure, suffered a reverse. Even had Tikhvin itself been taken, it could not have been held.

The strategic aim of severing Leningrad's rearward communications by reaching Lake Ladoga, and of following this up by linking up with the Finns, had to be abandoned. In several telephone conversations with the Führer to which I listened in, Field-Marshal von Leeb urgently asked to be given freedom of action, and to be permitted to withdraw this part of his front behind the line of the river Volchov in good time, in order to shorten his front and release manpower as a reserve. He met with no success, and the enemy recaptured the positions we could not hold; then he finally presented himself at the Führer's headquarters in person to ask to be relieved of his post, as he was too old and his nerves could no longer stand the strain. He was removed from his command, as he had asked; obviously it 'suited' Hitler better that way.

I know that the thoughts quietly coursing through Hitler's mind were thoughts for posterity: he sacrificed these two first-class commanders only to provide 'scapegoats' for the first setbacks; he had no desire to recognise that he himself was actually to blame.

These first crises, not really of very great significance, were virtually swamped by Japan's unexpected entry into the war and the wave of optimism that followed. I would vehemently dispute that Hitler either knew of it in advance or had had any influence on the Japanese; the best actor in the world could not have put on a performance like that. Hitler had been convinced of the authenticity of the [American-Japanese] talks in Washington, and Pearl Harbour had taken him completely by surprise.

Jodl and I were both present that night, as—the only time during the war—he came bursting in to us with the telegram in his hand. I gained the impression that the Führer felt that the war between Japan and America had suddenly relieved him of a nightmare burden; it certainly brought us some relief from the consequences of America's undeclared state of war with us.

Long before they had ventured to express their doubts to the Führer, the War Office had lost confidence in our ability to force a decisive victory by capturing the [Russian] capital before winter closed in. Not only were the soldiers showing strong signs of weariness—they had known no rest since the double battle of Vyasma-Bryansk—but the cold was steadily growing more intense and the lack of any winter clothing was taking a heavy toll.

Having recovered after a severe heart attack, kept secret at the time, Brauchitsch had gone to the front for several days, and—as I later learned from the commanders on the front—had talked over

162

with them the question of where—if as was feared our attack were not to succeed in breaking through—the front ought to withdraw to, to pass the winter and to build up reserves behind a shortened front, always assuming that such a measure became inevitable. In my view, it was the duty of the commander-in-chief to take such precautions in good time.

A renewed heart attack, coupled with a breakdown in this embittered officer's nervous system, obliged Brauchitsch to return to his sickbed for several days again. Halder, who continued to appear each day for the Führer's briefing conferences, naturally kept himself informed on the situation developing out there. It was evident that Hitler also recognised that a crisis was looming up, but he stubbornly resisted all the War Office schemes outlined by Halder.

In the meantime, the frost and cold had intensified, leading to heavy casualties among the troops. Hitler bitterly rebuked the War Office for having failed to see to the distribution of winter clothing, trench-heaters and so forth, in good time.

He knew full well that the transportation to the front [of the necessary winter equipment was impossible] during such a long-drawn-out struggle, when there was a shortage even of ammunition and provisions as a result of the prevailing transport crisis.* With each day that passed, the cold intensified, more men succumbed to frostbite, the tanks broke down as their radiators froze up, and finally it had to be accepted that there was no possible prospect of continuing the assault. Nobody who was not there can ever picture the Führer's frame of mind that day, for he himself had long realised that a military catastrophe was nigh, try as he might to conceal it from his staff; now he searched for scapegoats who could be blamed for the omission to provide for the troops' welfare and many other shortcomings.

Only the real reasons for the reverse were suppressed, evident though they were: he had underestimated the enemy's ability to resist and the risk of winter closing in early that year and expected too much of the troops' fighting capacity in the endless battles from October onwards; and finally they lacked sufficient supplies. I am convinced that Brauchitsch realised that some way would have to be found round the inflexibility both of the front and of the Führer; it could not be concealed from him that the guilty party would soon be looked for, and that his name would not be Hitler. As he himself told me that day, 19th December, 1941, he summoned up all his courage and had a row lasting almost two hours with Hitler. I myself was

* The incomplete sentence in Keitel's text has been completed by the Editor.

not there, but I do know that in the course of the argument he asked to be relieved of his post, giving as an additional reason his poor state of health (as was his duty in any case).

He came briefly to see me afterwards and said only: 'I am going home—he has sacked me. I can't go on any longer.' To my question—'What is going to happen now, then?'—Brauchitsch replied: 'I don't know: ask him yourself.' He was obviously very agitated and depressed. A few hours later I was summoned by the Führer; he read out to me a brief Order of the Day composed by Schmundt and himself, announcing that he was assuming command of the Army himself; the Order was to be circulated at once to the Army. A second, internal order subordinated the Army General Staff to the person of the Führer, while the War Office's administrative responsibilities were transferred to me, with the limitation that I was to be bound by the Führer's directives; this latter order went only to Halder as Chief of General Staff and was not given any wider circulation.

So, even though it was not made public at the time that the Führer's release of his Commander-in-Chief of the Army was by *mutual* consent, it was apparent that a scapegoat for the Army's defeats and for the growing crisis in the disastrous battle barely fifteen or twenty miles outside the gates of Moscow, had been found, even if not yet publicly identified.

5

The Russian Campaign
1941–1943

ENTERTAINED the gravest misgivings about the Hitler-Halder
regime's taking over the Army's new High Command, because I
had perceived how unsuited they were to each other. In our private circles, the Führer had often cracked jokes at Halder's expense
and labelled him a 'little fellow'. Even if this unattractive habit of
selecting absent officers as the butt for his humour was not all that
tragic with a man like Hitler—as there were few people he spared
from his mockery—it seemed to me questionable whether such a
team would ever yoke together well. I myself proposed to Hitler that
Jodl should be appointed Chief of the Army General Staff, as he had
come to know and respect him well; while I further suggested that
General von Manstein should take over as Chief of our military
operations staff in his place—in other words, he should be the
Armed Forces' Chief of General Staff, with a new definition of his
duties vis-à-vis myself as the Chief of the High Command. Quite
remarkably, Hitler did not reject the proposal out of hand but said
he would first like to discuss it with Schmundt, and turn it over in
his own mind. Without referring to any discussion between them,
Schmundt afterwards informed me that the Führer wanted to keep
Jodl in the OKW, and he had determined to work with Halder:
this would probably turn out all right, as whatever might be said
of him, Halder was honest, loyal, reliable and obedient.

One thing was quite clear to me (and nothing Schmundt said
detracted from this view): that great though Hitler's regard for
Manstein was, he feared him to a degree; he feared his independent
ideas and strength of personality. When I confided my proposal
to Jodl, he shared my view: 'With Manstein, it would never work
out.' Once the decision had been taken, I spared no effort to buttress
Halder's position with the Führer, to support and brief him on the
workings of Hitler's mind when I was aware of them, and to give

him sound advice. I did everything in my power to build up a lasting confidence between them.

In any event, it was in my own interests, for I was the one who always had to suffer and make good the consequences of each latent crisis of confidence. Gradually I was becoming fed up with being the target of everybody's obloquy, as though I was to blame every time Hitler found that the face of this or that general did not fit any more.

Towards the middle of December, after our return from the Reichstag session of 11th December [1941] in Berlin—Japan's entry into the war—the weather had drastically changed in a very few days from the period of mud and slime to that infernal cold, with all the attendant and catastrophic results for the troops, clad as they were only in improvised winter clothing. Worst of all, however, was that in addition to the road transport breakdowns, the railway system had come to a complete standstill: the German locomotives and their water towers had just frozen solid.

Confronted with this situation, Hitler's first order to the eastern front was: '*Stand fast, not one step back!*' This was because he had correctly realised that to withdraw even by only a few miles, was synonymous with writing off all our heavy armaments; in which case the troops themselves could be considered lost, because without heavy armament they were absolutely defenceless, quite apart from the fact that the artillery, anti-tank guns and vehicles were irreplaceable. In fact there was no other solution than to stand fast and fight, if the army were not to withdraw without weapons and suffer the same fate as Napoleon had in 1812. Obviously this did not preclude well-prepared and limited withdrawals to improved defensive positions, provided the movements were kept firmly in hand.

While on both sides of the front the great armies just froze solid, to the west of Moscow and in the central sector of Army Group Centre local crises began to blow up in the fighting.

Field-Marshal von Kluge personally telephoned the Führer one night in my presence with a bitter complaint about Colonel-General Hoepner, who had ordered his Army's front to be withdrawn some distance in defiance of the Führer's order, and who was in consequence gravely endangering the adjacent northern flank of von Kluge's Army. The Führer flew into an uncontrolled temper, and ordained Hoepner's immediate removal from the Army command and his discharge from the armed forces for deliberate and premeditated disobedience; Halder was at the War Office's headquarters at the time, so he was not present. The Führer fulminated all night long in our reading room, cursing at his generals who had not been brought up to obey. He would make an example of him—he would announce what he had done to Hoepner in an Order of the Day, as a warning to all those venturing to defy his express orders as their whims dictated.

A similar case emerged over Christmas [1941] and the New Year, involving Guderian. He was in command of the Second Tank Army as it attacked Moscow from the south, through Tula, only to freeze literally solid in the cold. The Army Group [Centre] planned, with the Führer's permission, to withdraw him westwards into the gap south of von Kluge's Fourth Army. Guderian, however, had worked out his own programme, involving a retreat southwards along his earlier route of attack, stage by stage, after he had blown up the greater part of his tanks where they had just frozen solid in the mud. Field-Marshal von Kluge had tried in vain to influence Guderian, but the latter was refusing to carry out the 'impossible' withdrawal order given to him. Von Kluge demanded the general's dismissal, which Hitler at once ordained: Guderian was summoned to see the Führer at his headquarters.

I was present during the interview between Hitler and Guderian [on 20th December, 1941]. He remained obdurate in face of all the Führer's exhortations and remonstrances, saying that he did not consider the Army Group's order either necessary or justified, nor did he accept the Führer's reasons; for him, he explained, the welfare of his troops was the primary consideration, he had tried to act accordingly and he was as firmly convinced as ever that he had acted properly. Finally the Führer gave it up, and retaining absolute composure he dismissed Guderian with the suggestion that he might like to go somewhere to convalesce after this enormous strain on his nerves. After this, Guderian went into retirement; he suffered grievously from his temporary inactivity.

The third case occurred in January 1942, in Colonel-General Strauss' Ninth Army on the left flank of Army Group Centre. This time it was the commanding general of the Sixth Army Corps, General Foerster, and one of his divisional commanders who—in my own view—had completely lost their nerve and were sent back home. I would prefer not to go into the details of the violent defensive battle and the regrettable circumstances surrounding these dismissals; it was obvious that there had been an injustice as a result of erroneous reports from the air force.

It would be a travesty of the truth, however, if I failed to stress at this juncture that the way in which we averted disaster can only be attributed to the willpower, steadfastness and unrelenting severity displayed by Hitler throughout. Had the narrow-minded and selfish emergency plan thought out by the tired and apathetic front-line generals of Army Group Centre—suffering fearfully in the terrible cold—not been blocked by the merciless and uncompromising opposition, by the iron will of the Führer, the German Army would inescapably and inevitably have suffered in 1941 the fate of [the French in] 1812.

I must express myself quite plainly on this issue, for I was an eye-witness of those terrible weeks. All our heavy armaments, all our tanks, all our motor vehicles would have been abandoned on the battlefield. The troops would have recognised that they were virtually defenceless, they would have thrown away their rifles and guns and run away, with a merciless enemy on their heels.

It was under this burden, which deeply worried all of us, that we spent a cheerless Christmas at the Führer's headquarters. I arranged a brief party in the guards' big mess-hall for the NCOs and troops attached to the Führer's headquarters, with their officers taking part as well; I made a speech about the struggle out on the eastern front, and our love for our Fatherland. There were dark shadows of anxiety on every face, as reverently but sadly we began to sing 'Holy Night, Silent Night'.

By early in January 1942 the whole eastern front had succeeded in regrouping from the attacking structure which had characterised it until early December to a relatively ordered defensive front. But there could be no question of a winter respite. The Russians were extremely active and at several places along our front, where it had been badly weakened by losses and breakdowns, and consisted of virtually only a few outposts, they went over to the offensive. Now the initiative was with the enemy; we were obliged to revert to defensive dispositions and paid the price with not insignificant casualties.

In February I had to force a new programme on Speer, the new Reichsminister for Armament and Munitions (Dr. Todt having been killed in an air crash on the airfield at the Führer's headquarters early that month); the programme called for the immediate release for front-line duties of a quarter of a million Army troops who had been made available for munitions production. That was the beginning of the struggle for manpower, a struggle that was never to end. During those first winter months, the Army had lost over a hundred thousand men, and twice that number in December 1941 and January 1942.

A reduction of divisional strength from nine to seven battalions was inevitable, while simultaneously considerable inroads were made into the non-combatant troops of the supply echelons, the army's 'tail', which were radically cut back. This first drive of mine in February 1942 marked the beginning for me of an unending and harrowing struggle with the civil authorities of the war economy, a struggle for manpower to maintain the armed forces' fighting strength and above all that of the army.

Compared with the army, the fresh manpower requirements of the navy and air force were minimal, while that of the *Waffen-SS* rose in a steeply climbing curve, an insatiable siphon skimming the cream of German youth. With the Führer's support, the *Waffen-SS* had enticed the most valuable sections of German youth into its ranks by means of open and concealed, legal and illegal propaganda methods, and by indirect pressure tactics too; the best elements of youth, who would have been perfect future commanders and officers for the army, were thereby lost to us.

All my protests to the Führer were in vain; he refused to have anything to do with my arguments. Merely to mention the subject resulted in an angry outburst from him: he knew our distaste and dislike for his *Waffen-SS* because it was an élite, he said, an élite which was being politically trained in the way he had always had in mind, something which the Army had refused to do; but it was his unalterable intention to channel as many of the finest young men of the whole country into the *Waffen-SS* as volunteered for it—there was to be no limit on the number of volunteers.

My protest that the recruiting methods were often highly questionable and even illegal, bribes for example, achieved nothing except to make him fly into an uncontrollable temper and demand proof for my statements—which of course I never supplied, to protect my informants, mostly fathers and high-school teachers, from persecution by the secret state police.

It was hardly surprising that the fighting quality of an army which had long lost its bravest young officers and leaders plunged only lower and lower if it was deprived of its most valuable reinforcements, and if to plug the gaps in its ranks it was supplied only with increasing numbers of formerly reserved munitions workers who thought that they had evaded the war and all its horrors long ago and who were now being sent back in droves and with decidedly mixed feelings to the front. In addition to these, the Army derived further reinforcements necessary for padding out its ever-shrinking units by means of the so-called 'combing-out drives' both in Germany and among the

169

innumerable formations and units of what was euphemistically termed the 'communications zone', a concept which did not entirely fail to merit its dubious repute. I do not intend to waste my breath on the worth of these reinforcements; obviously there were some valuable and honourable fighting men coming back to the front, especially those returning from military hospitals in Germany; but the greater part were less than enthusiastic about their posting. No wonder the troops' fighting spirit and readiness to sacrifice themselves went into permanent decline.

As a front-line soldier in World War One, the Führer had by no means shut similar thoughts out of his own mind; but he always found solace in his belief that the enemy would at least be in the same predicament, if not far worse, than us.

Speer always managed things so that the various employers of the war economy, including those of the public sector—the Reich Railways, the Post Office, and so on—had the right to release the men whose services seemed least indispensable, while they retained for themselves the most valuable employees; in this way they were able to comply numerically—at least approximately—with the quotas demanded. But obviously the workers most easily replaced are without doubt not the best soldiers either, and they are certainly not young and active men with military training.

Then Sauckel, the General Commissioner for the Utilisation of Labour, had to find replacements for the gaps caused in the war economy, mostly unskilled workers from Germany and the occupied territories. It was no less a person than Sauckel who not only recognised my own views on the problem but openly confided in me that in this 'business' it was the armed forces who were being cheated and that the munitions industry was not only unloading worthless manpower on to us but was in fact often concealing skilled workers—hoarding them and shielding them from call-up—out of their own naked selfishness, hanging on to them for possible exploitation later elsewhere. Sauckel put the number of men illegally evading military service in this way at a minimum of half a million, mostly men who would make the finest type of soldier.

What wouldn't these missing men have meant for the eastern front? It is simple arithmetic: one hundred and fifty divisions of three thousand men apiece, which would have increased the Army's establishment by fifty per cent. Instead of which, its dwindling units were padded out with batmen and camp followers and the like, while their positions in the Army's supply echelons were taken by volunteers from among the Russian prisoners of war.

The Russian Campaign

I have always been the first to realise that not only the maintenance of, but the greatest possible increase in munitions output is a
vital prerequisite for a war, because the replacement of worn-out
and obsolete equipment is the prerequisite for the maintenance of
the fighting-strength of troops; I fully realised that the longer the
war lasted and the more it began to resemble the static warfare of
the First World War, with its colossal expenditure of munitions and
material, the greater our own expenditure of munitions and armaments would be. But despite all that, I have always believed that in
the final analysis it is the fighting man using the weapons who is the
primary element in a battle-worthy army, and that its fighting spirit
depends on him. Without him the best weapons and the most
plentiful munitions in the world are poor compensation.

It was characteristic of Hitler's *modus operandi* that he achieved
maximum effort by playing off opposing parties against each other,
in this case playing off the Munitions Minister in the material
sphere against myself as Chief of the High Command in the manpower
sphere; he made demands on each of us which he himself knew to be
impossible and then left it to us to fight it out. I needed soldiers,
Speer needed munitions workers; I wanted to buttress our steadily
declining front-line strengths, Speer wanted to avoid declining
armaments production, and indeed to boost them in accordance
with the orders given him. Both targets were mutually irreconcilable
and impossible of fulfilment if the General Commissioner for the
Utilisation of Labour failed to provide the workers. Small wonder
that Speer and I both put the heat on Sauckel, for I would get no
soldiers if Speer received no replacements for those of his workers
called-up for military service, none of whom he would release before
their replacements arrived.

When Speer accused the armed forces before Hitler of employing
far too many people in their 'tail', in the home-based Army, in the
Air Force, convalescing in military hospitals, in convalescent units,
in the communications zones, and so on, his protests were applauded;
but when I declared that the war economy was hoarding and concealing manpower, so as to be ready for any eventuality—multiple-
shift working, extra contracts and the like—I was reviled, because I
as a layman could not possibly know anything about industrial
production; I was told to flush out the 'communications zones'—
there were hundreds of thousands of shirkers and slackers skulking
there. It was an unending tug-of-war because the bow had been
stretched too far, although the rational exploitation of military and
industrial manpower was in fact still not testing the extreme limits

171

of practicability. Human inadequacy and the selfishness of those involved were all against it.

I could write a book on just this one tragedy of the last three years of the war, without exhausting the subject. The consequences of the manpower shortage in the Army are clearly illuminated by two statistics: the Army's monthly wastage rate in normal times—apart from major battles—averaged 150,000 to 160,000 men, of which on average some 90,000 to 100,000 could be replaced. The recruits of one age-group averaged 550,000 during the last few years; so if by express order the *Waffen-SS* was to receive 90,000 volunteers out of that (and nothing like that number ever volunteered) and the Air Force 30,000 men, and the Navy the same number, then that was already almost one-third of the age-group gone.

Only as the season of spring mud began again in about April of 1942 did the sector attacks the Russians had been carrying out along our whole front until then begin to abate. It was obvious that their objective had been to leave us no real respite, by creating crisis points by attacking first here and then there, but with no visible major strategic target. The only really dangerous positions from the tactical point of view were the deep wedge driven south of Orel, and the Demyansk pocket. While the latter was eventually given up, the possibility did arise of our starting an encirclement action in the south, to the east of Poltava, especially as the ground and weather conditions would permit operations to commence there about four weeks earlier than along the central and northern sectors of the front, and the Russians obliged us by offering us a strategically worthwhile objective, by concentrating their troops and increasing their attacks there. Hitler accordingly decided to precede the summer operation he had personally planned by an independent offensive against the Russian wedge driving towards Poltava.

Quite obviously Hitler's plan of campaign—and he was its sole originator—could not involve any further resumption of the general offensive on the eastern front, in view of the drastic shortage of manpower and our responsibility for remaining on the defensive everywhere else; for this reason he had decided on a break-through on the northern flank of Army Group South, which had been under the command of Field-Marshal von Bock since Reichenau's death [on 17th January 1942]. After an armoured break-through towards Voronezh-on-the-Don, the Army Group, steadily reinforcing its northern flank, was to roll up the Russian front along the Don and advance on Stalingrad with this flank while the southern flank

172

THE BLACK SUMMER OF 1942

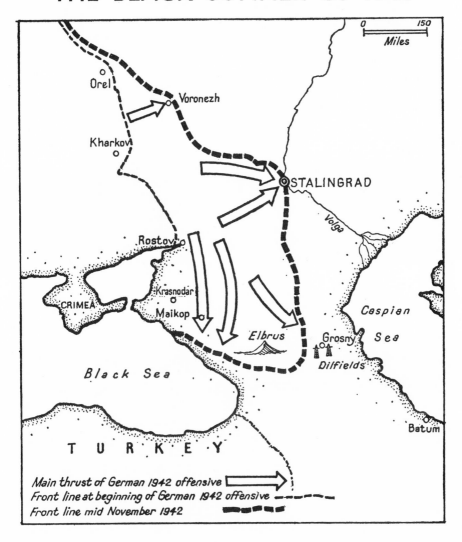

Main thrust of German 1942 offensive
Front line at beginning of German 1942 offensive
Front line mid November 1942

advanced on the Caucasus, overrunning the oilfields of its southern slopes and capturing the passes over the Caucasus.

While all the forces that could possibly be spared on the eastern front were to be withdrawn for this operation, particularly the tank armies, the Crimea was at the same time to be occupied in preparation for a crossing from the Kerch peninsula into the oil regions of the Caucasus; the War Office had been planning for this since March.

For Hitler the operation's first essential was to mislead the Russians about his real objective by means of the advance on Voronezh, about half-way between Moscow and the Donets region, so as to give them the impression of a deliberate wheel to the north and towards Moscow and trick them into holding their reserves there. Secondly, he planned to sever the various north-south railway links between Moscow and the industrial and oil regions, and then by suddenly and unexpectedly wheeling southwards along the Don, to overrun the Donets region itself, seize control of the Caucasus oil fields and block the Volga near Stalingrad to river traffic destined for inner Russia; this was because that river carried Russia's oil supplies, with hundreds of tankers from Baku. Our allied troops, those of Roumania, Hungary and Italy, were to screen the long northern flank of our Army along the natural obstacle presented by the river Don with their thirty divisions or so, which could be presumed to be shielded from the danger of attack by the river itself.

During my October [1941] visit to Bucharest for the victory parade held to celebrate the capture of Odessa, I had already discussed in detail Roumanian military aid for 1942 with Antonescu. Intoxicated with his recapture of Bessarabia and the occupation of Odessa—an old Roumanian dream—Antonescu was not difficult to bring to terms: again it involved a certain amount of horse-trading, with his troops being exchanged for armaments and munitions from us, but the sore spot was still the Vienna Award which had obliged Roumania to cede to Hungary what was, in fact, the greater part of Transylvania.

Antonescu was therefore demanding that Hungary should provide an equal contingent of troops for 1942. If the latter country did not make a decisive contribution, he foresaw a danger for Roumania, for the score would have to be settled with Hungary: the latter country was maintaining strong troop concentrations on the frontier with Roumania, so Roumania would have to do the same against

Hungary, which would considerably restrict the scale of her contribution to our attack on Russia.

I protested that during a war with the Soviet Union, which would liberate both countries from the immense danger presented by Bolshevism, any talk of hostilities between Roumania and Hungary was absolute madness; but my protests had no effect on him, even though the most immediate danger threatening both of their countries had only really been eliminated a very few weeks before. Or was it, in fact, just because of that that they were now so belligerent?

In any event, Antonescu pledged his further participation in our war on Russia with a contingent of fifteen divisions, if we would guarantee to modernise and completely re-equip them, which I naturally agreed to, hard though it would be for us. In fact, the Roumanian Army was easier to satiate, as it had originally been largely equipped with standard weapons from the French armament industry and we were able to satisfy their requirements many times over from the booty we had taken there.

The way my visit to Bucharest had come about was this: Hitler had rejected an invitation from them, and Göring had been reluctant to go as he had put Antonescu's back up over the question of Roumania's petroleum deliveries; the result was that I went as the representative of the German armed forces at the victory parade. I stayed as the young king's guest at the royal castle, where, together with Antonescu, I had an audience with the king and the queen mother (the wife of the exiled king, who had long found a suitable replacement for her in his mistress, Mme Lupescu). At twenty-one, the king was a tall, slim and good-looking youth, still rather awkward in his manner but not unlikeable; the queen mother was still a very attractive and worldly woman. Antonescu put an end to our superficial conversation with the remark that it was time for us to leave for the parade and its preliminary investiture ceremony.

Several times Antonescu asked me for my opinion on the march-past, which by German standards was more than ragged. I hastened to point out to him that, of course, one should not use our great German peacetime parades as a standard of comparison, as these troops now had come straight from the front; I said that what mattered was not the discipline of their drill but the expressions on their faces as they gazed upon their highest leaders; and *that* had made a very favourable impression on me.*

---

* In Keitel's original manuscript there follows a description of the conferring of the Order of King Michael on him, and details of various society functions during his visit; these have been omitted by the Editor.

As a result of my talks in Budapest, Mussolini's vanity was put to a sore trial with not only Roumania but Hungary too contributing to our 1942 campaign in Russia: he could not see Italy put to shame like that. Accordingly he offered us an unsolicited contingent of ten infantry divisions; it was an offer the Führer could hardly refuse. According to our general in Rome, General von Rintelen, they were to be élite divisions, including four or six Alpini divisions, or at any rate the best that the Italians had. Transport complexities made it impossible for us to move them up until the advent of the summer, as our railways had first to handle the German troop concentrations for the summer offensive.

The railway transport system was never really equal to the needs of the armed forces or a war economy, despite the fact that the German Reich Railways not only expended vast quantities of material on modernisation but also put its best railway engineers and directors to work on the system. The railway's performance during the winter of 1941–1942 can only be termed disastrous; from December 1941 to March 1942 it grew so critical that only the establishment of a special motor transport organisation staved off the complete collapse of the vital supply system for our troops. On 1st January 1942, Minister Dorpmüller [Reich Transport Minister] and his Under-Secretary, Kleinmann, spent the whole day from early in the morning until late in the evening at the Führer's headquarters. For hour after hour their conferences with the Führer and myself went on, and the Chief of Military Transport, General Gercke, was also called in. The situation demanded the adoption of special measures, particularly for the protection of the locomotives and of their water-tanking stations which were totally unsuitable for the sub-zero temperatures of the unusually cold spell. There were days when as many as a hundred locomotives broke down; German locomotives were just not designed for a climate like that; we had been forced to re-bed all the railways to the standard German gauge, because virtually no Russian rolling stock had fallen into our hands at all.

The Chief of Military Transport had complained bitterly—and rightly—about our Reich Railways for not replacing the locomotives as they broke down; their lack of protection from the frost was not his fault. During the evening, with the Führer in the chair, the only possible solution was arrived at: the Reich Railways would take over responsibility for the entire railway system in occupied Russia right up to the Army's railheads from which the supplies would be distributed to the front-line issuing depots direct; the network would no longer be the Chief of Military Transport's responsibility.

On the face of it it was a unique and quite remarkable solution, as the direction of the entire transportation system in the occupied territories was otherwise the Chief of Military Transport's pigeon. But General Gercke was wise enough to accept this suggestion of the Führer's because the Transport Minister had available quite different means of eliminating stoppages and because he, Gercke, would now be liable for them no longer. Instead the Minister was required to report to the Führer in person each day on how many trainloads he had turned over to the Chief of Military Transport at the rail-heads. The following figures will give some idea of the size of the problem: the Army by itself (i.e. not including the Air Force) had a requirement for 120 trainloads of supplies every twenty-four hours, assuming that no particular operations were in hand demanding increased munitions supplies and hospital transport; but with a supreme effort, the railway's carrying capacity could be brought up finally to only one hundred trains a day and that for only brief periods. Besides, there were violent fluctuations which could be attributed to the endless railway stoppages caused by the partisans; often there were more than a hundred stretches of railway line blown up in one night.

The spring offensive began in the Poltava region at the very last moment, before the deep Russian penetrations could break through our weak and increasingly extended defence forces. Field-Marshal von Bock wanted to use the reinforcements allocated to him for the counter-offensive—some of them still in the process of being moved up—to defend the area where the danger of a Russian break-through to the west seemed most imminent; but the Führer, as Commander-in-Chief of the Army, insisted on the counter-attack's being launched in such a way as to strike at the root of the enemy bulge and cut across it along its 'chord'; he would excise the cyst like that. Von Bock, on the other hand, feared that all this was being tried too late.

Hitler intervened and simply ordered the operation to be carried out as he had said. He was proved right, with the result that in this hour of crisis the battle turned into decisive defeat for the Russians who lost unexpectedly large numbers of prisoners to us.

There is not much time left to me, so I will refrain from depicting the progress of the Hitler offensive as it ground to a halt in the Caucasus and at Stalingrad—the prelude to the turn of the tide against us in the east. I would like to restrict my narrative to some particular episodes and personal experiences of that period.

The first, and completely inexplicable, event was the publication in the newspapers of the Western Powers of certain copies of our plan of attack. They reproduced at least one sentence of the Führer's 'basic directive' so accurately that there could be no doubt but that there had been treachery somewhere along the line. The Führer's mistrust of the staffs entrusted with the preliminary study found new sustenance: he renewed his charges against the General Staff, who, he said, could be the only source of this betrayal.

In fact, as was discovered during the following winter, the guilty party was a renegade officer on the Air Force operations staff, who had been employed in their Intelligence section and who had established contacts with the enemy's espionage network. During a big trial before the Reich Military Tribunal in December 1942, a number of sentences were passed, because a major organisation of traitors and spies had been uncovered in Berlin. Even though they were largely civilians involved, both men and women, the most important of the enemy's sources of military intelligence had been this Air Force officer, a Lieutenant-Colonel Schulze-Boysen, and his wife. But until this had been established, Hitler continued to heap abuse on the Army's completely innocent General Staff.

The second misfortune was when a divisional staff officer's aircraft crashed in no-man's-land on the eastern front; he had been carrying upon his person the order issued to General Stumme's Army Corps for its attack during the big offensive due to begin very few days later. The hapless officer had lost his way in the plane and, together with the documents, fell into Russian hands; he himself was shot out of hand on the spot. Hitler's indignation at the commanding officers concerned—the commanding general, his chief of staff and the divisional commander—resulted in a court martial before the Reich Military Tribunal presided over by Göring. It was thanks to him, and to my own collaboration, that the officers under sentence were all variously pardoned and later resumed their duties elsewhere. The worthy General Stumme was killed in action some months later while deputising for Rommel in North Africa.

After a three-day battle we succeeded in breaking through to Voronezh and the battle for the Don crossing into the city itself began; it was now that the first misgivings began to make themselves felt about von Bock's leadership of his Army Group, because in

Hitler's view he was digging in for a battle there instead of wheeling southwards (without bothering about the fate of Voronezh or about his flanks and rear) and winning territory along the Don as fast as possible.

In his quarrels with Halder I could again see a leadership crisis looming up and I advised the Führer to fly out in person to Field-Marshal von Bock to argue it out with him. My proposal was accepted. I accompanied the Führer on the flight, while Halder had provided a staff officer from the War Office operations department. As usual, the Führer outlined his basic strategy to von Bock and discussed with him, in an amiable way, the manner in which he wanted him to continue the operation.

On all sides there was a cordial atmosphere, which I must admit disappointed me, because the Führer only touched marginally upon the matter which was uppermost in his mind and which the day before he had so decisively branded as a blunder. This made me very angry and quite exceptionally I abandoned my invariable reticence and bluntly told Bock what it was that the Führer wanted, expecting that the latter would now speak his own mind more clearly too. But the moment passed unnoticed as everybody began to get up for their meal. I, nevertheless, seized the opportunity to tell the Army Group's Chief of Staff, General von Sodenstern, quite frankly why it was that the Führer had come in person and what was on his mind.

After the meal, which was marked by the same affable atmosphere as the conference itself, we flew back to the Führer's headquarters.

The actual outcome was a negative one: on the very next day, as Halder was addressing the war conference, Hitler again blew up about the recalcitrant and incompetent leadership of the Army Group: but the Führer himself was the one to blame, for I myself had witnessed how he had only beaten around the bush instead of clearly stipulating what it was he wanted. So we—Halder, Jodl and I—had to put up with the same scene all over again.

I have mentioned this episode only because I often experienced this weakness of Hitler's for 'parleying' about with his distant but senior generals. I gained the impression that he was embarrassed to a degree and was obliged to adopt an inappropriate attitude of modest reserve, with the result that the generals who only rarely met him face to face totally failed to appreciate the gravity of the situation and certainly did not dream that they were under suspicion of kicking over the traces and of failing to recognise Hitler, the Führer and Supreme Commander of the Armed Forces, as an expert in military affairs. In this particular respect Hitler—quite apart from his natural mistrust—was extremely susceptible and easily offended. So the germ of von Bock's dismissal was there; and a few weeks later Field-Marshal Freiherr von Weichs had replaced him.

For the operations in the Caucasus a newly-formed Army Group A had been foreseen, and its operations staff had already been trained. The question arose of a suitable Commander-in-Chief for the Group; Halder and I—quite independently of one another—proposed the name of Field-Marshal List. Hitler wavered and could not make up his mind, while refusing to divulge what it was he had against him. Finally, when it was high time for a decision to have been reached, Halder and I had a joint interview with Hitler about it, and after much hesitation he gave his consent. But the very first operations prosecuted by the Army Group as it advanced past Rostov and prepared to fan out into the Caucasian hinterland brought a wave of unjustified charges against List: all at once the story was that he had prevented the armoured units of the SS from breaking off towards Rostov, or that he had begun far too late and attacked too cautiously, and so on, although every one of us knew that he had operated according to the orders issued to him.

Some weeks later List came to report at the Führer's head-quarters at Vinnitsa; I myself was in Berlin, but on my return I was obliged to listen to Hitler's complaints that it was I who had been responsible for putting forward the name of this unsuitable man, as he had left the worst possible impression, one of complete lack of orientation, behind; he had put in his appearance carrying a map printed to a scale of one to a million, with none of his troops' dispositions marked in, and so on and so on. When I rejoined that he, Hitler, had himself expressly forbidden the carrying of such detailed maps when travelling by plane he rounded violently upon me, shouting that Göring had also been at the conference attended by List and had been very shocked at it all.

The disastrous flight which Jodl then made out to the mountain Corps, which was based predominantly on the Caucasus and fighting for the mountain passes leading out to the Black Sea, brought the crisis to a head. Jodl conducted a detailed interview with the commanding general of the mountain Corps General Konrad, and with Field-Marshal List, about the hopelessness of the situation, and upon his return he reported to the Führer that evening that he was obliged to subscribe to List's appreciation that the task he had been given was impossible of execution. I will skirt round the details—Jodl can and will relate them far better than I can. In any event, Jodl's contribution—which really represented nothing more than the views of Jodl himself and List—left the Führer speechless, and finally caused a terrible outburst of rage. Here again the damage had been done by the crisis of confidence and by his pathological delusion that his generals were conspiring against him and were trying to sabotage his orders on what were in his view pretty shabby pretexts. He had become obsessed by the *idée fixe* of capturing the coast road running along the Black Sea and over the western spur of the Caucasus mountains; and he believed that his generals were failing to appreciate the value of this strategy and were opposing him for that reason. What he did not seem to want to understand was that the very great supply and logistical difficulties entailed by the mountain paths made the operation absolutely impracticable.

As a result, his unbridled rage was directed against Jodl and myself —myself for having originally arranged Jodl's visit; I was ordered to fly out to List at Stalino next day and inform him that he had been relieved of his command of the Army Group and was to return home to await the Führer's pleasure.

I never found out who had been stirring things up against List, an army commander of the highest calibre who had particularly proved his value in France and in the Balkans. It is my belief that the witchhunt started on the political side, with Himmler or Bormann; otherwise it is inexplicable.

The consequences of this series of events have been related elsewhere already: Jodl was supposed to disappear, although I shielded him by saying I was responsible; although I had lost my reputation, my dismissal or posting elsewhere was denied to me, despite Göring's having promised to secure this from the Führer. We no longer ate our meals with him at one common table, and stenographers were permanently introduced among us as we conferred. It was not until 30th January, 1943, that he deigned to shake hands with Jodl and myself again.

Nor did the Chief of General Staff, Halder, escape unscathed during this *brouhaha* over List. The operations in and to the north of the Caucasus failed to satisfy Hitler's ambitious plans, and the Russian attacks on Army Group South to the west and south of Moscow had created a serious situation; they had in fact been designed to relieve the hard-pressed Russians on the southern sector of the front.

Halder rightly described the overall situation as anything but satisfying, despite the enormous territorial gains brought by our offensive. Halder, like Jodl and myself, was waiting to see where the Russians' strategic reserves would put in their appearance, in addition to these recognisable and recognised focuses of attack; in his opinion these reserves had still not been thrown into the balance. Furthermore, the Russian mode of warfare during our big offensive in the south had manifested a new character: in comparison with the previous encirclement actions, the numbers of prisoners that fell into our hands remained relatively small. The enemy was evading the traps we laid for him in time, and as a strategic defence was exploiting the sheer vastness of his territory, dodging our forces and avoiding disastrous actions. Only in and about Stalingrad and in the mountain passes did the enemy really offer his most stubborn resistance, as he no longer had to fear the prospect of tactical encirclement.

Even if the mass of the Sixth Army under Paulus did succeed—relying heavily on the strength of our allies along the river Don, who were reinforced by individual German divisions—in driving through into the Stalingrad area, his forces were too extended for more than localised offensives in the oil fields and near Stalingrad; the over-extended front was no longer capable of smashing its attacks through. Halder correctly perceived the danger to which the Don flank, which was being held south of Voronezh by the Hungarians and Italians, and to the west of Stalingrad by the Roumanians, was exposed. The Führer had never lost sight of the possible danger to the Don flank and his faith in his allies was only meagre, but he assessed the value of the river Don so highly as an obstacle, at least until it froze over, that he thought it justifiable to take this risk with them.

Although Hitler had tolerated co-operating with Halder more from common sense than from a sense of trust or even personal inclination, one could detect a marked estrangement between them, an increasing tension manifested partly by his abrupt treatment of Halder, partly by unfavourable criticism of him and occasionally even by violent quarrels. We all saw how Hitler ventilated his disillusionment over the way the offensive had seized up and about the cries for help from Army Groups North and Centre—desperately fighting and desperately on the defensive—cries which Halder was underlining and emphasising to him.

Hitler had to vent his ill-humour on somebody. In his dispute with Jodl and myself he had already shown his inability to control his feelings. His unbearable irritability had to a great extent been brought on by the hot, continental climate at Vinnitsa, which he could not stand and which literally went to his head, as Professor Morell several times explained to me. Medicaments were useless against it; and even the permanent humidifying installation in his bunker and in the conference chamber only temporarily alleviated his discomfort.

But quite apart from all this, every situation only hardened in us a tacit realisation that the enormous quantities of men and material we were pouring in with no hope of replacement bore no comparison to the meagre expenditure it had forced upon the Russians hitherto. Almost every day Halder was waiting with new statistics on the formations still available to the enemy as a strategic reserve and on the enemy's tank and spares outputs (data provided by General Thomas) and on the capacity of the enemy's armaments industry in the Urals (Thomas again) and so on; again and again the Führer was provoked to refute the statistics.

I was forbidden to circulate General Thomas' 'defeatist' reports any longer: they were pure fantasy, he refused to stand it, and so on. His criticisms of Halder became increasingly frequent: he was a pessimist, a prophet of doom, he was infecting the commanders-in-chief with his wailing and so on. It was then that I knew that the wheel had turned full circle again: a scapegoat was being sought, somebody else to be sent out into the wilderness.

When Hitler informed me in General Schmundt's presence that he was going to part with Halder, I broke the resolution I had made after the calamity over Field-Marshal List, never to put forward another name for any post whatsoever. I just could not bring myself to sit fast and turn a blind eye as things took their course: I energetically championed General von Manstein as Halder's successor; Hitler again rejected my proposal, this time with the excuse that he could not spare him from his present command. After much to-ing and fro-ing I proposed with much more firmness the name of General Paulus; I received a categorical 'No'. Paulus, he said, was going to take over General Jodl's office after the battle of Stalingrad; that had already been decided upon, as he did not intend to keep working with Jodl very much longer; he had already reached these decisions, and had talked it all over with Schmundt.

The latter was to fly to Paris next day and fetch General Zeitzler, the Chief of Staff to von Rundstedt as Commander-in-Chief, West; he was going to make Zeitzler his new Chief of General Staff. I considered Zeitzler quite indispensable in the west and urgently warned him against recalling him from there in the present situation; he was not the man the Führer was looking for, he didn't need him, I said; I added that I was in a good position to judge, and I knew Zeitzler too well, although I did consider him a brilliant Army and Army Group Chief of Staff.

None of my advice was heeded; it was obvious that the Führer and Schmundt were at one on this, and the latter executed his mission in Paris.

On the same day, Halder was summoned to Hitler in my presence. The Führer made a lengthy speech, in the course of which he explained that he could not work with him much longer and had resolved to find another Chief of the General Staff. Halder listened to the tirade without a word; then he rose and walked out of the chamber with the words: 'I am leaving.'

Two days later the Zeitzler era began, in close collaboration with Schmundt, who must, therefore, have been behind this choice. Zeitzler had rightly attracted the Führer's attention to himself: he had been Chief of Staff to an Army Corps in the Polish campaign, and during the campaign in the west he had been Chief of Staff to Kleist's armoured group at the time of the Sédan break-through to Abbeville; he had particularly excelled as the organiser of the Atlantic coastal defences, playing a considerable rôle in the success of the Dieppe defences at the time of the British raid there in the summer of 1942. When all was said and done I had, after all, a more than academic interest in who was selected as the Chief of the Army General Staff, because I wanted at length to see somebody who really enjoyed the Führer's confidence occupying the controlling office in the Army.

It could not be anything but a great release for me if I did not have to fight a daily battle against the Führer's distrust.

Jodl and I also hoped to achieve a fruitful collaboration with him, as Zeitzler had been Jodl's operations officer for several years and was not only familiar with the basic concepts of unified armed forces command but indeed one of its earliest champions. It was our first and most grievous disappointment when we saw exactly the opposite of what we had hoped taking place: Zeitzler not only dissociated himself from us, but was intent on excluding us to an increasing degree—and even more than hitherto—from the decision-making on the eastern front, by means of frequently briefing Hitler on the eastern front situation alone and *à deux*; it was obvious that he considered Jodl solely interested in the other theatres of war; and it was even more obvious that he feared our influence on the Führer—a very regrettable and narrow-minded point of view.

In North Africa, during the summer of 1942, Rommel's triumphant campaign with his one light infantry and two armoured divisions, and with the participation of Italian units and magnificent support from Kesselring's Air Group, brought unexpected victories. Now that he had organised the defence of the sector he had reached to the west of Alexandria, Rommel himself, who had in the space of one year been promoted from lieutenant-general to field-marshal, urgently needed to return to Germany to regain his health which had been badly affected by the tropical climate. One cannot help wondering what this daring and highly-favoured tank commander would have achieved had he been fighting with his units in the one theatre of war where Germany's fate was to be determined.

The Army's new C.G.S. was inheriting an onerous legacy: there was fierce and unprofitable fighting among the northern spurs of the Caucasus mountains, there was uncertainty along the weakened front in the steppes between the mountains and Stalingrad, there was very heavy fighting in and about Stalingrad itself and the gravest possible danger to our allies holding the front along the river Don. The uneasy question overshadowing everything was: where are the Russians going to launch their counter-offensive? Where were their strategic reserves?

The battle of Stalingrad swallowed up division after division, attracting them like moths to a candle flame: although the Volga had been reached to the north and south of, and actually within Stalingrad, fierce house-to-house fighting was raging throughout the city and its vast industrial sites. Painfully won advances, brilliant defensive victories to the north of the city between the loops of the Volga and the Don increased our determination to capture every corner of the city, and with it of achieving our tantalising and hidden aim—the victory over Stalingrad—which seemed at times so near. Certainly it was the ambition of every officer and every soldier of Paulus' army to crown their campaign with absolute victory: I will offer no opinion on whether and how far our Supreme Command [i.e. Hitler] was thereby already promoting the catastrophe that was to follow.

When the [Russian] counter-offensive began in November, perfectly positioned from the strategic viewpoint, first bowling over the [Third] Roumanian Army and thereby opening up deep into the flank of the Sixth Army, and when it was then on the point of surrounding Paulus' army in Stalingrad, only one decision could possibly have staved off disaster: giving up Stalingrad and using the entire Stalingrad army to fight its way out to the west.

I am in no doubt whatsoever that that would have worked out, that the Sixth Army would have been saved and the Russians probably defeated—admittedly at the cost of giving up Stalingrad and our position on the bank of the Volga. All the frightful events that followed in consequence of the complete encirclement of Paulus' army in Stalingrad by January 1943—the forbidden break-out for which it was too late, the vain attempt at supplying the army by air, the tardy counter-attack launched with too little strength to liberate the Sixth Army—all are graven deeply on my memory. I cannot paint the drama in its full intensity: for that I lack the material. . . .*

Giving up Stalingrad was inevitably a severe blow to our prestige; the wiping out of a whole army, and the situation brought about by its loss, meant a setback which was consonant with our having lost our 1942–1943 campaign, despite the genius with which it had been conceived and born. Small wonder that our critics became more vociferous, and the Russians received a tremendous boost for the prosecution of their war; we had played our last trump, and lost.

Whatever the outcome of an attempt to rescue Paulus' army from Stalingrad might have been, in my view there would have been only one way of staving off the total defeat which faced us in our eastern campaign: that would have been to authorise a strategic withdrawal of all our troops to the shortest conceivable front: a line from the Black Sea or the Carpathians to Lake Peipus. To have built and fortified such a front line as a line of defence, and to have held it with the forces still available and to have strengthened it adequately with such reserves as came to us, would—in my opinion —not have been impracticable.

K. 29th September
[1946]

At this point Field-Marshal Keitel's early memoirs are interrupted. Two days later the death sentence was pronounced upon Field-Marshal Keitel and he devoted his next ten days to feverishly describing the events in and around the Führer's headquarters in April 1945 as the final collapse of Germany began—the last eighteen days of the Third Reich. Keitel himself was hanged on 16th October, 1946, before he had time to revise any of his original manuscript.

* In Keitel's original manuscript there follows an incomplete and fragmentary sentence on the theme of Stalingrad, which could not be reconstructed; it has been omitted by the Editor.

186

6

Extracts from Keitel's Wartime Letters to his Wife

EDITOR'S NOTE: According to Lieutenant-Colonel K.-H. Keitel, Lisa Keitel (née Fontaine), the widow of the field-marshal, burned all the letters she had received from her husband. But among the papers of Dr. Nelte, Keitel's defence counsel, there are seven letters written by Keitel to his wife during 1943 and 1944, some in pencil and some in ink, letters which for some no longer ascertainable reason were filed with his other correspondence dating from the period of the Nuremberg trial. It can be noted how the field-marshal's typically correct military upbringing prevented him from going into service matters in greater detail in these, his private letters:

Führer's Headquarters,
3rd August, 1943.

The telephone is not safe enough for me to discuss the war and the dangers of the air offensive against our cities. Hamburg has been a catastrophe for us, and last night there was yet another very heavy air raid on it. The same must be expected for Berlin as soon as the nights are long enough for the longer flying time involved. That is why I want you to leave Berlin as soon as possible in view of the enormous danger there now is of fires breaking out; fires are far more dangerous than high explosive. [*Keitel added a number of personal instructions for his wife, which she disobeyed; she stayed in Berlin, despite a heart complaint, even after her home at No. 6 Kielganstrasse had been bombed out in November 1943.*] I am afraid of vast *conflagrations* consuming whole districts, streams of burning oil flowing into the basements and shelters, phosphorus, and the like. It will be difficult to escape from the shelters then, and there is the danger of tremendous heat being generated. This will not be cowardice, but the sheer realisation that in face of phenomena like these one is completely powerless; in the heart of the city you will be quite powerless. . . .

Apart from this there is not much to report: there is a state of flux and we can only wait and see what will happen with the new developments in Italy. Badoglio has reassured us that they will go on fighting, and that it was only on this condition that he accepted office. Nobody knows where Mussolini is. . . .

Führer's Headquarters,
29th August, 1943.

Nobody can tell when there will be any respite for peaceful contemplation in our lives again; for the time being we have war—we have already been at war for four years now! Nobody knows when the Bolsheviks will crumple to their knees, but before then there can never be peace! Anyway, you have more than enough leisure now to reflect on things, while I am stunned by the burden of my work and the much bigger burden of worries and vexations. On top of that, we are coming into the winter again now, something that is very evident to us, cold and rainy as it is today. At present all hell is loose on the eastern front, but I am counting on a respite when the mud begins to soften, probably in four to six weeks at the earliest, in the middle of October. When that happens I expect we will shift camp to the south again [i.e. to the Berghof at Berchtesgaden]. In the middle of this week there is the state funeral in Sofia; I have to represent the German Armed Forces, I'll probably be flying down there. . . .

On the eastern front it was the period of the desperate fighting retreats all along its southern sectors, with the German troops of Army Group South, including those under the command of Field-Marshals von Manstein and von Kleist falling back on the line of the River Dnepr. On 28th August, King Boris II of Bulgaria—the champion of maximum collaboration with the Axis powers in the Balkans—had met a mysterious end in Sofia; officially it was announced that he had died of cerebral apoplexy, but it was more probably caused by poisoning: certainly he died very conveniently for the Soviets! A regent took over the government as King Simeon II, his father's successor, was still under age. On 22nd September, 1943, Field-Marshal Keitel celebrated his 61st birthday.

Führer's Headquarters,
25th September, 1943.

Despite everything there was no shortage of letters and congratulations for me on the 22nd, and the nuances in them are not uninteresting: one is forced to notice how several, in fact I can say how *many* have been of a particularly cordial and pleasant character, as opposed to those who are satisfied with mere formalities. . . . . First I had an early breakfast with the adjutants and the train commandant, with eggs, roast duck and a cold meat salad, altogether very sumptuous. At eleven o'clock I called on the Führer privately to receive his birthday greetings; he invited me to dine with him during the evening, when I had returned from my hunting expedition. At eleven-thirty I drove off by car through Wehlau to Pfeil, a forestry station east of Königsberg, in the Labiau district. I was very well looked after: Master of the Hunt Scherping [*of the Reich Forestry Commission and the Prussian Provincial Forestry Department*] was there to meet me, in fact he was the one who had got me the invitation from Göring to go elk-hunting. After about half an hour's chatting, we set off for the hunting grounds, about another ninety minutes' drive out towards Tilsit.

Our hunt was quite dramatic. There were two elk that were fair game in the Tavellenbrück game area at Ibenhorst. I could not get near the elk, which I caught sight of soon after we began our stalk. There was nothing to be seen amongst the giant hydroceles and the dense alder and pastureland, and the going was very heavy. I finally took a pot shot from a thousand feet away and, of course I missed at such a range. We carried on patiently stalking and two hours later the elk showed up only five hundred feet away and collected its first bullet from me; I immediately fired again, and the elk just dropped to the ground. It is an enormous beast, about seven feet high and weighing about nine hundred pounds; in any event, my enterprise was rewarded. A very nice Master, and very charming women. I got back here only late in the evening, and was able to change quickly into uniform for dinner with the Führer.

26th September, 1943.

I don't suppose I have ever had so much work to do as in the last few weeks and the last few days, even my adjutants found it indescribable and can only goggle at the way I eat my way through it. Every evening it takes me until very late, or even early next morning, to clear it all away. But as long as my sleep does not suffer, short though it now is, it makes no difference. Felix Bürkner [*formerly Inspector of Riding and Driving, who had lost his job because of difficulties caused by his non-Aryan background*] wrote me at great length! There is a completely incomprehensible opposition to him from Schmundt, who refuses to give him a job under any circumstances. It is *impossible* for me to protest to the Führer about it.

The Memoirs of Field-Marshal Keitel

There is no doubt that Keitel was weighed down with work in the weeks following 8th September, 1943, when Italy had withdrawn from the Axis Pact, involving considerable re-dispositions in Italy and the Balkans. During 1942 and 1943 Keitel began to suffer from blood-circulation difficulties, and it seems that this was the result of the overwork as much as of a previous lung disorder.

On 17th July, 1944, Field-Marshal Erwin Rommel, Commander-in-Chief of Army Group B on the invasion front in Normandy, was badly injured during a strafing attack on his car while returning from a front-line tour of inspection. He was implicated in the 20th July conspiracy, and on 14th October, 1944, he was called upon by the Chief of Army Personnel, General Burgdorf, accompanied by his official expert on officer questions, Lieutenant-General Maisel, and obliged to commit suicide by swallowing poison. Hitler had given him the choice of either committing suicide or facing the People's Court. By the time the following letter, with its oblique reference to Rommel, had been written, the situation on the eastern front was relatively stable, with an autumn defensive campaign in the Gumbinnen and Goldap areas of East Prussia, and the Fourth Army (General Hossbach) meeting a renewed attack by the Second White Russian Front.

Führer's Headquarters,
24th October, 1944.

How far I will get with this letter I cannot predict, but at least I ought to make a start on it. All that there is to report is that my health is good, and the Chief Medical Officer, Dr. Lieberle, was satisfied with my blood pressure yesterday and is unable to do anything with my struggling and nervous heart because organically there is nothing wrong with it. . . .

In the meantime quite a lot has been happening: Rommel has died after all from the multiple skull injuries he received on a car journey, through a blood-clot; it is a heavy blow to us, the loss of a commander well favoured by the Gods. And now yesterday Kesselring has also been injured in a motor accident. I don't know anything in detail about it yet, but in any case he will be out of action for some months even if he does pull through. They drove into the back of a gun in the dark; he has head injuries and was unconscious for a time. I hope he gets over it all right.

There is fighting now on East Prussian soil, where the Russians have broken through on both sides of Rominten heath. I think we are going to be able to iron things out, but first we have to bring more troops up, and that is in hand. Our presence here [*i.e. at the Führer's headquarters in East Prussia*] has a very soothing effect on the population, I am certain of that. The Russians certainly won't dream that we are still here, which is an added safeguard for us. There are more than enough troops around us to protect us!

By early November, Keitel had, according to the testimony of his family, lost all hope of a favourable outcome to the war ; indeed, as early as August 1941, after the death of his youngest son at Smolensk, he confided to Karl-Heinz his eldest son (according to the latter's recollection), that the war could not now be won 'with normal means'. According to Keitel's own memorandum on the 'Blame for the German Collapse', dated 8th June, 1945 (papers of Dr. Nelte), the Field-Marshal saw the attack on Russia in 1941 as a risk hard to justify. Questioned whether the attack had been necessary, he answered only 'It is for a politician to answer that'. The war could have ended in 1941, he added, only if a quick victory had been won in the east ; after Stalingrad there remained only the hope of preventing the invasion in the west and thereby avoiding a war on two fronts 'which would be the end of us sooner or later'. Keitel further added, 'If despite all this the Führer still carried on fighting, then the only reason can have been that he thought that there was nothing else awaiting the German people anyway than the annihilation with which it had been threatened.' The following letter was written to his wife on the occasion of her birthday on 4th November, 1944.

Führer's Headquarters,
1st November, 1944.

Tonight I am driving to Torgau for the Reich Military Tribunal where I am to appoint the new President [General Hans Karl von Scheele] and have a talk with the gentlemen as their chief. I will only be touching the outskirts of Berlin on my way back, inviting people to meet me there to confer with me, and putting them down again at Fürstenwalde. . . .

After all the vicissitudes of our last years, we must always hope that happier days are ahead. Really, we have a thirty-year war behind us, lasting from 1914 with only very few carefree interludes. Our generation and our children's generation have deserved to be able to live their lives in such a hard-won peace. . . .

7

The Bomb Plot
20th July 1944

EDITOR'S NOTE: On 20th July, 1944, a suitcase bomb exploded in the Führer's headquarters in East Prussia. Hitler himself survived, but several officers were killed. The bomb had been planted by Colonel Count von Stauffenberg, Chief of Staff to the Commander-in-Chief of the Reserve Army. The plan was to establish Colonel-General Ludwig Beck as a 'Reich Administrator', after Hitler's death, with Field-Marshal von Witzleben, who had been on sick leave since 1942, as Supreme Commander of the Armed Forces; others involved at the Berlin end were the Chief of the General Army Office, General Olbricht, the City Commandant, General von Hase, and numerous General Staff officers. In addition Field-Marshals Rommel and von Kluge (C.-in-C. West) were aware of the conspiracy. After the bomb blast, a Top Secret signal went out at 4.45 p.m. containing the code-words 'Internal Unrest', according to which Field-Marshal von Witzleben transferred executive authority in all occupied areas to the front-line commanders-in-chief (i.e. West, South-west and South-east) and on the eastern front to the various Army Group commanders. At 6.0 p.m. a further signal went out to the German military districts numbered I to XIII and XVII, XVIII, XX, XXI and to military district Bohemia-Moravia, according to which executive authority was transferred to the commanding generals. The order was completely obeyed only by the deputy commanding general of defence district XVII (Vienna) apart from the military governor of France in Paris, while in military districts XI (Kassel) and XIV (Nuremberg) steps were put in hand to comply with the order. But during the evening Keitel telephoned the military districts from the Führer's headquarters announcing that the orders from Berlin were forged, and the uprising was crushed. Von Staufenberg, Olbricht and Beck were shot that same night, while von Witzleben was executed on 8th August, and von Kluge committed suicide upon his recall as C.-in-C. West on 19th August, fearing that he was to be called to account for his complicity; the military governor of France, General von Stülpnagel, was hanged (after a vain suicide attempt) on 30th August and Rommel himself was forced to commit suicide in October 1944.

Dr. Otto Nelte, Field-Marshal Keitel's defence counsel at Nuremberg, prepared a questionnaire for him to answer as a preliminary for the hearing, and the part of the questionnaire dealing with the bomb plot of 20th July, 1944, is reproduced here to throw light on the Field-Marshal's attitude to the conspiracy, which he himself had no time to deal with explicitly in his memoirs.

What in your view were the deeper motives behind the Putsch?

Dissatisfaction with Hitler, both with his political system and with his direction of the war. As it seemed quite out of the question that Hitler would go of his own accord, the conspirators resolved to eliminate him. By this they hoped to release the soldiers and officials of their oath of allegiance to Hitler at the same time. What kind of political system—if any—was intended to take his place I don't know. I never heard of any so-called government programme; as for the military side, I do not believe it was intended to end the war by surrender. There was an order signed by Witzleben as 'Supreme Commander of the Armed Forces', but it was rejected by all its recipients. Finally, there were similar orders issued to the military districts, which were not obeyed.

Were there any indications, or had Intelligence been received indicating that a revolutionary movement was in existence?

Not that the OKW or I knew of. Hitler had received no reports or warnings and he did not speak with me about it either before or after the murder attempt. During the investigations it was established that some officers in the War Office and in military Intelligence had known of the planned murder attempt, but they had not reported it.

I would like to refrain from asking you for details of the Putsch, *as they are of no consequence for your defence. Would you just tell me one thing: did any front-line commanders take part in the* Putsch?

No. Which front-line commanders—if any—had any cognisance of the planned *Putsch* was not established. As far as I know, none of them. General Beck's attempt at establishing contact [with Army Group North] failed and was thrown out.

What part did you play in the affair?

I was present when the bomb exploded, and on the orders of the Führer—who was not deprived of his governmental or executive

193

authority for one instant—I issued all the necessary instructions to all the fighting services and to the subordinate military district commanders.

I have brought up this subject of the 20th July, 1944 plot in this examination of you only because during an earlier hearing someone has accused you of being guilty of, or an accessory to, the death of Field-Marshal Rommel. Rommel was heavily incriminated by the testimony of one of the main conspirators, a lieutenant-colonel on the staff of the military governor of France, von Stülpnagel. The Führer showed me the protocol of the testimony and ordered the Chief of Army Personnel to summon Rommel to his presence; Rommel refused to come, as he was too ill to travel. Thereupon the Führer ordered his chief adjutant and the Chief of Army Personnel, Burgdorf, to go and see him, taking with them the incriminating protocol and a letter which I wrote at Hitler's dictation. In this latter it was submitted to Rommel that he should report to the Führer if he believed himself innocent; if he could not, then his arrest was inevitable, and he would be obliged to answer for his actions before a court. He might like to consider what the consequences of that would be; on the other hand there was another way out for him to take.

Having perused the protocol and the letter, Rommel asked whether the Führer was aware of the protocol's existence; then he asked General Burgdorf for time to think. Burgdorf had personal orders from Hitler to prevent Rommel committing suicide by shooting himself; he was to offer him poison, in order that the cause of death could be attributed to the brain damage he had suffered in the motor accident; that would be an honourable demise and would preserve his national reputation.

As they drove off together to the doctor in Ulm, Rommel swallowed the poison and died. The real cause of death was concealed, on Hitler's express wish, and Rommel received a state funeral with full military honours.

It is of interest to consider the preliminary interrogation of Field-Marshal Keitel by the American Colonel Amen, published in Nazi Conspiracy and Aggression, Supplement B, p. 1256 et seq. In this painfully thorough interrogation, one thing which the American officer obviously completely failed to grasp becomes very plain, unfamiliar as he would have been with the Prussian Code of Honour : the field-marshal's actions were based solely on the normal consequences any German officer (and especially a senior one) must draw upon the failure of an attempt at an action based—in Keitel's

194

view—upon dishonourable motives; every opportunity must be given to the German officer to choose this way out. During his interrogation he expressed his unlimited admiration of Rommel's military achievements and courage, and he obviously considered poison in this case a better means of suicide than the traditional bullet in the head, because he feared a gigantic scandal— not so much for the Third Reich as for Rommel and the officer corps—if Field-Marshal Rommel's suicide or, alternatively, his being sentenced to death by the People's Court became common knowledge. Hence the—for the Americans—incomprehensible attitude displayed by Keitel.

8
The Last Days under Adolf Hitler
1945

As one of the few people to have survived the events of April 1945 both within and without the Reich Chancellery, I would like to relate some of my recollections, beginning with those of 20th April, Hitler's last birthday.

Berlin and the city's eastern suburbs were already under sporadic long-range gun fire from small-calibre Russian artillery; a few enemy bombers and spotter planes had been wheeling over the eastern end of the city, particularly at and shortly after dusk, but they kept a respectful distance between themselves and our anti-aircraft batteries on the flak towers, which in addition to acting as anti-aircraft defences were engaging the Russian long-range batteries with accurate gunfire and repeatedly silencing them. Fighting had already reached the outermost suburbs of east Berlin, as General Busse's Ninth Army had been routed near Frankfurt-on-Oder and Küstrin, and our defence of the Oder had collapsed.

The Chief of the High Command [i.e. Keitel himself] and his Chief of operations staff [Jodl] and their immediate lieutenants were still working in the command post which had been built in Dahlem's Föhrenweg by War Minister von Blomberg back in 1936, while the OKW operations staff which had relinquished its nearby quarters at the Air Zone Command building in Kronprinzallee, had moved in [with the Army General Staff] to the War Office's bunker at Wunsdorf (in Zossen). It was there too that Jodl and I had our emergency billets, I myself being billeted at Number 16 Föhrenweg, the former home of the champion boxer Schmeling.

Towards midday of 20th April, the British and American air forces executed their last massive air raid on the centre of Berlin, the governmental quarter. Together with my wife, Grand-Admiral Dönitz and his wife, and our adjutants, we watched this violent and horrible spectacle from a small mound in the garden of the Grand-

196

Admiral's service quarters: he had returned to Berlin the night before from *Coral*, his operational headquarters near Eberswalde, as it was now threatened by the Russians' advance.

During this final heavy bombardment in perfect and sunny weather the already badly afflicted Reich Chancellery building escaped further damage; our own fighter squadrons did nothing to beat off the attack on Berlin, and the anti-aircraft defences were powerless against an enemy attacking from such a height. The raid lasted almost two hours, the bombers parading overhead in tight formation as though it were a peacetime air display, dropping the bombs in perfect unison.

A war conference had been laid on from four o'clock onwards that afternoon in the Führer's bunker at the Reich Chancellery. As Jodl and I entered the bunker, we saw the Führer accompanied by Goebbels and Himmler going up to the Reich Chancellery's day-rooms; I rejected an adjutant's suggestion that I should tag along with them, as I had not yet had the opportunity of greeting the Führer. I learned that a number of boys of the Hitler Youth had been paraded upstairs in the Reich Chancellery to receive decorations for gallantry, including several Iron Crosses, for their superb work in A.R.P. and anti-aircraft units during the enemy air raids.

After the Führer had returned to the bunker, Göring, Dönitz, Keitel and Jodl were individually summoned to his small sitting room next to the conference chamber to congratulate him on the occasion of his birthday. All the other people taking part in the conference were greeted by the Führer with just a handshake as he entered the chamber, and no further attention was paid to its being his birthday.

When I found myself alone face to face with the Führer, I found myself unable to congratulate him: I said something to the effect that both his merciful escape from assassination on 20th July and his continued survival until today, his birthday, to maintain in his hands the supreme command at this grave moment when the very existence of the Reich he had created was threatened as never before, inspired in us the confidence that he would draw what seemed the inevitable conclusion now: I said that I believed he should begin surrender negotiations before the Reich capital itself became a battlefield.

I was about to continue in this vein when he stopped me with the words: 'Keitel, I know what I want; I am going to go down fighting, either in or outside Berlin.' To me that sounded like an empty slogan, and he could see I was trying to dissuade him from the idea; he held out his hand to me, and said: 'Thank you—call in Jodl, will you. We will speak later about it.' I was dismissed from his room. What he discussed with Jodl I never learned.

The war conference took its usual course in the oppressive confines of the bunker chamber; the War Office's General Krebs described the situation on the eastern front, and Jodl the remaining theatres. In the meantime, Göring and I withdrew to the private rooms and discussed his intention to evacuate his operational headquarters to Berchtesgaden, as Karinhall was already in grave danger and *Kurfürst*, the Air Force operations staff's headquarters, was already being cut off from time to time from the signals networks. Göring was planning to go by car, in which case it was high time for him to leave, as between Halle and Leipzig there was only one main road south known to be clear of enemy spearheads. I advised Göring to go, and he asked me if I would suggest to Hitler that the Air Force operational headquarters should be transferred to Berchtesgaden.

Despite the critical situation—in the Italian theatre—the war conference passed calmly and without the otherwise frequent unbalanced outbursts. The Führer made a number of clear and objective decisions; his excitability was well in rein. When I put forward the proposal that Göring should be despatched to the south before the communications were severed altogether, he agreed and went so far as to suggest this himself to Göring.

My motive in doing this centred admittedly on my own absolutely firm belief at that time that the Führer and the OKW operations staff would—as had been provided for in our orders—also be transferring their supreme command to Berchtesgaden, even if not until the situation in the fighting around Berlin was consolidated; if necessary they would have to flee by air and at night. The aircraft for this were already standing by, and everybody not absolutely vital to the Führer's headquarters in Berlin had already been sent off to Berchtesgaden by special trains and convoys of lorries. The same went for the OKW and the War Office, which had both been split up and resolved into a joint Northern Command Staff (for Dönitz) and a Southern one, at Berchtesgaden. Dönitz was to assume command of all branches of the armed forces in northern Germany as soon as central and southern Germany were cut off from the north by the linking-up of the American and Russian troops to the south of Berlin. Hitler himself had signed the orders for this, as he himself planned to take over in the south while remaining in radio communication with Dönitz.

On our return to Dahlem, on 20th April, I informed Jodl of my decision to fly out to Berchtesgaden everybody with whose services we could possibly dispense; my own special train had already moved there two days earlier. With my adjutant Szymonski in command, my private aircraft made a pefect daylight take-off in the hands of Air-Staff Engineer Funk [Keitel's pilot] and a full crew, taking General Winter, Dr. Lehmann, Frau Jodl and my wife to Prague where a service car was waiting to take them on to Berchtesgaden. The plane was back at Berlin-Tempelhof and at my disposal again that evening. All this was done to ease the pressure and prepare the way for the imminent migration of the Führer's headquarters to Berchtesgaden, a move which at that time was beyond any question.

On 21st April, General Schörner, commander of the biggest and strongest Army Group on the Eastern Front [Army Group Centre] operating from down in the Carpathians to almost as far as just south of Frankfurt-on-Oder, arrived to make a personal report on the situation to the Führer. They met in complete privacy, and as Jodl and I entered the Führer's bunker that afternoon Schörner was just taking leave of him. It was obvious that the Führer had been greatly encouraged by their talk, for he uttered a few optimistic remarks which Schörner echoed, and then invited us to congratulate Germany's latest 'Field-Marshal'.

As the war conference progressed, it became very obvious that Schörner had imbued the Führer with an exaggerated confidence in his own front and leadership, and that Hitler was now clutching at this like a drowning man at a straw, despite the fact that in the final synthesis it was only a limited section of the front that was putting up any show of resistance. Things were getting hopeless in the west and in Italy; the Russians were at the gates of Berlin. . . . The Führer's mood brightened still further as, unexpectedly for us, General Wenck, commanding the newly-formed Twelfth Army, put in an appearance during the conference to brief Hitler on the position of his divisions, and on his operational intentions and the timetable for his surprise attack on the American formations operating in the Harz region and advancing on the Elbe. As General Wenck has survived and is in American captivity, I will leave it to him to describe what were his aims, intentions and prospects at some date in the future; I myself have no charts or papers to refer to. The Führer particularly valued Wenck as the energetic but cautious staff officer for which he had come to know him; he had been the closest colleague of the Chief of General Staff, Guderian, and his right-hand man and permanent representative, and he had been hand-picked by the Führer for the command of the newly-raised

Twelfth Army. This latter would, it was hoped, bring about a change in the position between the mountains of central Germany and the Elbe, by mopping up the enemy forces—believed to be only weak —in the Magdeburg–Lüneberg–Brunswick area and joining up with the armoured group which had crossed the Elbe south of Lauenburg and which was fighting in the vicinity of Uelzen.

In view of the improvised nature of his formation, the complexity of the situation, which was tying down our forces on every hand, and the numerical weakness of the army in question, I was unable to comprehend either the Führer's optimism or that of General Wenck. I am convinced that Wenck did not honestly hope to gain more than a local success, and certainly not a strategic victory. But in this case too the Führer's manifest self-deception was only increased by the generals in whom he had trusted and this in turn inspired hopes in him which were to prove fateful to us. Only people who—like me—have seen and heard the hundreds of cases where even senior commanders did not dare to stand up to the Führer at times like this and tell him what they thought and what they considered feasible, have any right to reject the accusation of 'feebleness' among the Führer's closest advisers.

As Jodl and I drove back together in my car that evening after the war conference, as was our custom, we both expressed our amazement that the Führer had seemed so optimistic, or at least had been able to talk so confidently. Schörner and Wenck must have infused him with this new spirit. Could it really be that he did not see how hopeless our position was? No, he must have seen it, but he refused to admit it could be true.

At our usual time on the afternoon of 22nd April, we went to the war conference. I saw at once that leaden clouds lay heavily over the atmosphere; the Führer's face was yellowish-grey and he was of stony countenance. He was extremely nervous, his mind kept wandering and twice he left the conference chamber for his private room next door. In our absence, the situation on the eastern front and the acute worsening of the position round Berlin had been outlined at midday by General Krebs, who had taken General Wenck's place as representative of Guderian, Chief of the General Staff, who had been sent on permanent leave some weeks before.

Not only was there street-fighting in the eastern suburbs of Berlin now, but as a result of the rout of the Ninth Army to the south, the Russians had already reached the Jüterbog area, and the Army's biggest and most important central munitions dump was thus in grave and immediate danger; we had to be prepared to write it off. There was also increasing enemy pressure on the northern outskirts of Berlin, although on both flanks of Eberswalde Colonel-General Heinrici's Oder front still stood fast. Jodl and I learned of this worsening of our position in the battle of Berlin only at the Reich Chancellery. The commandant of Berlin had received personal orders from the Führer that midday for the the safeguarding of the Inner City and the government quarter.

Jodl kept the war conference as short as possible. Army Group West [i.e. the formations under the C.-in-C. West, Field-Marshal Kesselring] had in southern Germany already been pushed back into the Harz from Thüringia, there was fighting in Weimar, Gotha, Schweinfurt, and so on; in northern Germany they had been pushed back to the Elbe and the region south of Hamburg.

At the end of the conference, I asked for an interview with the Führer accompanied only by Jodl. A decision could not be postponed any longer: before Berlin became a battle-ground of house-to-house street-fighting, we had either to offer to surrender or to escape by flying out to Berchtesgaden at night to commence surrender negotiations from there. I had the conference chamber cleared, and found myself alone with Hitler, as Jodl had just been summoned to the telephone. As so often in my life, Hitler cut me short after my very first few words and broke in to say: 'I know already what you're going to tell me: "the decision has got to be taken now!" I already have taken a decision: I will never leave Berlin again; I will defend the city with my dying breath. Either I direct the battle for the Reich capital—if Wenck can keep the Americans off my back and throw them back over the Elbe—or I will go down with my troops in Berlin, fighting for the symbol of the Reich!'

I told him bluntly that that was madness, and that in the present situation I was obliged to demand that he fly that very night to Berchtesgaden to ensure the continuity of command over the Reich and the Armed Forces, something that could not be guaranteed in Berlin where communications might be severed at any moment.

The Führer explained: 'There is nothing to stop you flying to Berchtesgaden at once. In fact I order you to do so. But I myself am going to stay in Berlin. I have already announced that to the German people and the Reich capital on the radio an hour ago. I am not in the position to retract.'

At that moment, Jodl came in. In his presence, I explained that I had no intention whatsoever of flying to Berchtesgaden without him, Hitler; that was quite out of the question. It was not just a matter of the defence or loss of Berlin, but of the command of all the armed forces on every front, which could not be guaranteed from the Reich Chancellery if the situation in the capital worsened any more. Jodl fervently agreed, and explained that if their signals communications with the south were to break down altogether— and the big cable had already been cut in the Thüringian Forest— then there would be no further possibility of directing the operations of the Army Groups of Schörner [Centre], Rendulic [South], the Balkans [north-west Croatia], Italy [south-west (C), under Colonel-General von Vietinghoff-Scheel] or West [Field-Marshal Kesselring]; radio communication alone would not suffice. The split-command organisation would have to be put into effect at once and the Führer would have, as planned, to fly to Berchtesgaden to remain in command.

The Führer called in Bormann, and he repeated to the three of us the order to fly to Berchtesgaden that night, where I was to take command, with Göring as his personal representative. All three of us announced that we refused to do so. I said: 'In seven years I have never refused to execute an order from you, but this is one order I shall never carry out. You cannot and should not leave the Armed Forces in the lurch, still less at a time like this.' He replied: 'I am stopping here, and that is that. I have deliberately announced this without your knowledge so as to commit myself. If there has got to be any negotiating with the enemy—as there has now—then Göring is better at that than I am. Either I fight and win the battle of Berlin—or I am killed in Berlin. That is my final and irrevocable decision.'

I saw it was useless to continue this argument with Hitler in his present mood, and I announced I would drive at once from the Reich Chancellery to the front to see General Wenck, cancel all the orders covering his operations, and direct him to march on Berlin and join up with the Ninth Army units fighting to the south of the city. I would report to him, the Führer, at noon next day on the new position and on Wenck's movements, and then we should be able to look ahead from there. The Führer at once agreed to my proposal; obviously, it brought him a degree of deliverance from the frankly horrifying position in which he had put both himself and us.

On his orders I was provided with ample victuals; as I partook of a bowl of pea soup before my departure, I went over the other measures to be taken with Jodl. He suggested to me that the supreme command should be safeguarded against the event that the Führer really did adhere to his plan as outlined to us in the emotional scene shortly before. We both at once agreed that in that case it would be impossible to command from the Führer's Reich Chancellery bunker, but on the other hand that we would not go to Berchtesgaden and thereby give up both the Führer and contact with him; but we would under no circumstances remain at the Reich Chancellery or even in Berlin ourselves, as we would thereby lose all contact with the various fronts.

On this basis, I authorised Jodl to make the necessary dispositions for the combined OKW and War Office command staff foreseen for Berchtesgaden to transfer all the remaining units still in Wunsdorf under the command of Lieutenant-General Winter (deputy-chief, OKW operations staff) immediately to Berchtesgaden, to safeguard the operational command in the south, while the Northern Command Staff should that same evening be assembled at Krampnitz barracks, near Potsdam, to which locality we two would also transfer with our immediate lieutenants. Overall command should remain for the time being with the Führer, keeping in contact with the Reich Chancellery all the time, and with the daily war conferences continuing as before. This left the way still open for the solution we had originally planned, for we were both firmly resolved to dissuade the Führer, come what may, from his mania for succumbing in Berlin. Jodl undertook to apprise General Wenck, possibly by radio, of my advent and of the order I intended to issue to him; then we separated.

I drove straight from the Reich Chancellery, accompanied by my staff officer Major Schlottmann, and with my ever cheerful driver Mönch at the wheel. We wandered all round Nauen and Brandenburg in the greatest difficulty as they had recently been ploughed up by an air raid and only a desert of ruins remained; the direct street leading south to Wenck's headquarters had been hopelessly blocked. I finally found Wenck shortly before midnight at a lonely forester's house. Our finding the place at all was pure chance, because I met a despatch-rider who guided me to General Koehler's headquarters first of all, and General Koehler provided me with a driver who knew the forest lanes leading to Twelfth Army headquarters.

In a *tête-à-tête* with General Wenck, I outlined the situation that had developed during the previous afternoon in the Reich Chancellery, and made it clear to him that my last hope of fetching the Führer out of Berlin rested solely on the success of his breaking through to the capital and linking up with the Ninth Army. I was thinking in terms of nothing less than abducting the Führer—if necessary by force—from the Reich Chancellery if we were to be unable to bring him to his senses, something which I hardly dared to hope after his calamitous performance during the previous afternoon. Everything depended, I told him, on the success of our operation, whatever the cost.

Wenck called in his chief of staff; with a map, I sketched in the situation round Berlin as best I knew it from the previous day; then I left the men alone and set about my supper in the hall of the forester's house, while Wenck dictated the new order to his army I had asked him for, to take back to the Führer. About an hour later, I drove off again with the army order in my pocket, having offered to hand Wenck's order to General Koehler on the way back, and to brief him personally and visit his divisional commanders during the night as well. I wanted to bring my own personal influence to bear on all these troop commanders and bring home to them both the rough significance of the task lying ahead of them and the assurance that if things went wrong, it would augur ill for Germany. Wenck was—and stayed—the only one to learn my innermost thoughts and of my intention to abduct the Führer from Berlin before the capital's fate was sealed.

At dawn, after a tiresome search, I reached the command post of the closest division to the front; it had already issued orders to attack in line with the changed situation and our intentions. I found the divisional commander some way back in a village, while there were sounds of battle some way off in the distance. I demanded that he should accompany me immediately to his most advanced regiment, so that he could exert some personal influence on his troops and because I wanted to speak to the regiment's commanding officer myself.

It was a division that had recently been raised in the capital from units and unit leaders of the Reich Labour Service. Naturally, it was not a battle-hardened troop, but its officers and men were fired by a magnificent spirit; but their commanding officers, obviously energetic and war-hardened soldiers, belonged more than normally at the head of their troops and not to rearward command posts, for only their personal example could compensate for the lack of training and self-confidence of their subordinate officers. After I had brought home the importance of their task to the attacking officers, both by my own presence and by a speech to them, I called in briefly on General Holste's headquarters on the way back to Krampnitz; he was responsible for safeguarding the line of the river Elbe against a crossing by the Americans from the West. I discussed the position in detail with Holste—an old regimental comrade from the 6th Artillery Regiment, whose enthusiasm and vitality I could vouch for—and stressed to him the importance of his rôle, which was the prerequisite for the success of Twelfth Army's operations (to which formation I forthwith subordinated him): Holste was absolutely convinced by the burden of reports from the troops and enemy Intelligence that the Americans were making no preparations to attack eastwards over the Elbe.

Towards eleven o'clock that morning [23rd April, 1945] I checked back into Krampnitz—dead tired, of course—and after consulting with Jodl called at the Reich Chancellery to report to the Führer. As we were ordered to report to him at two o'clock, I was able to get in a good hour's sleep first.

In contrast to the previous afternoon, I found the Führer very calm, and this kindled new hopes in me of bringing him to reason and persuading him to forget his unfortunate plan. After General Krebs had described the position on the Eastern Front, where things had not noticeably worsened, and Jodl on the other fronts, I confidentially reported to him—with only Jodl and Krebs in attendance —on my visit to the front.

First of all, I handed to him the Twelfth Army order issued by Wenck; the Führer scrutinised it carefully and retained it. Although he passed no comment on it, I gained the impression he was completely satisfied. I outlined in detail the outcome of my talks with the troop commanders and gave him my own impression gained on the spot. In the meantime news had arrived of the progress of the attack being mounted by General Koehler's Army Corps towards Potsdam to their north-east. The Führer enquired whether contact had already been established between them and the Ninth Army, which I was unable to answer. Nor did General Krebs have any reports to that effect from the Ninth Army, whose radio traffic was being monitored by the Reich Chancellery's signals office. Krebs was again ordered to direct the Ninth Army to establish contact with the Twelfth Army and mop up the enemy forces between them.

Finally I again requested a private interview. The Führer said he wanted Jodl and Krebs to be present too; it was at once clear to me that he intended to take the same stand as before, only in front of witnesses this time. My renewed attempt to move him to leave Berlin was categorically rejected. Only this time he gave me his explanation in perfect calm: he explained that the very knowledge of his presence in Berlin would inspire his troops with a determination to stand fast, and would keep the people from panicking. This was unfortunately now the pre-condition of success for the operations presently in hand for the relief of Berlin and for the battle that would follow for the city itself. One factor alone would offer any hope of realising this success, which was still possible: that was the people's faith in him. He would therefore personally direct the battle for Berlin in a fight to the finish. East Prussia had been held only so long as he had kept his headquarters at Rastenburg; but the front had collapsed there as soon as he failed to support it by his presence. The same fate would lie in store for Berlin; that was why he would neither modify his resolution nor break his pledge to the army and to the city's population.

This theme was put over without a trace of excitement, and in a firm voice. After he had finished, I told him I would drive out to the front at once and visit Wenck, Holste and the others, to harangue their troop commanders and tell them that the Führer expected them both to defend Berlin and to liberate him. Without a word, he extended a hand to me and we left him.

On some pretext or other, I was able shortly afterwards to speak to Hitler once more, but quite alone, in his private chamber next to the conference room. I said that our personal contact with him might be severed at any moment, if the Russians were to come down from the north and cut the communications between Krampnitz and Berlin. Might I know whether negotiations had been commenced with the enemy powers, and who would be conducting them? At first he said that it was still too early to talk of surrendering, but then he began to insist that one could always negotiate better once one had achieved some local victory; in this case the 'local victory' would be in the battle for Berlin. When I said I was not satisfied, he told me that he had in fact been conducting peace talks with England via Italy for some time now, and that very day he had summoned Ribbentrop to discuss their next steps with him; he would prefer not to go into closer detail with me just then but he certainly would not be the one to lose his nerve. That, said the Führer, was all that there was to be said on the subject for the time being.

I told him that I would return next day from my visit to the front to brief him on developments in the situation. Then I withdrew, not suspecting that we should never see each other again.

I drove back to Krampnitz with Jodl. On the way we frankly agreed that we could not leave things as they were—we discussed the possibility of abducting the Führer from his bunker, possibly even *by force*. Jodl told me that he had been occupied with similar thoughts since the previous day, although he had not ventured to

The Last Days under Adolf Hitler

give voice to them. While they had been in the Reich Chancellery's bunker today he had examined the prospects for putting such a plan into practice and had had a look round: the plan was quite out of the question in view of the strong SS guards and of the Security Service bodyguard who had sworn personal oaths of allegiance to Hitler; without their collaboration any such attempt was doomed to disaster. Men like General Burgdorf, the military adjutants, Bormann and the SS adjutants would all stand fast against us too. We gave the idea up.

Jodl further thought that we ought to wait for the outcome of the steps he had undertaken with Göring; on the evening of the 22nd he had described the afternoon's events in the Reich Chancellery in the closest detail to General Koller, the Chief of Air Staff, and stressed that the Führer had resolved to stay in Berlin either as victor or victim; Jodl had sent Koller to Göring in Berchtesgaden to put him rapidly in the picture on the crisis which had thus blown up. Only Göring could intervene now, as he was indeed competent to. I underwrote Jodl's action at once, and was grateful that he had taken the initiative there in a direction which had not occurred to me myself.

When we checked into Krampnitz, our whole organisation—that is the OKW operations staff plus War Office (North), which Jodl had combined into a Northern Command Staff under his own command—was on the point of moving off. Having received an unconfirmed report of Russian cavalry scouting down towards Krampnitz from the north, the commandant had already had the huge munitions dump blown up, without waiting for any orders to that effect, and had ordered the evacuation of the barracks. Unfortunately I had no time to call to account this hysterical gentleman who had just wiped out Berlin's munitions supply. . . .*

General Wenck had moved his Army headquarters considerably further to the north, and was occupying another forester's house when I arrived shortly after dusk. He had endeavoured to establish contact with one of his armoured divisions on the other side of the Elbe, but without success. I urgently appealed to him to devote his operations now more than ever solely and entirely to Berlin, and to bring his own personal influence to play, for the Führer's fate hinged upon the outcome of this last battle and not upon tank raids on the other bank of the Elbe.

* In Keitel's original manuscript there follow further charges against the Commandant of Krampnitz, which could in any case not have been defended for lack of manpower, something the Field-Marshal overlooked in his anger; the passage has been omitted by the Editor.

A telephone call from Jodl was waiting for me there; he broke the news to me that during the night he had unfortunately been obliged to evacuate Krampnitz because of the proximity of the enemy, against which he would have been able at that time to mount only two companies of tanks. He was therefore transferring the OKW's headquarters—that is, our operational headquarters—to a forest encampment at Neu-Roofen, between Rheinsberg and Fürstenberg; the camp had originally been fitted out with signals and communications equipment for Himmler, but was lying empty and was 100 per cent available to us. I agreed at once, of course, with the added proviso that radio contact with the Reich Chancellery was to be maintained and that the Führer should be informed of our move.

I realised at once that there was no guarantee that the daily war conferences in the Führer's bunker would continue any longer, as the enemy would probably deprive us of the Krampnitz route to Berlin next day. But there was now no other course of action open to us.

After I had tried to bring home to General Wenck the gravity of the situation and the importance of the task given to him, of re-opening access to Berlin, and after I had ordered him to report in person to the Reich Chancellery to put the Führer in the picture, I drove out into the night to call on Holste's headquarters, reaching it shortly before midnight. With Holste I went over the details of the task now facing him: by weakening his rear, which was confronting American forces which apparently had no plans to cross the Elbe, Holste was to gather all his forces together and screen the northern flank of Wenck's Twelfth Army against any danger or actual interference from the Russians.

At the time there was still some prospect of re-establishing access to Berlin through Potsdam and Krampnitz if:

1. the Twelfth Army's drive resulted in the complete liberation of Potsdam and its communications with Berlin;
2. the Twelfth and Ninth Armies could link up south of Berlin; and
3. the attack being made on the Führer's personal orders by SS General Steiner's Armoured Corps from the north could batter through to the Berlin–Krampnitz road in territory admittedly unfavourable for tank operations, cramped and easy as it was for the enemy to block.

General Holste's only problem was to establish contact with Heinrici's Army Group and Steiner's Armoured Corps to the north-west of Berlin: if he succeeded in doing that, then by exploiting the impassable Havelland marshes he could plug the gap with only moderate forces. I assured Holste that orders to this effect would go to Heinrici's Army Group, and drove back out into the night; in the early light of dawn I passed through Rheinsberg, a quiet and peaceful town, and after a considerable search reached our encampment at Neu-Roofen, where Jodl and his immediate staff had just arrived themselves, towards eight o'clock. The camp was so well hidden in the forest, some way away from the village and the road, that only local guides could find it for us.

The painful awareness of our physical detachment from the Reich Chancellery and of our dependence on wireless and telegraphic communications strengthened me in my resolve to assume responsibility myself for decisions—in contrast to earlier—as soon as I could no longer receive telephone messages from there; during the morning I telephoned the Reich Chancellery, and spoke first to one of the military adjutants and then to General Krebs, asking for a line to the Führer as soon as he was available.

Towards midday that 24th April, I made a personal report to Hitler on my latest visits to the front; I mentioned the favourable progress being made by the Twelfth Army in its drive towards Potsdam and added that I intended to put in an appearance at the Reich Chancellery towards evening. He forbade me to drive to Berlin by car, as the access roads were no longer adequately safeguarded, but he raised no objection to my flying to Gatow, the Air Warfare School's landing ground, and being collected from there. He turned the receiver over to Colonel von Below and I arranged my flight at once with him; I was to arrive shortly before dusk.

I summoned my trusty Ju. 52 from Rechlin to the landing ground at Rheinsberg, where I planned to take off for Berlin. Directly after this telephone conversation, the first war conference under my direction was held: General Dethleffsen (General Staff) outlined the position on the Eastern Front, and Jodl the remaining theatres of war. We were still in touch with all our formations, so without exception the various reports from the fronts were all to hand as usual. Immediately afterwards, Jodl apprised the Führer by telephone of my proposals, and obtained his agreement to them. General Krebs, the Deputy-Chief of the Army General Staff, was at the Reich Chancellery end, and Jodl imparted his innermost thoughts to him.

That evening I drove through Fürstenberg to the command post of SS General Steiner's Armoured Corps just to the south, hoping to ascertain the situation there and the prospects of his attack. By that time, only one of the two armoured divisions which had been regrouping in New Brandenburg, had arrived; the second was still being moved up. While Steiner had succeeded in fighting his way out of the narrow lakelands and winning the space for his tank formations to deploy in, he had attracted the enemy's attention by the thrust and as a result the chance of a surprise break through—which otherwise would beyond any doubt have succeeded—had been lost.

Upon my return to the camp, it was time to depart for my flight to Gatow. My adjutant had already laid everything on, when a telephone call came from Colonel von Below, forbidding me to take off before dusk as enemy fighters were interfering with air movements at Gatow. I postponed my flight until ten o'clock that evening, but this plan was scotched as well: after a beautiful spring day, fog closed in and the flight was abandoned. I put it off again until the evening of 25th April.

Very early on the 25th, I again drove out to the front, visiting General Holste's headquarters first of all. After I had been briefed on his Corp's situation, and had telephoned Wenck—who had again transferred his Army Headquarters—to be brought up to date by him, I dictated to Jodl my own appreciation of the situation for forwarding to the Führer: General Wenck had admittedly reached Potsdam with his battle group; but it was only on a narrow front forced like a wedge up between the lakes to the south of the town, and he lacked reserves, and above all extra strike-capacity, as considerable sections of his forces were tied down on the multiplying battles round the Elbe crossings (without any map I cannot give their exact locations) to the north of Wittenberg, so that he could not release them for an attack on Berlin itself or a joint movement with the Ninth Army, which latter was now apparently comprised only of remnants. To execute both operations properly, the Twelfth Army just was not strong enough.

In this situation, I authorised General Wenck—whatever the danger on the Elbe front—to release at least one division for the main Berlin operation and to apprise the Führer of this decision by radio on my behalf.

When I was about to drive through the little town of Rathenow on my way back to camp, about halfway between Brandenburg and Nauen, German troops blocked our path and announced that

THE BATTLE FOR BERLIN, 1945

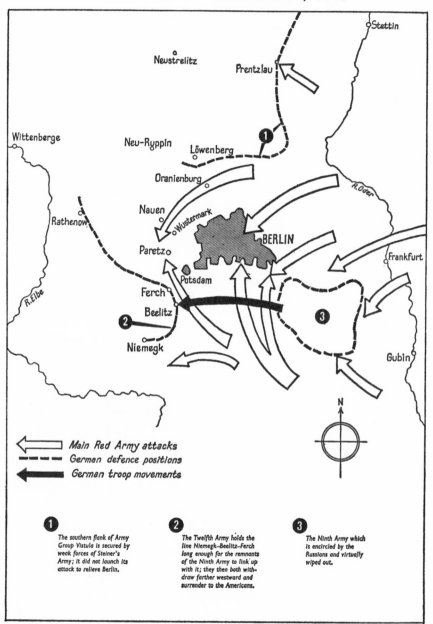

Main Red Army attacks
German defence positions
German troop movements

1 The southern flank of Army Group Vistula is secured by weak forces of Steiner's Army; it did not launch its attack to relieve Berlin.

2 The Twelfth Army holds the line Niemegk–Beelitz–Ferch long enough for the remnants of the Ninth Army to link up with it; they then both withdraw farther westward and surrender to the Americans.

3 The Ninth Army which is encircled by the Russians and virtually wiped out.

Rathenow was being attacked by the Russians and was under enemy gunfire. As I myself could detect no sound of fighting anywhere, I drove down the absolutely empty road further into Rathenow. A *Volkssturm* [People's Levy] company had excavated a three-foot-deep trench in the market square, affording them a field of fire of barely a hundred yards over to the houses on the far side. Nobody knew anything about the enemy, except that an attack on the town was anticipated. I explained to the company commander the lunacy of his actions; I had the company mustered, addressed a short speech to them, and ordered the company commander to lead me to the city commandant.

On the way, I saw in various places every kind of artillery, field howitzers, infantry guns, 3.7 cm anti-aircraft guns, and so on, drawn up in courtyards, limbered up and obviously camouflaged against detection from the air; their tractors and crews were standing idly round them. It seemed that there was sporadic gunfire from an enemy battery aimed at the outskirts of the town.

I found the commandant in a house some way off, issuing orders to some ten or twelve officers gathered round him. He was an active pioneer-troop officer, and my appearance not only amazed him but threw him into complete confusion. He told me that he had ordered the evacuation of the town and the mining of the bridge at its eastern end [sic] as the enemy was about to attack. I shouted at him that he must be out of his mind to decamp just because of a few rounds of long-range gunfire: what signs had he actually seen of the enemy? where was his battle-reconnaissance unit? what had they reported to him? and what, above all, was the whole point of having the artillery that was lying around in every courtyard of the city? I ordered the whole party out of the house and walked with them to the outskirts of the town where the enemy was supposed to be attacking; apart from a few puffs of shell bursts, there was nothing to be seen. Under my supervision, orders were issued for the defence of the town, the artillery was brought out and dug in, and this major was transferred to a command post from which he could see for himself out over the broad open spaces upon which there was no sign of an enemy.

I made it plain to him that if he surrendered the town to a few cavalry patrols it would cost him his neck, and that I would visit him again next day and expect to find the defences properly organised. He was to send a despatch rider to General Holste at once to report to him my intervention and the orders I had issued to him. I drove back down the line of retreat this brave commandant had earmarked for himself, and found mile after mile of columns of troops of every kind already in retreat, convoys of lorries laden with guns, machine-guns, ammunition, and so forth. I stopped the lot of them and packed them off back into the town under the command of a few elderly military police officers I had culled from the rest. In view of the Havelland marshes to the east of it and the barren terrain, offering no hope of cover, Rathenow could never be seriously attacked from the east. But a vital line of communication to the northern part of Holste's Corps and to Heinrici's Army Group led [westwards] through this town to the territory east of the Elbe. Right up to 29th April, Holste reported to me every day that every enemy endeavour to take Rathenow had been beaten off. After that I am not aware what happened.

Late that afternoon, I returned to camp at Neu-Roofen, and once again laid on a flight to Berlin for the coming night. As Jodl had already briefed the Führer by telephone on the developing situation, I decided to eschew telephoning him myself in view of my planned flight to Berlin. Unfortunately, the Reich Chancellery again forbade me to land at Gatow as this was already under intermittent enemy gunfire; for this reason Heerstrasse, the highway between the Charlottenburg Gate—where the Technical Institute was—and the Brandenburg Gate had been equipped as a runway for aircraft to land, and from dusk onwards an airlift of Junkers transport planes had been arranged to bring in every kind of munitions ordered by the Reich Chancellery and the commandant of Berlin as well as two companies of SS troops who had volunteered for action in the city. For this reason, my arrival was scheduled for after midnight, so that I could still take off again before dawn. From midnight onwards we waited at Rheinsberg airfield for clearance to take off; but we were instead categorically forbidden to make the flight, as fires had broken out in Berlin and were causing such a smoke haze over the Tiergarten area that it was impossible to land.

Not even a personal telephone call from me availed anything; I was informed that because of the haze several aircraft had already crashed, and the 'runway' was blocked. When I again argued the point with the Reich Chancellery upon my return to camp, suggesting I flew in at dawn, I was told the Führer himself had forbidden me to, because on the previous evening Colonel-General von Greim had been badly injured as his plane came in to land just before dusk. Afterwards, I had a long and detailed telephone conversation with General Krebs: he told me on this occasion that Göring had been dismissed by Hitler from all his offices and from his rights as Hitler's successor, as he had requested the Führer's authority to begin surrender negotiations with the enemy. Krebs said a radio signal had been received to that effect from Göring in Berchtesgaden on the 24th and the Führer, beside himself with rage about it, had ordered his SS guards at the Berghof to arrest Göring: he was to be shot.

I was horrified by this news, and could only rejoin to Krebs that there must be some misunderstanding, as on the evening of the 22nd the Führer had himself commented in my presence that it was a good thing that Göring was in Berchtesgaden, as he was better at negotiating than he, Hitler, was. Apparently Bormann was listening in to the telephone conversation between Krebs and myself, for suddenly his voice came on the line, shouting that Göring had been sacked, 'even from his Reich Chief Huntsman job'. I made no reply; God knows, the situation was too grave for sarcastic remarks like that. I went to see Jodl to talk over this new development with him; he could only explain the query contained in Göring's signal by reference to the mission on which he had sent General Koller. Koller would also have notified Göring of the Führer's earlier comment. Now we realised why Colonel-General von Greim had been ordered to the Reich Chancellery anyway: to take over command of the German Air Force, as Göring's successor.

I did not sleep a wink that night, for this latest move of the Führer's had suddenly illuminated for me the fearful mood prevailing in the Reich Chancellery, and above all the ascendancy of Bormann. He alone could have had his infamous finger in this; he had exploited the Führer's frame of mind to bring his protracted feud with Göring to such a victorious conclusion. What would happen if as it now seemed the Führer was voluntarily to meet his end in Berlin? Had he deliberately chosen to kill off Göring with himself at the last moment? My resolve to fly to Berlin on the evening of the 26th, come what may, began to harden: if Greim had done it, then so could I.

On 27th April, towards midday, Grand-Admiral Dönitz put in an appearance at our camp at Neu-Roofen; he had also radioed Himmler to attend. The four of us, including Jodl, discussed the situation privately, after both our guests had sat in on the war conference. It was obvious to us that the Führer was determined to stand fast and fight in Berlin, and that our duty would be not to abandon him so long as there remained any chance of backing him out. The fact that at least the Americans were still making no attempt to cross the Elbe downstream of Magdeburg and the additional circumstance that there had been sufficient consolidation of the front of Schörner's Army Group for him to detach forces from his northern flank to secure against a Russian encirclement of Berlin from the south, as the Führer had commanded, contrived to impart to the situation—at least round Berlin—a more hopeful countenance, however grave the overall war picture might be. We took leave of one another.

I resolved to give the Führer one last option during the coming night: *get out of Berlin;* or transfer Supreme Command to Dönitz in the north and Kesselring in the south; the OKW staff under Lieutenant-General Winter, deputy-chief of the OKW operations staff, had already placed itself at Kesselring's disposal. But both commanders must be given complete discretion to act as they saw fit: it was not possible to go on like this.

Although once again every preparation was made for me to fly to Berlin that night, once again I had to give up the endeavour at the last moment. There was said to be absolutely no question of any aircraft flying to Berlin and landing along the east-west Axis that night.

Not only transport planes, but fighters and spotter planes were turning back from Berlin: the city was shrouded in smoke, fog and low cloud, and even low-flying planes had failed to see the Brandenburg Gate. Even the now Field-Marshal Greim's take-off had been abandoned.

This was the position when I telephoned the Führer, and proposed that at least the altered command structure I considered necessary should be approved. He rejected such a measure as uncalled-for: he had no intention of relinquishing command so long as there was no interruption of wireless communications. He equally rejected the subordination of the Italian theatre and the Eastern Front—the Army Groups commanded by Schörner, Rendulic and Löhr—to Kesselring: Kesselring had more than enough on his plate with the Western Front. He [Hitler] would hold Berlin as long as he himself was in command there; I was to look after munitions supplies, he asked no more than that of me. I kept my demand for him to leave Berlin to myself; he had gathered that from our conversation anyway, and I hesitated to mention it at all specifically by telephone.

After Dönitz and Himmler had departed, [on 28th April] I drove over to Colonel-General Heinrici, commanding officer of the Vistula Army Group, to put myself in the picture on the defence of the Oder, which he was directing from Schorf heath right up to

Stettin. Hitherto, this front had been directed by General Krebs from the Reich Chancellery on account of its coherence with the defence of Berlin; responsibility for the defence of Berlin had been detached from the Army Group and turned over to the commandant of Berlin, who in turn received all his orders direct from the Führer.

For some days General Heinrici had been pressing a demand for Steiner's armoured group and particularly Holste's Corps to be subordinated to him: he planned to use them at least as a screen for his southern flank. Colonel-General Jodl had repeatedly refused this request, for the obvious reason that Wenck's Army would be wholly exposed on its northern flank and at the rear. Towards one o'clock I joined Heinrici at his command post in a forest encampment to the north-east of Boitzenburg, the estate of Count Arnim. Heinrici and his chief of staff General von Trotha gave me a thorough breakdown of the situation, which had worsened considerably as a result of the Russians' break-through south of Stettin, as there were insufficient reserves immediately available to plug the gap. I agreed to examine whether we might be able to assist, but I again rejected once and for all this renewed demand for control of Holste's Corps, giving all my reasons for doing so. In fact, I demanded that his Vistula Army Group should now finally be subordinated to the OKW, and ordered him to make immediate war reports to our operational headquarters. We parted like old friends, in complete concord.

That evening, Heinrici telephoned me to report that the gap torn in his front had become worse; he asked me to place at least one armoured division from Steiner's group at his disposal. I promised him a decision as soon as I had spoken with Jodl and with Steiner himself. I established that SS General Steiner had arranged for the 7th armoured division, which was still in the process of being moved up, to carry out its attack as ordered only during the coming night. I ordered the division to be ready to stand at my disposal, so that it could if necessary be diverted to another direction. To have to abandon Steiner's attack, on which the Führer had laid such great hopes, came very hard to me. But in view of the situation on Heinrici's front, with the enemy being able within two to three days to sweep round to the rear of Steiner and the southern flank of the Vistula Army Group, Jodl and I were convinced that the only proper course of action now was to throw the 7th armoured division across the gap from the south, and into the Russians' flank. So I released the 7th armoured division to Heinrici, but with stringent conditions attached to its line of attack and its objective, in order that I could gather it up again afterwards whatever the outcome, as a reserve. The orders were confirmed by Heinrici; Jodl apprised the Führer of what had been done. It must have been a bitter disappointment to him.

Early on 28th April, at four o'clock in the morning, I drove over to SS General Steiner. I had hoped either to find the headquarters of the 7th armoured division there, or to ask him where it was; I also wanted to discuss with Steiner how and if he was going to execute his attack, even without the 7th division. But it turned out that the division had been intercepted by the [Vistula] Army Group itself, and had never even reached the assembly area I had designated; nobody had reported to Steiner for orders.

After Steiner had explained to me how he planned to resume the attack after regrouping, even without the 7th armoured division, I drove down the approach road I had ordered for it, without seeing a soul in sight. It began to dawn on me that either the division had been delayed or else it was being operated elsewhere.

As I drove along another road, I encountered squads of infantry and horse-drawn artillery. When I asked after the 7th armoured division and what was happening here, I learned that two nights before the southern flank of Heinrici's Army Group—without having sighted the enemy at all—had taken to its heels westwards across the Schorf heath, and would be flanking Fürstenberg during the course of the day, 28th April; there the artillery was to be dug in again.

I nearly had a fit! During our conversation the afternoon before, Heinrici had not breathed a word to me about this orderly retreat—in full sway even then. So the 7th armoured division had also been deployed quite differently—and that was the reason for his having pressed for Holste's Corps to be subordinated to him as well.

At about eight o'clock I returned to our operational headquarters, to confer with Jodl on this completely altered situation, whereby we and our camp—at the very latest by the next day—would have been delivered up unawares and defenceless to the Russians. I ordered Heinrici and General von Manteuffel to attend on me at a rendezvous north of New Brandenburg and then drove off while Jodl had a first, very harsh altercation with the [Vistula] Army Group's chief of staff. On my drive north, I finally found the 7th armoured division and after a long search the divisional headquarters. At that moment the Army Group's liaison officer, an engineer staff-officer, was there and he was just outlining to the divisional commander by means of a map the next stages of the retreat, and the distances envisaged for each day. That was all I needed: to overhear the Army Group's general plan of retreat like this, something of whose existence neither the OKW, the Führer nor General Krebs had even suspected. The actual orders had been issued that evening, after my departure from the Army Group's headquarters, so it had already been decided on by then. Their promulgation *without* the permission of either the OKW or the Führer himself was the consequence of my frank discussion with Heinrici, who had drawn the conclusion that the Führer was no longer in any position to intervene and that he could thus do as he thought fit, his primary purpose being to get his Army Group across to the Elbe and surrender it to the Americans. All this I learned only later, from Heinrici's successor; today I know that his chief of staff, General von Trotha—whom I dismissed that very evening—was the originator of the master plan.

Anyway, in accordance with its orders the 7th armoured division dug in to a purely defensive position in order to relieve the enemy pressure on [Heinrici's] units as they retreated from their front; to the great astonishment of the surprised divisional commander, I flew into a temper about this way of using an armoured division: it wasn't for this ignoble rôle that I had reached the agonising decision to withdraw the armoured division from General Steiner's command at the very moment of its decisive attack to the south, on which not only the Führer but we had placed so much hope in view of what General Wenck had attained with the Twelfth Army.

As soon as the divisional commander had briefed me on the situation that had arisen through the collapse of the front—it was similar in enormity to the Russian break-through across the Oder—I brought it home to him that as a tank officer defensive operations were no concern of his, and that his real strength would lie only in counter-attack. He naturally agreed, but pointed out that to put his division on a footing for such an attack now would cost much time, and that he would take so long merely to regroup that the attack would go off at half cock. Despite his plea, I ordered him to use his weapon in the manner for which it had been designed: anything else was futile.

Early that afternoon, the encounter with Colonel-General Heinrici took place, with General von Manteuffel present. Our discussion was strained, as I could not rebuke Heinrici savagely enough for having concealed his plan to retreat from the High Command and myself. He did not admit that it had amounted to so much as a retreat but talked only of the necessity of withdrawing his southern flank through the Schorf heath to the other side; besides all the troop movements and operations designed to shorten his front had been firmly under control. The plan that had been shown to me at the headquarters of the 7th armoured division had only been a guide prepared for the engineer-troop headquarters for road-blocks and demolitions, if it should come to a collapse, and so forth. After I had outlined to these gentlemen the overall situation and the position of Wenck's Twelfth Army, SS General Steiner's command and Holste's Corps, and described the already critical situation resulting north and north-west of Berlin from their arbitrary withdrawal of their southern flank which had gravely endangered the rear of Steiner's armoured corps, Heinrici gave his word to heed my orders from now on, and promised to knuckle down under the overall command. We parted at least superficially properly, with me appealing to him to abide by our long-standing friendship and by his pledge.

That evening, I did not get back to camp until after dusk. In Jodl's view, the position north of Berlin, on that southern flank, was more acute than ever. I had a long telephone conversation with General Krebs in the Reich Chancellery after the Führer had referred my call to him, so that I was unable to speak with Hitler personally. It was a very bad telephone line, and it kept breaking down. The chief of military signals who was in our camp with us explained to me that our only radio contact now was established between a wireless aerial suspended by a captive balloon near our camp, and the Radio Tower in Berlin; all the telephone lines had broken down. As long as the Radio Tower remained in German hands for transmitting and receiving signals, and the captive balloon stayed in one piece, our communications with the Reich Chancellery were assured. In addition, we still had radio contact with the radio office in the Führer's bunker.

Jodl proposed to me that we should evacuate our operational headquarters next day [29th April]. At first I rejected this proposal, as I had no desire to risk the further separation from the Führer which the implicit loss of radio [speech] communication would involve, unless it was absolutely necessary. That our stay there was approaching its end was admittedly becoming obvious from our own artillery: a heavy battery had begun to open fire right by us soon after dusk, and kept up a sporadic barrage all night. During the course of the evening, Jodl had been lucky enough to get through to Hitler by radio, and he had reported our discoveries about Heinrici's front to the Führer, and received his complete agreement to all my dispositions against any further retreat by Heinrici's Army Group, and to my order for a counter-attack by the 7th armoured division, and so forth.

At about midnight, Colonel-General Heinrici telephoned me complaining bitterly about Jodl's rebukes to his chief of staff [von Trotha], and announcing that in view of the continued worsening of the situation of which he had learned during our conversation, he had ordered his Army Group to resume its retreat. I told him that his attitude—for which there was no valid justification whatsoever—was flagrant disobedience. He countered that in that case he would no longer accept responsibility for the command of his troops, for whom he claimed he alone was responsible. I replied that in my view he was no longer suitable to command an Army Group, and that he was to consider himself dismissed: he was to relinquish his command to the senior Army commander, General von Tippelskirch. I told him I would inform the Führer that I had relieved him of his command, and terminated the conversation.

At that moment, Jodl came in and began to inveigh against the Army Group's chief of staff, whom he considered totally incompetent; I would have to intervene with Heinrici, as we could not put up with methods like these any longer. I told him I had sacked Heinrici, and he told me he thought my action fully justified. By wireless telegraphy I informed the Führer I had dismissed Heinrici, and why; General Krebs acknowledged the signal that night on behalf of the Führer.

On the morning of 29th April, the noise of fighting to the east of our operational headquarters grew louder. During the night Jodl had already made the necessary preparations for evacuation, with the chief of military signals; it was only a question of one move to Himmler's former operational headquarters in Mecklenburg, which was already equipped with an adequate signals installation. Himmler had willingly declared his readiness to vacate the headquarters for us, and to accommodate our advance party; we were at liberty to follow when we pleased.

As a result of the rain during the night of 28th to 29th April, we had had to haul in the captive balloon, so that for a time our radio communication with Berlin was interrupted. We were unable to send it aloft again until about midday, as its canopy had become heavy with rain. On the 29th, however, there was a scorching sun and a clear sky, and the enemy's air force was out in unusual strength over our camp and the front, now only about seven miles away.

As soon as the balloon was aloft, I asked for a telephone line to the Reich Chancellery. First there was a conversation between me and the commander of Greater Berlin, who was apparently there in the Reich Chancellery. General Weidling, the artillery general who had formerly commanded the Oder front near Küstrin at the time of its collapse there, came on the line; this was the same general of whom distorted reports had reached the Führer from SS quarters to the effect that he and his staff were in full flight to the Döberitz camp, while their troops were fighting fierce battles between the Oder and Berlin. Hitler had such little confidence in his generals that he had furiously ordered General Krebs to see that the general was arrested and shot out of hand for cowardice in the face of the enemy. As soon as he had learned this, General Weidling had none the less immediately presented himself at the Reich Chancellery and demanded to speak to the Führer. As General Krebs afterwards told me, an interview had forthwith taken place with Hitler in the Reich Chancellery, with the result that the Führer had sacked the officer who had been city commandant up to then and appointed Weidling commander of Greater Berlin, with unlimited powers; he had assured him of his supreme confidence in him.

I have mentioned this instance only to show how easily the Führer's confidence in his Army generals was shaken, and how he almost invariably reacted without any reservations upon receiving unfavourable aspersions on them from his obscure Intelligence sources in the SS. In this particular instance, only the firm resolve of the general concerned had avoided a grave and imminent miscarriage of justice.

Shortly after my conversation with Weidling, a radio-telephone conversation did take place between Jodl and the Führer himself, and I listened in with an earphone. The Führer was very calm and objective, acknowledged once again the steps I had taken, and said he would like to speak with me as soon as Jodl had finished making his war report to him. Even as Jodl was still conferring with him, there was a loud bang outside, and the conversation was completely interrupted. A few moments later the chief of military signals came into our room and announced that the balloon had just been shot down by Russian aircraft: there was no spare, so *plain-language* communication could not be restored.

Devastating though this revelation was for me, it did help me decide to order the evacuation of our headquarters immediately after lunch: there was no question now of restoring the plain-language radio link, but telegraphic signals could be transmitted by wireless from anywhere. I was furious not to have spoken with the Führer myself, although Jodl had been able to discuss the most vital points with him. We sent a last signal reporting that we were moving out, and requested them to send all further signals on to our new operational headquarters, which we should have reached by that evening.

Towards midday, the sounds of battle grew louder, and enemy air activity increased, with bombing attacks particularly on the Rheinsberg bottleneck and strafing of the retreating convoys blocking the streets. We split the OKW up into a number of road parties, and gave each one a different route to follow. Jodl and I stayed with our immediate staffs at the encampment until the very last moment; my adjutant had that morning reconnoitred a forest lane specially for us, taking us in a wide detour round the villages round Rheinsberg and the choked highways. At seven o'clock we moved off, leaving only the last signals troops and the wireless station to follow. As we learned from them next day, Russian patrols combing through the forest would unquestionably have surprised us in the camp barely an hour later had we still been there; as it was, only one signals truck and some telephone sets fell into their hands, before they could be dismantled.

In beautiful spring weather we drove along the narrow, hidden lanes through the dense forest, circling the villages and hamlets, towards Waren, to meet General von Tippelskirch and discuss with him his Army Group's further operations.

I was obliged to *order* him to assume command, as he repeatedly begged me not to confer it on him; I disclosed to him that I had already summoned Colonel-General Student from Holland as the new commanding general, but that he was to remain in command until the former arrived. I learned from him that SS General Steiner had taken over command of his Army (for the time being!) having transferred his armoured corps' command in turn to Colonel Fett of the OKW, who had originally been allocated to him as an Intelligence Officer.

After I had briefed Tippelskirch thoroughly on how I wanted him to operate the Army Group, he asked to be rid of his Group's chief of staff; Jodl willingly agreed after his scene with von Trotha, so I ordered the latter's dismissal as well.

We drove on to our new operational headquarters at Dobbin, the estate of the famous Dutch oil magnate Deterding (who had died in 1939).

When we arrived we met Himmler; he planned to move out with his staff early next day, so the sleeping quarters provided for us were cramped and crowded. But at least we were in wireless communication again, and we at once took over the radio office, which almost immediately began furnishing us with signals. A signal had arrived for me from the Führer, signed by him; it contained five questions:

1. Where are Wenck's spearheads?
2. When will they renew their attack?
3. Where is the Ninth Army?
4. Where will the Ninth Army break through to?
5. Where are Holste's spearheads?*

Over dinner, I conferred with Jodl on our reply, and myself wrote out a first draft. Only after a lengthy discussion did we hand in our reply to the radio office for despatch during the night.

I had been brutally frank, and made no attempt to gloss over the seriousness of the situation now and the impossibility of liberating Berlin any more. The southern flank of the Vistula Army Group had swung round so far to the west as a result of their retreat-movement that Steiner's armoured corps had been obliged to call off its attack and take over the screening of the Group's southern flank to the north-west of Berlin together with Holste's Corps; otherwise they would find themselves being attacked from the rear or even cut off. All that we knew of the Ninth Army was that about ten thousand men had battled their way through the forests with no heavy artillery at all and joined up with the eastern flank of the Twelfth Army. They were no real reinforcement for General Wenck, as his attack had become hopelessly bogged down among the lakes just south of Potsdam. I wrote at the end of the signal, 'Relief of Berlin and reopening of access to it from the west impossible. Suggest a break-out through Potsdam to Wenck, or alternatively that Führer should be flown out to the south. Am awaiting decision.'

Towards midnight Field-Marshal von Greim the new commander-in-chief of the German Air Force arrived at Dobbin, his right ankle heavily bandaged; he had taken off from Berlin with his chief pilot, Hanna Reitsch, on the 28th and had landed safely at Rechlin; he had driven out to me from there direct, to report on events in the Reich Chancellery. He had spent several days there with the

---

* The correct text of this signal has been inserted here to replace Keitel's remembered version, which is slightly different.

Führer; he told me about Göring's dismissal and the reason for it—as I described earlier—and added that the position in Berlin was very grave, although the Führer was confident and composed. He said he had had long talks with him, but despite their old friendship had been unable to persuade him to leave Berlin. Greim added that he had been commissioned to contact me and confer with me on the situation. He would be flying to Berchtesgaden on the 30th, and taking over command of the Air Force there.

On 30th April, we remained at Dobbin. My hope of receiving a reply from Hitler was not realised; the correct reception of my signal was acknowledged word-by-word to our radio office, so it had been correctly picked up at the Reich Chancellery and passed on to the Führer. I could only construe the lack of any reply to my final sentence as being tantamount to a refusal.

At four o'clock in the morning, on 1st May, we moved out of Dobbin. I had had a hot bath and I had been able to sleep in a bed with clean white linen for a few hours. On the day before, the estate management had evacuated the estate, leaving it to one of the stewards: the modern villa where we lived next to the old château —which had been converted into a barracks for foreign workers— was being run by a publican's wife even after our departure; each evening she had handed round a few bottles of wine, but the Russians would have drunk the whole cellarfull afterwards, I suppose.

I had laid on a war conference for ten o'clock in the barracks at Wismar, where the actual working party, comprising both War Office and OKW, had been accommodated since the 29th already. Afterwards, I received Colonel-General Student in the mess; he had arrived by plane at noon. I briefed him on the position, and went over with him the tasks which would lie to him now, stressing the importance of keeping open the Baltic ports for the shiploads of refugees and troops pouring in from East Prussia. Finally, Jodl discussed with him which orders were to be issued first and the light in which his staff saw their new and various tasks.

Student took over command with a genuine resolve to clarify the situation and to damp down the unwarranted mood of panic that was prevailing. During our drive to Wismar, we had unfortunately witnessed terrible scenes of the disorderly flood of refugees, convoys of vehicles and supply columns, which we had ruthlessly to drive through. Twice we ourselves had to jump out of the car because *British* aircraft were strafing the columns with machine-gun and cannon-fire. For hours on end we were jammed in these queues of vehicles, two and three abreast, and all getting in each other's way. I had a marvellous military policeman in an open car who managed again and again to inject some degree of order into this chaos, and to pilot us through.

At midday that day, 1st May, we drove in several separate groups to the headquarters building that had been provided in northern Neustadt for the northern OKW group in a naval barracks where there was space for everybody to work, and where a complete signals network had been installed. I expected to find Grand-Admiral Dönitz there, but I was disappointed: he had set up headquarters with his staff at a naval hostel near Plön. I drove out of Neustadt alone to see him: it was about an hour's drive away.

At Plön, the Grand-Admiral was in the middle of a conference with Field-Marshal Busch, who was commander of the coastal front from about Kiel right down to Holland as far as I recall. Apart from Busch, I met Himmler there as well; he had tried to join forces with Dönitz there. I have no idea what his real intentions were, but it seemed that he wanted to place himself at our disposal for further duties and brief himself on the situation.

Towards evening, Field-Marshal von Greim called on Dönitz in Plön with his chief pilot, Hanna Reitsch. He had postponed his flight to southern Germany for a day to discuss with Dönitz any requests the navy had to make of the air force. From Hanna Reitsch I learned that SS Lieutenant-General Fegelein had been shot on the Führer's orders, after he had been arrested by a police patrol, drunk and in civilian clothes, in a Berlin night-club.

I had a lengthy conversation with Dönitz about the hopeless situation. He showed me a signal from Bormann, to the effect that according to his testament, the Führer had designated Dönitz as his successor, and that an officer with the testament itself was on his way out to us by plane. I realised at once that my signal from Dobbin on the night of 29th to 30th April had removed any doubts the Führer might still have entertained about the hopelessness of his position, and that the testament, and Bormann's advance notice of it to Dönitz, had been the consequence.

Both of us were convinced that in Berlin the final scene could come at any moment, although Field-Marshal Greim judged the progress of the Battle for Berlin considerably more favourably, from what he had personally seen and heard in Berlin up to the evening of the 28th. Deeply disturbed, I drove back to Neustadt, being unfortunately badly delayed on the way by several heavy British air raids on the villages around the naval headquarters just before dusk.

I was terribly worried that my signal might have drawn too black a picture, with the result that the wrong conclusions had been drawn. But I finally accepted that it would have been irresponsible to varnish over the unpalatable truth; my frank signal had been the only correct course of action. Jodl expressed the same opinion when I talked things over with him upon my return and told him all that I had learned at Dönitz's headquarters.

During that same night, 1st to 2nd May, I was telephoned by Dönitz to come for an interview with him at eight o'clock that morning; I accordingly left Neustadt in good time. Dönitz received me at once, and privately showed me two new signals:

(a) from Goebbels with a list of members of the new Reich Cabinet, allegedly drawn up by the Führer, in which Goebbels was to be 'Reich Chancellor'. It began with the words, '*Führer deceased yesterday*, 3.30 *p.m.*. . . .'
(b) from Bormann, that the case in question had occurred, and Dönitz thus took over as successor.

So that was it! Goebbels' wording made it obvious that Hitler had taken his own life, otherwise it would certainly have read, '*killed in action*' and not '*deceased*'. The testament, which was supposed to have been flown out to us by an officer, had not arrived.

Dönitz immediately made it plain that as the Führer's successor—the new Head of State—he had no intention of having a Cabinet or list of Ministers dictated to him by anybody; I underwrote that view wholeheartedly. I gave him as my opinion that this was an obvious attempt by Goebbels and Bormann to confront him with a *fait accompli*. The afternoon was spent on composing proclamations to the German people and the armed forces. In a situation like this, it was clearly impracticable to swear-in the whole of the armed forces afresh: I proposed as a formula that the oaths of allegiance sworn to the Führer automatically transferred their validity to Dönitz as the new Head of State the Führer had selected.

During the course of the morning, Himmler also appeared, and had a number of private interviews with Dönitz. It had already struck me that he did not figure on Goebbels' list of Ministers. I gained the impression that he regarded himself as a natural member of the new Dönitz Cabinet, because he asked me what the armed forces' feelings towards him were. I rather gathered that he had his eye on the office of War Minister. I avoided replying, but advised him to discuss the matter with Dönitz; I could hardly go over the head of the Supreme Commander of the Armed Forces. I added that I would be asking Dönitz to relieve me of my duties, as soon as he had ruled on the question of the command of the armed forces, as new commanders-in-chief would have to be chosen for both the Army and the Navy now.

As soon as Dönitz learned that Himmler was there, he had me called in once more for a private interview, to tell me that Himmler had placed himself entirely at his disposal, having apparently entertained some hopes during the previous days of taking over as Hitler's successor himself. He asked me what I would think of Himmler's being in a new Cabinet; I could only reply that I considered Himmler insufferable. We both promised to keep this absolutely to ourselves. Dönitz planned to have Count Schwerin von Krosigk, the then Secretary to the Treasury, as his personal adviser and Foreign Secretary; he intended to discuss the composition of the new Cabinet with him.

As soon as the proclamations were ready to be broadcast, I left Dönitz's headquarters and drove back to Neustadt with the intention of reporting to Dönitz again early next day, 3rd May. On my arrival, I analysed the new position with Jodl; both of us had only one thought now—to bring the war rapidly to an end as soon as the evacuation of East Prussia and the operations designed to salvage our armies on the eastern front permitted. We decided to go over these points with Dönitz next day.

We were strengthened in our resolve by a lengthy telegram Field-Marshal Kesselring sent us for Dönitz's eyes on the evening of 2nd May: Kesselring reported the surrender of the Army Group in Italy, which was already ratified, and he added that while he had been taken by surprise by Colonel-General von Vietinghoff's unauthorised surrender negotiations, he was accepting full responsibility for them and he underwrote the latter's action. Now that the Italian front had collapsed, the position of Colonel-General Löhr's Balkan Army Group had become dangerously exposed, and there was no hope of salvaging it.

Armed with this Intelligence, I drove back to Dönitz in Plön early on 3rd May; his own radio office had already picked up Kesselring's signal. Dönitz was equally determined to put an end to the war as quickly as possible, and he accordingly called me in as soon as I arrived. I proposed that the northern OKW group should be transferred to his headquarters immediately. As there was not enough room for that in Plön, and the Supreme Command's overall control had to be established without delay, Dönitz ordered that the Supreme Command was to be moved to Flensburg, with immediate effect. I summoned Jodl to Plön with our immediate staffs, while the combined OKW/War Office organisation set out for Flensburg. After Jodl's arrival, we both had a long conference with Dönitz, who completely underwrote our own views on the situation.

That evening, Dönitz drove out to Rendsburg, where he had sent for Admiral von Friedeburg to disclose to him personally that he was to be named the new C.-in-C. of the German Navy. We stayed thenight in Dönitz's old headquarters, and followed him to Flensburg on 3rd May, leaving at four-thirty that morning. In Flensburg-Mürwick, offices and sleeping quarters were made available to us in a naval barracks; Jodl, I and our immediate staffs moved into the same building as the Grand-Admiral, with offices next door to his own.

Jodl's chief of staff for the OKW theatres was now Colonel Meyer-Detring, while as chief of the operational division, General Dethleff-sen handled the War Office affairs. I would thus prefer not to go into the military situation: these two officers were in a better position than I to judge the situation at the time, and will no doubt both write their own memoirs in due course.

It will be enough to say that measures were immediately put in hand to finish the war in accordance with clear instructions issued by the Grand-Admiral, while at the same time ensuring that as many refugees and troops from the eastern front as possible were saved by funnelling them back into central Germany. It was obvious to us that when the time came we would be asked to capitulate on the spot and without further ado: so it was a matter of expediting the transfer of what was still over three million troops from the eastern front to the American occupation zone, to prevent them falling into Russian hands. This was also the object of the negotiations begun as early as 3rd or 4th May on the Grand-Admiral's initiative between Admiral von Friedeburg and the British Commander-in-Chief, Field-Marshal Montgomery.

When the latter refused to make special agreements with us, the negotiations were followed by the instrument of surrender proposed by von Friedeburg and signed by Colonel-General Jodl at General Eisenhower's headquarters early on the morning of 7th May; its only concession lay in the extension of the term to midnight of the 8th.

From Eisenhower's headquarters Jodl sent me a signal which, although in guarded language, left me in no doubt about the possibilities accorded by this two days' grace, and I was able to signal the units on the eastern front—and especially General Schörner's Army Group, still fighting in eastern Czechoslovakia—authorising their withdrawal westwards within the desperately limited time of not more than 48 hours. This directive went out before midnight on the 7th. Colonel Meyer-Detring had already taken an appreciation of the situation and a copy of the directives we were drawing up out to the Army Command in Czechoslovakia by means of a gallant flight straight out to the front.

General Hilpert's Army Group in the Baltic provinces (Courland) had been put in the picture by Major de Maizière; he was authorised to send all his sick and injured troops home with the last transport ship leaving Libau. De Maizière brought me the last greetings from my son, Ernst-Wilhelm, to whom he had spoken just before his return flight to Flensburg. Field-Marshal Busch (north-western front) and General Böhme (Norway) had already attended personally on the Grand-Admiral to receive instructions. We were still in uninterrupted radio contact with Field-Marshal Kesselring, commanding in the south in conjunction with the southern OKW group commanded by Lieutenant-General Winter of the OKW operations staff.

A number of members of the government had reported at Flensburg-Mürwick, including the new Foreign Secretary, Count Schwerin von Krosigk; Reichsminister Speer had also arrived, and General von Trotha, the Chief of Staff I had sacked from Student's Army Group (ex-Heinrici's), had somewhat remarkably attached himself to him.

Himmler was also trying to maintain his position *vis-à-vis* Grand-Admiral Dönitz. After a conference with Dönitz, I undertook to ask Himmler to resign and refrain from making further visits to the Grand-Admiral's headquarters. He had initially been entrusted with certain police duties, but he was relieved of these as well. For a Dönitz government Himmler was quite untenable, and on Dönitz's behalf I made that quite clear to him.

The following instance shows how little insight Himmler had into the political situation, and the burden that he was to us: from an unspecified headquarters he sent to us an Army officer who had previously been on his staff—and whom he simultaneously discharged—with a letter to be forwarded to General Eisenhower. The officer had been authorised to apprise me of the letter's contents:

it contained in a few words an offer to surrender voluntarily to General Eisenhower, if he was assured that in no circumstance would he be turned over to the Russians. Himmler had already voiced this intention once to me in Jodl's presence, during our last interview with him. As the officer who brought the letter never returned to Himmler, the latter never learned that his offer was not forwarded to Eisenhower as we destroyed the letter on the spot. Besides, Himmler had directed his courier to inform me (for Dönitz) that he was planning to go to ground in Northern Germany; he would remain 'submerged' for the next six months or so. The rest of the story—with his arrest a few weeks later, and his suicide by taking poison while in custody—is well known.

On 8th May, after Jodl's return from Eisenhower's headquarters at Reims, I was commanded by the Grand-Admiral, acting as Head of State and Supreme Commander of the Armed Forces—to fly by British transport aircraft to Berlin, with the preliminary instrument as signed by Jodl and Eisenhower's Chief of Staff. Admiral von Friedeburg accompanied me as the Navy's representative, and Colonel-General Stumpff, the last C.-in-C. for Home Defence, on behalf of the Air Force. In addition to these, I took with me Vice-Admiral Bürkner, Chief of the OKW's Military Intelligence department, and Lieutenant-Colonel Böhm-Tettelbach, because not only did he speak fluent English, but he had also passed the Russian-interpreter examinations.

We flew by British transport plane to Stendal first. There a squadron of civil aircraft had been mustered by the British Air Chief-Marshal who was General Eisenhower's representative. After a sort of victory flight round Berlin, we all landed, with my plane last, at Tempelhof airport. A Russian guard of honour had been drawn up for the British and American parties, with a military band; from our landing area we were able to watch the ceremony from afar. A Russian officer had been detailed to accompany me— I was told he was General Zhukov's chief quartermaster—and he drove me in one car while the rest of my party followed in other cars.

We drove across Belle-Alliance-Platz through the outskirts of the city to Karlshorst, where we were put down at a small empty villa not far from the Pioneer and Engineer School's barracks. It was about one o'clock in the afternoon. We were left absolutely to ourselves. Presently a reporter came and took some photographs, and after a while a Russian interpreter came: he was unable to tell me at what time the signing of the Instrument of Surrender was to take place; I had in any case been given a German copy of it at the airport.

I was, therefore, able to compare the version signed by Jodl with the wording of this new one; but I observed only minor divergences from the original. The only basic modification was the interpolation of a clause threatening to punish troops who failed to cease fire and surrender at the time provided. I told the interpreter officer that I demanded to speak to a representative from General Zhukov, as I would not sign such an interpolation unconditionally. Several hours later, a Russian general arrived with the interpreter to hear my objection; I believe he was Zhukov's Chief of Staff.

I explained that I was objecting because I could not guarantee that our cease-fire orders would be received in time, with the result that the troops' commanders might feel justified in failing to comply with any demands to that effect. I demanded that a clause should be written in that the Surrender would come into force only twenty-four hours after the orders had been received by our troops; only then would the penalty clause take effect. About an hour later, the general was back with the news that General Zhukov had agreed to twelve hours' grace being given, instead of twenty-four. He ended by asking for my credentials as the representatives of the victorious powers wished to inspect them; I would receive them back shortly. The signing was to take place 'towards evening', he added.

At about three o'clock that afternoon we were served a magnificent meal by Russian girls. Our patience was being sorely tried. At five o'clock we were taken into another building and served afternoon tea, but nothing happened. They brought back my credentials and told me everything was in order, but apparently they still did not know at what time the Surrender was going to be signed. At ten o'clock my patience was exhausted, and I officially demanded to know when the signing was going to take place; I was told it would be in about an hour. During the evening I had our modest baggage fetched from the plane, as the return flight which we had taken for granted was now impossible.

Shortly before midnight—that is, the time the surrender was due to come into force—I was conducted with my lieutenants into the mess hall of the barracks. As the clock began to strike the hour, we entered the big hall through a side door, and were led across to the long table directly facing us, where three seats had been kept free for my two companions and myself; the rest of our entourage were obliged to stand behind us. Every corner of the hall was packed, and brilliantly lit by spotlights. Three rows of chairs running the length of the hall and one across it were crowded with officers; General Zhukov took the chair with the plenipotentiaries of Britain and America on either side of him.

As soon as Zhukov's Chief of Staff laid the Instrument in front of me, in three languages, I asked him to explain why the qualification I had demanded to the penalty clauses had not been inserted in the text. He went across to Zhukov, and after conferring briefly with him, under my close scrutiny, he came back and told me Zhukov had expressly agreed to my demand for the penalty measures not to take effect for a further twelve hours.

The ceremony began with a few introductory words; then Zhukov asked me whether I had read the Instrument of Surrender. I replied, 'Yes.' His second question was whether I was ready to recognise it with my signature. Again, I answered with a loud 'Yes!' The signing ceremony began at once, and, after I had been the first to sign it, the attestation. Finally, I and my party left the hall by the door close behind me.

Now we were returned to our small villa again; during the afternoon a table had been set up, groaning under the weight of a cold buffet, with various wines, while in the remaining rooms clean beds had been prepared for every one of us, one bed each. The official interpreter said that a Russian general was coming, and that dinner would be served upon his arrival. A quarter of an hour later Zhukov's chief quartermaster appeared and asked us to begin; he asked us to excuse him as he could not stay. The meal was probably more modest than we had been accustomed to, he apologised, but we should have to put up with it. I was unable to refrain from answering that we were not at all accustomed to such luxury and such lavish feasts. He obviously thought he was only being flattered by this remark.

We all thought that the kind of *Sakuska* with which we were served was all there was to this hangman's breakfast; we were all feeling very replete when we learned that there was a hot roast meat course to follow, and finally they gave us all plates of fresh frozen strawberries, something I had never eaten before in my life. It was obvious that some Berlin gourmets' restaurant had provided this dinner, as even the wines were German brands. After the meal, the interpreter officer left us; apparently he had stood in for the host. I laid on our aircraft for six o'clock next morning to take us back, and we all turned in.

Next morning, at five o'clock, we were given a simple breakfast. As I was about to leave at about half-past five, I was asked to wait for Zhukov's Chief of Staff who wanted to have a talk with me about our return flight. We all stood around our cars, waiting to drive off. The general requested me to remain in Berlin; they would endeavour to provide me with the opportunity to issue from Berlin our cease-fire orders to the troops on the eastern front, just as I had demanded when we discussed the terms of the penalty clauses the day before. I replied that if they would guarantee radio communication, I would at once issue the further signals; they would have to hand over the German cyphers to me. The general disappeared again to ask Zhukov for a decision. He returned with the news that it would not be possible after all for me to despatch these signals; but General Zhukov still invited me to remain in Berlin nevertheless.

Now I saw what they were up to. I insisted on flying to Flensburg at once, as I would have to transmit the amended surrender conditions to the troops as quickly as possible from there; otherwise I would not accept the consequences for what happened. He was to inform his general that I had signed in good faith and had been relying on General Zhukov's word as an officer.

Ten minutes later the Chief of Staff was back again with the news that my aircraft would be ready to take off in an hour. I climbed quickly into my car with Bürkner and Böhm-Tettelbach and the interpreter; these gentlemen had all detected that an attempt was being made to detain me much more clearly than I had myself—at first, at least.

They told me that the Russians had obviously had too much to drink and that the victory feast was still in full sway at the mess as we drove safely off.

The interpreter asked what route I wanted to take to the airport. We drove past the City Hall, the castle and along Unter den Linden, and Friedrichstrasse. There were horrifying traces of the battle to be seen between Unter den Linden and Belle-Alliance-Platz. Large numbers of German and Russian tanks blocked Friedrichstrasse at several places, and the street was strewn with the rubble of collapsed buildings. We flew straight back to Flensburg, relieved to be in a British aircraft and in the air. We landed at Flensburg at about ten o'clock.

We had arranged to exchange official delegations with Montgomery and Eisenhower, to ease the business between us. On Saturday 12th May, the American delegation arrived at Flensburg and were accommodated aboard the *Patria*, a luxury steamship;

the first conference was arranged for eleven o'clock on Sunday morning. Dönitz was required to go aboard the *Patria* first to be received by the Americans, while I was to make my appearance half an hour later.

After Dönitz had left the ship, I was received by them; the American general disclosed to me that I was to surrender as a prisoner of war, and would be flown out at two o'clock that afternoon, in two hours' time. I was to turn over my official business to Colonel-General Jodl; I was to be permitted to take one companion and a personal batman, as well as 300 pounds of luggage.

I stood up, saluted briefly with my field-marshal's baton and drove back to headquarters with Bürkner and Böhm-Tettelbach, who had both accompanied me during this 'audience'. I took leave of Dönitz who had already been briefed on what was to happen and selected Mönch and Lieutenant-Colonel von Freyend as my companions, thereby ensuring a considerably less arduous captivity for them. I handed my personal papers and keys to Jodl and entrusted Szimonski with one or two personal objects for my wife, with a letter to her, to be flown down to Berchtesgaden in the courier plane. Unfortunately the British seized everything from the brave 'Schimo' subsequently—even my keys and bank pass-book, and the letter to my wife as well.

We took off for a destination that was not disclosed to us, and after flying right across Germany landed early that evening at Luxembourg airport; there I was treated as a prisoner of war for the first time, and transferred to Park Hotel at Mondorf, which had been converted into an internment camp. Seyss-Inquart had arrived before me.

In Flensburg I had been my own master; as I drove in my own car to the airfield together with General Dethleffsen, in those two unguarded hours I could have put an end to my life and nobody could have stopped me. The thought never occurred to me, as I never dreamed that such a *via doloris* lay ahead of me, with this tragic end at Nuremberg.

I began my term as prisoner of war on 13th May, 1945, at Mondorf; I was transferred to a prison cell at Nuremberg on the 13th August, and am awaiting my execution on 13th October, 1946.

Finis, 10*th October,* 1946.

234

9

Afterthoughts

KEITEL'S THOUGHTS ON SUICIDE

Suicide: how often I have found myself seriously confronted with this as a possible way out, only to reject it because—as suicides have always demonstrated—nothing is changed and nothing bettered by such action. Quite the contrary, the armed forces, whose counsellor and mediator I had so often been, would have labelled me a deserter and branded me a coward.

Hitler himself chose death rather than accept responsibility for the actions of the OKW, of Colonel-General Jodl and myself. I do not doubt that he would have done us justice and identified himself wholly with my utterances; but for him—as I learned only later —to have committed suicide when he knew he was defeated, shunning thereby his own ultimate personal responsibility upon which he had always laid such great stress and which he had unreservedly taken upon himself alone, instead of giving himself up to the enemy; and for him to have left it to a subordinate to account for his autocratic and arbitrary actions, these two shortcomings will remain for ever incomprehensible to me. They are my final disillusion.*

EXTRACTS FROM LAST LETTERS

To his eldest son, Lieutenant-Colonel Karl-Heinz Keitel, 12th January, 1946.
You will already know what has happened to me. The Trial will last for weeks yet; it is a severe ordeal for my nerves, but my final duty to the Nation and to History . . .

To his counsel, Dr. Nelte, 21st May, 1946.
My defence has entered a new phase and under wholly altered circumstances as a result of Grand-Admiral Raeder's devastating

* From a note written by Keitel for his defence counsel at Nuremberg on 24th October, 1945, on The Responsibility of the Chief of the High Command.

attack on my character and on my rôle in office. One can defend oneself against attacks and allegations of an *objective* nature, or from *strangers*, or at least one can earn the Tribunal's respect for trying to defend oneself; but Raeder *never* mentioned any shortcomings to me [during the war] despite his clear duty to do so if he really had serious cause to believe that my behaviour compromised the interests of the armed forces. In Berlin I was often present at ministerial discussions with him when the most diverse matters were brought up, and I sat in on most of his Naval Conferences with the Führer, so he had numerous opportunities either to tell me plainly or hint to me what dangers he saw in my official demeanour, especially as I approached him on several occasions for advice, in an endeavour to build up his confidence in me.

After everything that has now been said about me to the Tribunal I have seen my character so grievously smeared by a very senior representative of the armed forces—who can after all only be taken seriously—that I can no longer expect to meet with any understanding from this Tribunal as far as the unbridgeable antithesis between what I honestly desired myself and my sheer, shattering inability to do or refrain from doing anything at all on my own initiative [as Chief of the High Command].

As far as I can see my defence will now be less easy than ever to conduct. I fully appreciate the noble motives that have inspired you to act for my defence here, but if I can in any way lighten your burden in making up your mind, then I would like you to know that I would fully understand it if you were now to entertain the most earnest second thoughts about whether you ought to drop the defence of such a questionable figure as myself.*

I feel too ashamed of myself to be able to tell you this personally.

To Luise Jodl, wife of Colonel-General Jodl, 9th June, 1946.
I feel that I must and should write to tell you how delighted I have been with the course of the defence during this last week.

* All this refers to a document written by Grand-Admiral Raeder while interned in Moscow, for his own private purposes; Colonel Pokrovsky, for the Soviet prosecution, tried to introduce this into the Trial against Keitel as Exhibit U.S.S.R.-460; naturally the document was also made available to the defence. It dealt with the Grand-Admiral's views on Keitel (and, in fact, both officers were very akin in character). Raeder had sharply criticised Keitel for his 'failure'; written for his own use, the document had not been intended for publication, but his Soviet custodians naturally took it away from him (see IMT, Vol. XIV, p. 243). It was refused a public reading. It had never occurred to Grand-Admiral Raeder, ¦who was basically a very honourable and upright officer, that they might ride rough-shod over his rights like that; in his hearing of 25th May, 1946 (an affidavit by Colonel Pokrovsky) he tried to weaken the effect of his statements about Keitel, by stating that naturally nobody had any prospect of stopping long with the Führer if he was 'to have a dust-up with the Führer every other day'.

[Your husband's] constancy and dignity, and the way he has preserved his honour as a soldier, were as impressive as his clear and
irrefutable answers were convincing. The great effort you have
made with your co-operation has also repaid itself a hundredfold.
The things I have not managed to say or had forgotten to mention
are now a matter of record, and the things that were most incriminating for me he has been happily able to refute. I will recall
this historically unforgettable day with the deepest satisfaction and
sense of gratitude.

To his defence counsel, 1st October, 1946.

The death sentence has come as no surprise to me, but I am very
deeply upset about the way it is to be executed. I beg of you under
these circumstances to avail me of your selfless assistance once more,
to help me make a plea for my execution to be changed to a soldier's
death by firing squad. I consider it pointless to ask more than that.
My faith in your defence, and in the multifarious suggestions you
made to me, is completely unshaken. No other defence counsel
applied himself to client in such a selfless, tireless and personal way.

*From Frau Lisa Keitel to Dr. Otto Nelte, the Field-Marshal's defence
counsel, 1st October, 1946.*

I have just finished writing a last letter to my husband; I hope
you will still be able to get it to him. We heard the judgment, but
it was only as we expected. I hope that my husband's plea for a
military execution will be granted him and Jodl. Otherwise, please,
no plea for clemency.*

Keitel to his eldest son, Karl-Heinz, 3rd October, 1946.

This will probably be my last letter to you. According to my
calculations, the death sentence will be executed in fourteen days'
time, in other words once it has been confirmed. It has been a great
help to me in facing up to the Tribunal as I did that I have for a long
time been aware of what my fate would be. I regret nothing that
I said at my Trial, and I would never take back a word I said; I
spoke the pure truth, the whole time, to every question and on every
occasion. That is something I can still be proud of, and for all time
in history.†

---

* As far as can be ascertained, Lisa Keitel's last letter to her husband never reached
him.
† On 13th October, 1946, three days before his execution, the Field-Marshal sent one
last letter of good wishes to his son; he commented that only the women of the family
had written to him, and added: 'Enough said. What cowards we men are.'

The Memoirs of Field-Marshal Keitel

Vice-Admiral Leopold Bürkner to Keitel, 4th October, 1946.

Field-Marshal! It has been written that 'by his works ye shall know him'; all the good that you have done in your past life and even in this hapless war will not crumble into nothingness, even if at present it may seem so. In any event, I would like to thank you for all the good you did for me and doubtless to your many subordinates; these latter will be thinking of you now, just as I am doing. It is hard to believe that the last word will have been spoken about your onerous office.

Keitel to the Allied Control Council for Germany, 5th October, 1946.

I will willingly give up my life in the expiation demanded by my sentence, if my sacrifice will speed the prosperity of the German people and serve to exonerate the German armed forces from blame.

I have only one plea: to be granted a death by firing squad.

I hope that those members of the Allied Control Council who have been soldiers will have some understanding for my guilt, which was born of a virtue recognised in every Army of the world as an honourable and necessary basis for being a good soldier. Even if I failed to recognise the proper limits that ought to have been set upon this soldierly virtue, at least I do not feel I have therefore forfeited my right to atone for this error by the mode of execution that is the right of the soldier in every other army in the world upon whom sentence of death is pronounced as a soldier.*

*Field-Marshal Keitel's request to be executed by firing-squad was rejected by the Allied Control Council for Germany and, together with Alfred Jodl, he was hanged at Nuremberg on 16th October, 1946.

PART III

The Indictment

10

The Indictment
by
Walter Görlitz

I N 1945 the 'International Military Tribunal' at Nuremberg, representing the United States of America, the French Republic, the United Kingdom of Great Britain and Northern Ireland, and the Union of Soviet Socialist Republics, charged Field-Marshal Wilhelm Keitel, the former Chief of the Armed Forces High Command, with having participated in a conspiracy, with having committed crimes against peace, war crimes and crimes against humanity, or alternatively with having 'authorised' or 'directed' such crimes. He was accused of complicity in the murder and ill-treatment of civilian populations in occupied territories, and of ordering their deportation as slave labourers; he was accused of having ordered the execution of hostages, and the persecution of specific sections of the population for political, racial or religious reasons. An additional charge against Keitel and his twenty co-defendants was the accusation of having looted public and private property.

Of the men who really held power during the Third Reich, very few ever reached the dock at Nuremberg: the most prominent among the defendants was Reichsmarschall Hermann Göring. Adolf Hitler, Führer, Reich Chancellor and Supreme Commander of the Armed Forces and of the Army; Heinrich Himmler, S.S. Reichsführer, Reich Minister of the Interior, Chief of the German Police and Commander-in-Chief of the Reserve Army; and Dr. Joseph Goebbels, Reich Minister for Public Enlightenment and Propaganda, had taken their own lives and could therefore not be called to account. Reichsleiter Martin Bormann, Head of the Party chancellery and éminence grise of the Third Reich, had been 'missing, presumed dead' since 1st May 1945.

The leaders of the Third Reich had accumulated a mountain of guilt upon their beings; they were responsible for crimes unique in their enormity. And the culpability of the German leaders was not lessened one whit by the fact that the International Military Tribunal met to pass judgment only upon those war crimes with which they could charge the vanquished Germans, while turning a blind eye on all the war crimes committed by every one of the other belligerent parties.

The civilised world was crying out for revenge. The legal basis for such a trial, an innovation in the history of civilised peoples, had been established by the London Charter of 8th August 1945 for the 'Prosecution and Punishment of the Major War Criminals of the European Axis', an Agreement drawn up as a result of lengthy and complex preliminary talks over the years 1942 to 1944. The charter itself represented an important violation of one of the western world's fundamental legal doctrines: *nulla poene sine lege*. Legal teaching on the one hand and the demands for the expiation of the terrible crimes against justice on the other seemed to be difficult to reconcile.* But the National Socialists' war methods had involved such violations of international law that they cried out for requital even if the legal basis for such requital had first to be fashioned *post facto*. Nevertheless there was a real weakness in the Nuremberg Tribunal, and that was that here it was the victors who were sitting in judgment only upon the war crimes of their vanquished.

On 19th October, 1945, Field-Marshal Keitel was handed the Nuremberg indictment; he considered it a foregone conclusion that he would be found Guilty, although he pleaded Not Guilty from the dock.

The field-marshal's defence counsel, Dr. Otto Nelte, had originally been an industrial lawyer at Siegburg; in his speech for the defence on 8th July, 1946† he stressed that his client was concerned not with minimising the rôle he had played during the Third Reich, but to try to clarify the picture of his character. As Nelte put it: the defendant was fighting to save not his neck but his face. At the end of his exposition, the defence counsel declared that from the point of view of international law there was no answer to the question of under what circumstances, how far, and indeed if, a general was obliged to adopt a standpoint opposed to that of his own government. Accord-

* For the text of the indictment, see the *International Military Tribunal* proceedings, Volume I.
† For Nelte's defence speech see IMT, Vol. XVII, p. 654 et seq. and Vol. XVIII, p. 7 et seq. See also Dr. Nelte's pamphlet, '*Die Generale. Das Nürnberger Urteil und die Schuld der Generale*' (Hanover, 1947).

ing to Nelte, obedience and loyalty had been Keitel's only guiding principles. He did not ask for his acquittal, he pleaded only for his client's tragic dilemma to be recognised and understood.

*　　*　　*　　*　　*

In a memorandum compiled by his defence counsel during interviews with him on the subject of wars of aggression and the problem of Hitler's influence over his senior officers, Keitel wrote a number of telling comments on the German officer's position:*

> While the education of a professional officer is thorough, it is only one-sided; the intellectual and political education of the professional soldier is as a rule less complete. This has nothing to do with any question of intelligence and I do not mean to denigrate the officer corps in any way, but I want to stress the fact that the training of a good soldier was fundamentally different from an education for a purely liberal or academic profession. The officer's profession is not a liberal profession: a soldier's cardinal virtue is obedience, in other words the very opposite of criticism; the cardinal virtue of the liberal professions is the free interplay of forces for which criticism as such is a pre-condition.
>
> The consequence of all this is that the so-called 'manic' intellectual does not make a suitable officer, while on the other hand the one-sided education of the professional soldier described above results in a lack of ability to make a stand against theses which are not part of his real territory.
>
> Nothing is more convincing to a soldier than success.

There emerges from this a picture of the professional soldier of which the field-marshal himself was the very embodiment. It is in perfect accord with his character when Keitel admits that the head of state, in other words Hitler, did enjoy just such successes at first, but adds that it would have been out of the question for any 'honourable officer', indeed it would have been 'disloyal' for any officer to have broken faith with a head of state as soon as the wind changed.

In his defence speech Keitel's counsel stressed that the concepts of loyalty, of patriotism and of obedience are vital to every country's existence, and there we have the key to the field-marshal's attitude as a senior officer and gentleman. We know only one thing today of him, and that is that even as chief of Hitler's military chancellery he was never once able to prevail upon Hitler to change his mind on decisive matters, despite Keitel's often superior understanding of

* Papers of Dr. Nelte, file 1/7: Reserve (a)/General Questions on the planning of Wars of Aggression.

them; a second point is that although during the Third Reich there were often bitter and unscrupulous intrigues around the key positions of the government's power structure and at times even inside the Officer Corps, there were never any intrigues with the declared aim of replacing Keitel as Chief of the High Command, for his was the most thankless office that there could ever be. Of all the senior officers who lambasted the Chief of the OKW for his 'criminal weakness' towards the Führer, nobody felt any compulsion to replace him in that office.

* * * * *

In the book *Gespräche mit Halder*—'Talks with Halder'—Colonel-General Franz Halder, Chief of the Army General Staff from 1938 to 1942, was quoted as saying that one phrase keeps echoing back in his memory from the war conferences at Hitler's headquarters: 'You, Herr Feldmarschall. . .!' The phrase was invariably addressed to Keitel, in Hitler's half-Austrian, half-Bavarian dialect. Halder, upon whom Keitel throws a favourable light in these *Memoirs*, continued that Hitler had exploited Keitel as a rubbing-post to work his inner tensions off on. According to the same book, Halder once asked Keitel why he put up with it, and Keitel explained: 'Halder, I am only doing it for you. Please understand me!' And, according to Halder, there were tears in his eyes as he said this. The former Chief of the General Staff added: 'That is how he came to be involved in such criminal actions; but he was certainly not wicked *au fond*, as one occasionally reads of him.' A further incident lends weight to this assessment: during the 1944 Ardennes offensive, Lieutenant-General Westphal, chief of staff to the Commander-in-Chief West, took the Chief of the OKW to task over the critical fuel situation of the attacking forces. Keitel regretted that he had nothing to spare; Westphal did not let him go so easily: surely the OKW must have some reserves. . .? Keitel thereupon admitted that naturally he still had some in reserve, but . . . And, deeply distressed, he told Westphal, who had been a pupil of his at the Hanover Cavalry School: 'Oh, I have been turned into such a scoundrel. . .'

Keitel, who had acquiesced quite without forebodings to his appointment as Chief of the Armed Forces High Command, saw only gradually the thorns in the crown that had been placed upon his head. As time wore on, he was burdened with the additional functions of War Minister—without any kind of legal prerogative—together with those of the now non-existent War Minister's under-secretary and his chief of staff.

Even his most malevolent critics have not disputed his organisational prowess. Unfortunately, the head of state for whom he now
had to work—and indeed for whom he wanted to work, as it was
to him a duty and an honour—did not value simple structures and
the unambiguous delimitation of military spheres of competence as
highly as Keitel did. On the contrary: while Hitler certainly needed
a head of his 'military chancellery'—to whom he deliberately
accorded no independent command authority—he also deliberately
wanted the innumerable spheres of competence to overlap so that
he could establish his own authority over every sphere according to
his own whims. Keitel was the administrator of all the military—
and above all Army—matters that needed administering. Upon his
not entirely blameless shoulders there fell an enormous burden of
work, and he bore the brunt of all the opprobrium directed by Hitler
at such of his compliant and conscientious colleagues as upset him
in any way, even by their looks.

The field-marshal has himself dealt with the strange and entangled
thicket of OKW spheres of jurisdiction in these *Memoirs*, but the
point which must be repeatedly stressed is that he possessed no
command authority himself. As modern warfare necessitated the
mobilisation of every field of a nation's endeavour, the Chief of the
OKW, who was in Hitler's eyes the formal representative of the
Armed Forces, became entangled in innumerable matters which
were no real concern of his. And as the Chief of the OKW was an
officer with a strongly marked sense of duty, he felt unable to reject
any of these demands upon his time.

It is appropriate to recall once more the terms of the Führer's
decree of 4th February, 1938:

> The authority of command over all the armed forces is from now on
> to be exercised by me, directly and in person.
> The hitherto Armed Forces Office of the Reich War Ministry is
> transferred to my immediate command as 'The High Command of the
> Armed Forces', my own military staff.

Thus spake Adolf Hitler in 1938, before any annexations and
before any conquests; it was a natural climax in the process of
accumulation of all the influential offices of power of the old traditional state, from Reich Chancellor and Reich President down to the
Supreme Commander of the Armed Forces, because, as observation
would seem to confirm, this is apparently the *modous vivendi* of such
autocratic systems. One consequence of this could not be ignored,
a point which was stressed by Professor Hermann Jahrreiss, a German

constitutional and legal expert at the time of the Nuremberg Trial, and that was that if the Führer-State, the autocracy, came into existence in what was ostensibly a constitutional and legal manner, then the will of the autocrat became *law*.*

It was indicated to Keitel's candidate for the Command of the Army, General von Brauchitsch, during the 1938 national crisis, that one of his duties would be to associate the armed forces more closely with the National Socialist State; he had as little objection to this as did Keitel. For them the problem was not so much National Socialism as such, as Hitler himself. For these soldiers the decisive factor was not the prevailing political system but the personality at its head.

From memory, Keitel has quoted a speech delivered by Hitler on 30th January, 1939, apparently to a number of senior officers. (The recollected version is among his defence counsel's papers.) Hitler expanded upon the lack of fortune which had dogged Germany's attempts hitherto in her search for world-power status. The armed forces, he continued, would have to stand fast until 1942. The 'main conflict' with Britain and France was inevitable and he would instigate it all in good time. With strong words he censured the 'pessimistic element' in the military commands, the 'intellectual-mindedness' which had existed since Schlieffen, the one-sided intellectual 'over-breeding'. According to Hitler, there would have to be an 'absolute and radical' change. The Officer Corps was steeped in pessimism (an allusion to its demeanour during the Sudeten crisis). Hitler cited the Adam case and commented indignantly: 'What a state we are in if such a spirit is being spread from above'. He demanded a new system of officer selection: in future he wanted only officers who had faith in him. Verbatim, he said: 'I want no more warning memoranda from anybody' (a reference to the war of memoranda waged by General Beck in 1938). It was to be Brauchitsch's task to give the officer corps new purpose. He closed with the appeal: 'I beseech you all to try and recognise the task before us.'

That was really all that Hitler ever did have to ask of them. During his preliminary American hearings, Keitel later explained that it gradually dawned on him that Hitler often did not mean his words to be taken as violently as he had spoken them, and that Hitler had often deliberately exaggerated in speeches to his officers —a symptom of his inward uncertainty. The realisation brought little solace to Keitel then.

* The Nelte Papers: Hermann Jahrreiss' legal opinion on the Führer-State.

In these preliminary hearings of October, 1945, which have been published (*Nazi Conspiracy and Aggression*, Supplement B, p. 1284 et seq.) under the title 'Keitel's Analysis of Hitler's Character and Traits' he gave *inter alia* a number of illustrations of Hitler's fixation that he always had to regard everybody with the utmost suspicion.

The first concerned Hitler's relationship with the Army's oldest and most respected officer, Field-Marshal von Rundstedt. Von Rundstedt, Commander-in-Chief of Army Group South, was on 3rd December, 1941, at his own request relieved of his command by Hitler because he had refused to obey a number of orders from Hitler demanding the impossible of him. In 1942, after the illness and resignation of Field-Marshal von Witzleben, he was recalled and appointed Commander-in-Chief West (Army Group D).

When the Allied invasion forces succeeded in June 1944 in their invasion operations, as was only to be expected, Field-Marshal von Rundstedt was again sent into the wilderness by Hitler, and Keitel heard Hitler say of him: 'He is an old man, he has lost his nerve. He isn't master of the situation any longer, he'll have to go.' Some eight weeks later, Hitler was telling Keitel: 'I would like very much to see Field-Marshal von Rundstedt and have a talk with him to see how far he has recuperated his health.'

Rundstedt was ordered to call at the Führer's headquarters in East Prussia, where he waited for three days, and finally asked Keitel in rather a disgruntled voice what kind of game it was, and why they had sent for him. Keitel had no other recourse than to ask him to be patient. He had asked Hitler what plans he had for the field-marshal; Hitler had replied: 'I'll tell you tomorrow.' On the following day, Hitler had waved Keitel away saying: 'I have no time for him today.' It was not until the third day that he said: 'Come round this afternoon at such-and-such a time, bringing Field-Marshal von Rundstedt.' (In fact, as we now know, Rundstedt's successor on the western front, Field-Marshal von Kluge, had committed suicide as he expected to be called to account for his complicity in the conspiracy of 20th July, 1944).

Hitler disclosed to Rundstedt: 'Herr Feldmarschall, I would like to entrust you once more with command of the Western Front. Rundstedt replied, 'My Führer, whatever you may command I will do my duty to my last breath.'

The tight and all-embracing shackles of a soldier's duty and his attitude to the head of state were as binding upon von Rundstedt as they were upon Keitel; von Rundstedt belonged to those senior officers whom Keitel harshly described—at least once he was in

247

captivity—as 'Yes-Generals'. And all the rage that Rundstedt was able to summon up for angry outbursts about Hitler on the telephone did not prevent him from presiding over the Court of Honour that passed judgment upon the generals and staff officers who had lifted their hands against the Führer or were suspected of having done so.

On 5th September, 1944, Rundstedt replaced von Kluge's immediate successor, Field-Marshal Model, as Commander-in-Chief West. After Hitler's interview with Rundstedt in the Führer's headquarters, Hitler said to Keitel: 'You know the respect Rundstedt enjoys not only in the army, but in the other services too, in the navy and air force, is absolutely unique. He can get away with anything, and I have nobody who enjoys quite the same respect as he.'

After Hitler's last grand offensive, the second Ardennes offensive of December 1944, had collapsed he reverted after some hesitation to his old assessment of Rundstedt: he was too old, he had lost his grip, he was unable to control his generals, and so on. He, Hitler, would have to let him go again. Keitel added to this that Hitler always prided himself on being a perfect judge of people, but in fact he never was.

Keitel gave another illustration of Hitler's character, an interview with Hitler on armament problems. Hitler had asked him: 'How many light field howitzers are we producing monthly?' Keitel had replied: 'About a hundred and sixty, probably.' Hitler: 'I demand nine hundred!' And he continued to inquire: 'How many 88-mm anti-aircraft shells are being turned out monthly?' Keitel: 'About 200,000.' Hitler: 'I demand two million!' When Keitel protested: 'How on earth can we do that? Every single round has to have a clockwork time-fuse, and we have not enough of those. We only have a few factories turning out clockwork fuses for them', Hitler replied: 'You fail to understand me; I will talk it over with Speer, and then we will build the factories and within six months we will *have* the fuses.'

That was Germany's supreme warlord, the man with whom the Chief of the High Command of the Armed Forces not only had to work, but wanted to work, because in his view there could be no question of ducking out.

*   *   *

Keitel's *Memoirs* show the extent to which the compartmentalisation of every sphere of jurisdiction within the OKW was carried out. And they also show how much the field-marshal really was only Hitler's *chef de bureau*. On the other hand, the multiplicity of organisations immediately subordinated to the Führer and concerned with economic policy and war administration, above all in the eastern territories, meant that matters lying far beyond the scope of the armed forces were constantly being dragged up to the field-marshal by the SS, the Party and the Todt Organisation or by the vast apparatus built up since 1942 by the Reich Plenipotentiary for the Direction of Labour, Gauleiter Sauckel. If he was to remain the master of all these fields, if he were not to lose sight of the whole vast complex, he was obliged to concern himself actively with thousands upon thousands of problems without even the slightest real prerogatives of command. It took immense energy on his part to master all this work, but he devoted himself to his office with all the vitality he had. The only thing he failed to realise was how indispensable he had in fact become, even to Hitler; that, he was probably too modest to see. He was too little aware of his own value.

There were probably times when Keitel's adjutants asked why such an expert on farming had not been made Minister of Agriculture. His interest in agriculture endured despite all his desk work, and a job which gave him no respite, no mealbreaks, and only a brief midday pause and time for a modest stroll. Probably there were times when they asked themselves, and him as well, why he stayed on at all, when the orders he had to issue really demanded of any soldier that he should offer his resignation. Even if we ignore the fact that Hitler would never have permitted Keitel to go because he realised that without this *chef de bureau* he would have been unable to manage anything as far as military administration was concerned and even if we also ignore the fact that Keitel considered it unethical to resign one's office in wartime, the field-marshal was perfectly aware of what would happen if he did go. No Army general would be taking his place: 'The next one after me is Himmler!'

Grand-Admiral Dönitz, Commander-in-Chief of the Navy from 1943 onwards, has testified that he avoided stopping too long at the Führer's headquarters because of Hitler's extraordinary powers of persuasion.* Even Reichsminister Speer, a sober and cultivated man with no kind of inclination towards mysticism, found Hitler's powers of suggestion very sinister at times; but this was the man with whom Keitel had to work for nearly seven years.

Among the service Commanders-in-Chief and the other senior officers serving in Hitler's immediate vicinity there was a house rule to the effect that it was prudent to express one's opposition to the Führer only *à deux*. That was also Grand-Admiral Raeder's belief,

* IMT, Vol. XIII, pp. 243-4.

according to his testimony at Nuremberg; he added that Hitler's chief adjutant General Schmundt had advised him on this course. Hitler took a dim view of any collective opposition to his plans: his abysmal distrust being what it was he began to suspect that his 'generals' were conspiring against him. Even Keitel observed this rule, and indeed followed it so strictly that in the great controversies like that over the dropping or modification of illegal orders, he even refrained from asking his chief legal adviser, Dr. Lehmann, to accompany him when he saw Hitler.

Colonel-General Jodl, the chief of the Armed Forces Operations Staff, compared the Führer's headquarters in east Prussia with a concentration camp. Life within the Security Zone Ia at the 'Wolf's Lair' did indeed mean going without much that was part and parcel of everyday life. The enormity of the burden of purely formal work that fell upon a man like Keitel left him no time to form any effective overall picture of what was going on outside. Steering the mighty and inflated bureaucratic apparatus of the war administration consumed all his day and half his night as well, especially as the daily war conferences with Hitler swallowed up many hours by themselves. It is true that he came into contact with many individual matters from other fields of the war and war administration, quite outside his own office, but what he saw were only kaleidoscopic glimpses. What his supreme warlord did not want him to know, he did not find out; and that included a great deal, not only in the field of grand diplomacy but also the peculiar kind of warfare being waged by the SS Reichsführer, Heinrich Himmler. The result of his unnatural life, tied to a writing desk at the heart of the war machine, was an unhealthy isolation from the everyday life of the outside world.

An officer as highly placed as he was probably seemed from the outside to be a powerful man, although in actual fact the field-marshal would not have been able to march off so much as a company of soldiers on his own orders. He dissociated himself from gossip, rumours and the like. His adjutants gained the impression that he dissociated himself religiously from any kind of criticism of Hitler or of conditions under the Third Reich. He refused, at least in most of the cases, to cover up for officers in his command who had fallen foul of the secret police for making critical remarks about the Führer or the Party, for example; on the other hand, he himself would never denounce any officer who came to him with frank opinions or criticised his own attitude to him or raised complaints about conditions in Germany.

The Indictment

The office which Keitel held could isolate its occupant and divorce him from the realities of life. Of course, the question arises, why did he not throw off this thankless burden of office? The head of the OKW's central office, Lieutenant-General Paul Winter, once reminded him of the old Markwitz maxim: 'Opt for disobedience if obedience brings no honour.' But Keitel viewed the position differently. Firstly, he honestly believed that it was his duty to hang on to the office to prevent the SS from coming to power. And secondly, he knew full well that with the collapse of any hopes of a quick victory over Russia in 1941, their last hopes of any overall victory had gone; yet to throw off his office at a time of misfortune would have been the negation of all his principles. He stayed on to the bitter end, submitting to the processing and issuing of orders which he himself would never have issued.

* * *

The orders with which we are concerned here fall, considered logically, into two groups. There will be little point in totting up a list of counter-recriminations here, or in insisting that the other sides were equally guilty of breaches of international law, as for example in the Allied air offensive against the civilian population of Germany: it can certainly be argued that two wrongs do not make a right.

The first group of orders embraces those whereby, months before any attack was launched on the Soviet Union, the character of the German mode of warfare was decisively altered. They include: the directive entrusting 'special duties' to the SS Reichsführer and his police and secret-police organs and units in the front-line and rearward areas; the order modifying the liability of German troops to courts martial in the *Barbarossa* zone, in other words in the projected fighting areas in Russia; and the so called 'Commissar Order'. These three orders were issued in March, May and June of 1941, and they provided respectively for: the introduction of police squads, or more accurately of squads comprised of the National Socialist political police, of the SS and its security service into the fighting organisation for the purpose of carrying out mass murders of political or racial communities; an order to the troops that punitive actions conducted against the civilian population of the eastern territories foreseen for occupation were not normally to be made the subject of courts martial; and an order to the troops that the political commissars, who did after all belong to the Red Army machine, were to be sorted out from the bulk of Russian prisoners of war and liquidated. All these orders turned upside down the heritage of centuries

251

of military tradition. For the troops the order modifying their liability to courts martial was probably the most far-reaching.

Field-Marshal Keitel, who personally objected to the whole idea of an attack on the Soviet Union, has admitted in his *Memoirs* that these were 'highly controversial' innovations. He himself was against committing these measures to paper at all, but somebody nevertheless wrote them down in black and white. Most of the senior generals were opposed to the Courts Martial and the Commissar Orders. But at Hitler's last two major Russian campaign speeches delivered to his senior commands in March and June of 1941, nobody spoke out openly against these revolutions in conventional warfare, although most of them did afterwards privately reproach the Chief of the OKW for not having protested and prevented them. So they passed the buck to one another, instead of openly admitting that when it was a question of moral weakness, in fact, none of them had any right to reproach anybody.

As far as the 'special duties' of the SS Reichsführer's organisation in the east were concerned, Hitler once indicated brusquely to Keitel that these were no concern of his, they were purely police concerns. The security service's 'action squads'—allocated to each of the three army groups fighting on the Eastern Front—and the security service's special squads—formed for 'dealing with' the commissars and the so-called fanatical communists found in the reception camps for Russian POWs—carried out the mass-murder orders. It is illuminative of Hitler's reasoning that it was not until the autumn of 1941 that he lifted his veto on the employment of Soviet prisoners in the Reich, because of the shortage of manpower. He had feared that they would collaborate with communist cells among the German labour force or else they would re-instil communistic ideas in them. The Commissar Order was complied with to a varying degree, particularly during the first—decisive—months of the war in the east; but it was then gradually and quietly dropped, so that by 1942 it was no longer valid. As an honourable man, Field-Marshal Keitel did not try to deny his moral complicity in the issuing and forwarding of these orders, although not of their origination. But these special orders did their damage: they opened up abysses which could never be bridged again.

The second group of incriminating orders, including the Partisan Warfare decree of September 1941 and the 'Cover of Darkness' and 'Commando' Orders, and the OKW's Italian Orders of the autumn of 1943 (which remarkably did not rate any mention at Nuremberg, although they did come into the American trial of the so-called 'South-East' generals) were possessed of a different character: they resulted not from Hitler's objective planning processes, but from his reactions to the multifarious manifestations of partisan and guerilla warfare and sabotage squads operating behind the front lines.

Although prior to the Reich's attack on the Soviet Union on 22nd June, 1941, the war had seen some stirring of what might be called national and restorational resistance movements, in the occupied territories and above all in Poland, the communist partisan guerilla bands blossomed out everywhere with the collapse of the Nazi–Soviet *entente*; the Western Powers gave them active support with Britain as their base and buttressed the nationalist and democratic forces in Poland, Norway, the Netherlands, France and Belgium. Everywhere 'white' and 'red' partisan bands sprang up, very often not easily distinguishable from each other at first, but with a tendency to establish 'Common Fronts': units which in Poland and in Serbia, and in the closing stages of the war in France as well, as willingly made war upon each other as on the enemy.

In the Soviet Union itself partisan warfare was highly organised behind the German front lines as they initially swept eastwards across Russia. The partisans received massive reinforcements as soon as the population realised—thanks to the activities of the Security Service's 'action squads' and of the German regimes at once set up by the Party officials—that they had only exchanged the terror of the Communist Party for the new terror of the National Socialists.

During the summer of 1941 the inadequately occupied and pacified Balkans, and above all southern Serbia, the Sandshak, Bosnia and Herzegovina, saw the emergence of guerillas under the leadership of a communist official of Croatian origin, Joseph Broz, who went by the *nom de guerre* of Tito in Party circles. In view of the weakness of the Germans and the indifference of many of the Italian security forces, and of the circumstances that most of the German divisions were tied down on the Eastern Front, Hitler resorted to his usual expedient, brutality, in a September 1941 order on combatting communist guerillas. The order abounded in ruthless sentiments and grim equations: it demanded that for every German soldier killed, fifty or a hundred hostages were to be shot; and of course the order was issued *via* the OKW. If we disregard for the moment the question —which has never been satisfactorily clarified in international law— of whether and when and under what circumstances an occupying power is entitled even to take hostages, let alone to kill them (although it has always been the custom of belligerent powers!) this kind of ratio of hostages to victims was obviously excessive.

In addition, the Soviet Union made repeated and successful attempts to parachute agents into both the Reich territory and the occupied or allied countries; an example of this would be the dropping of the Soviet Colonel Radinov into Bulgaria on 11th August, 1941, to take over control of the 'anti-fascist' partisan units fighting in this kingdom co-operating in the Balkans with the Reich. Radinov himself was soon captured and executed, but that did not kill off the 'Fatherland Front'; it gave it added momentum.

All this may go some way to explaining the prevailing situation. The decree contained in the OKW order of 16th September, 1941 relating to the 'Communist Resistance Movement in the Occupied Areas'* came long before the guerilla activity had reached its climax, which is clear proof of the futility of all such orders: they were only grist to the mill of the partisan movement.

The order relating to the communist resistance movement referred to the occupied territories in the east and south-east. It contained the typical Hitler justification:

> It is to be borne in mind that a human life is of no value in the countries concerned and that a deterrent effect can be achieved only by unusual severity.

Keitel went to some trouble to get the hostage-ratio reduced, but Hitler reinserted his own original figures, of from fifty to a hundred per German life. In accordance with the regulation Keitel had imposed upon himself, he put his own signature to the order, but with the preliminary formula:

> The Führer has now directed me that henceforth . . . etc.

By which the Chief of the High Command intended it to go on record that lengthy disputes had preceded the issuing of the order.

In contrast to the above order the second such 1941 order, the infamous so-called 'Cover of Darkness' decree of 7th and 12th December, 1941, was intended for the western territories and above all for France, which from the military and organisational point of view was technically under a military government subordinated not to the OKW but to the War Office, and more particularly to the

---

* The document, reference number WFSt./Abt.L (IV/Qu) Nr. 002060/41 g.Kdos., is among the papers of Dr. Nelte.

Army's Quartermaster-General. In France, too, communist subversive activities had strongly increased with the outbreak of the war with the Soviet Union. All these activities were actively supported by Britain, who parachuted sabotage and command units into France, Belgium, Holland and Norway, mainly in close collaboration with the governments-in-exile of the occupied countries, and of the armed units they had formed. One of their greatest triumphs was the assassination in May 1942 of the Deputy Reich Protector of Bohemia and Moravia and head of the Reich Main Security Office, SS-General Reinhard Heydrich; this operation was carried out by Czech agents parachuted into Bohemia from a British aircraft and resulted in Hitler's Commando Order in the autumn of 1942.

The *modus operandi* of the communists in France was characterised by one of their first murders, that of the military commandant of Nantes, Lieutanant-Colonel Hotz. Here they were able to remove a capable officer, who was particularly popular with the local population, and thereby caused actual damage to the occupying power; secondly, an officer well-fitted to prevent any flowering of their underground movement was eliminated; and thirdly, the stupidity of Hitler's occupation regime being what it was, it could be expected that the execution of hostages would follow which again would not have any effect on the communists as by ancient custom the hostages were always rounded up from among the most prominent citizens.

The Nantes assassination was not an isolated incident. According to a note written by Keitel for his defence counsel* Hitler insisted that they alter their methods of combating such attacks, not only on people but also on industrial plant, railway installations, high-tension lines, and so on: death-sentences, he now said, only created martyrs and they were to be pronounced only in those cases which could be established beyond any shadow of doubt. Otherwise, all suspects in cases which could not be cleared up at once were to be transferred immediately to Germany after a court martial investigation of the charges; in Hitler's terminology, they were to be hauled across the frontier under 'cover of darkness' (*bei Nacht und Nebel*). The hearing was to be kept secret, especially from the defendant's next of kin, while the cases themselves were to be disposed of in Germany.

There were bitter disputes around this order. Keitel and the head of his legal department both had the most cogent objections to it.

* Folder III/15, among the Nelte Papers: *Nacht und Nebel*, a handwritten note by Keitel dated 12th February 1946.

During the debates Hitler reproached Keitel that nobody could suggest that he, Hitler, was not a full-blooded revolutionary or that he did not know how to set about starting revolutions; so who was there to know any better than he how to set about suppressing them?

Keitel finally issued the order, with the significant preamble that it was 'the carefully weighed and considered will of the Führer that . . .' and so forth. By this sentence he meant it to go on record that much controversy had preceded the issuing of the order, but that the Führer's will had proved unshakeable. Keitel himself believed that by insisting on a preliminary court martial review of the evidence on whether to pass judgment at once or transport the defendants to Germany, and by instructions that the secret state police were to deliver the prisoners to the courts immediately they had arrived at their German destination, he had built sufficient safeguards into the order to maintain the correct legal procedures. He himself doubted whether the order as a whole would have any effect. In fact it led to a series of disputes both with the French authorities and with the German Armistice Commission in France as the French asked for the next-of-kin to be notified at least in the event of death-sentences. That this order gave the secret state police the opportunity to channel large numbers of prisoners into the concentration camps was unknown to Keitel until he learned of it for the first time at the International Military Trial at Nuremberg.

In his note on the genesis of the 'Cover of Darkness' decree, he commented:

> *Obviously*, for my name to have been linked with this decree is highly incriminating against me, although it is a clear case of an order issued by the Führer . . .

But it was no part of the Chief of the High Command's responsibilities to modify the terms of application of such decrees. For him to have had the authority to require reports on the procedures adopted in at least the first such cases would have required his being granted a much broader insight into the methods of the secret state police and the concentration-camp system than he ever actually commanded. He assumed that the OKW's orders were being obeyed to the letter.

Quite apart from the strategic air offensive against German cities, the methods whereby Britain initially prosecuted her war against her Continental enemies—involving the dropping of paratroop commandos supported by sabotage units comprised of members of the armed forces of the governments-in-exile, and major or minor armed reconnaissances of the French and Norwegian coasts—evoked new and explosive reactions from Hitler.

One consequence was the OKW's ordinance issued on 4th August, 1942, on 'Combatting Lone Parachutists', signed by Keitel, and the 'Commando Order' of 18th October, 1942, which Hitler himself signed.

The OKW ordinance defined that where there were security-police and security-service agencies in the Reich and in the occupied territories, the combatting of parachutists was to be left to them. Parachutists captured by members of the armed forces were to be handed over to the security service; if it transpired that the prisoners were enemy servicemen, then they were to be turned over yet again to the Air Force authorities. Hitler found this ordinance too feeble.*

After the August 1942 Anglo-Canadian landing at Dieppe, an armed reconnaissance for possible later invasion operations, it was reported that the enemy had shackled German prisoners of war and that regulations existed to kill the prisoners if they were found to be too much of a burden for the Allied troops to withdraw with them. Hitler's anger was particularly roused by this: against fierce opposition, above all from Colonel-General Jodl, the 'Commando Order' was formulated, decreeing that all members of commando or sabotage units were to be killed. They were to be wiped out either in the course of the fighting or while trying to escape, whether they were armed or not. Any prisoners were to be turned over to the security service where they had been apprehended by security patrols, and the security service was to hand them over to the armed forces. If such people were to surrender voluntarily to military units, they were to be shown no mercy. Any officers contravening this order were threatened with the direst punishments.

That was a blow to every accepted military tradition.

Keitel describes how both he and Jodl intended to refrain from reporting any further on such incidents, in order to let the thing blow over. Thereupon Hitler himself drafted the order. It was complied with only to varying extents, as by its very nature it needed to be constantly brought up to date. For example, with an order dated 30th July, 1944, Keitel was obliged expressly to forbid the application of the Commando Order to members of enemy military missions operating with partisan groups in the south-eastern and south-western military regions, the Balkans and Italy respectively.†

* Folder III/16, Nelte Papers: Commando operations, re: Nuremberg Documents PS-553, the leaflet of 4th August, 1942, and PS-503, the Führer's order of 18th October, 1942. Keitel's answers to questions put by Nelte on 23rd March, 1946.
† Nuremberg Document PS-537.

On the other hand it did have tragic consequences in the initial stages: when for example on the night of 20th November, 1942, a glider which had been flown across from England crashed at Egersund in Norway, together with its towing aircraft, a Wellington bomber, causing the death of several members of the crew, the remaining fourteen men, who were all more or less severely injured, were taken prisoner and on the orders of the commanding officer of the 280th infantry division they were all shot in accordance with the Commando Order.*

Even more violently did Hitler react to the overthrow of the fascist government in Italy and the crossing of the legitimate government under King Victor Emanuel III and his Prime Minister, Marshal Badoglio, into the Allied camp. He decreed that officers of the Italian armed forces, who were in accordance with his orders to be interned, were to be treated as 'insurgents' if they offered armed resistance, and shot. This cost the lives of both General Antonio Gandin, commander of the Acqui infantry division on the Greek island of Cephalonia, and known to Keitel from his dealings with the Italians, and his deputy; both fell to the bullets of a German firing squad.

Everywhere the picture was the same. Hitler reacted explosively to any methods adopted by the enemy of which he disapproved, and often they were methods of a very illegal nature. In the state of excitement into which he then worked himself it was virtually impossible to point out obstacles of an objective or legalistic nature. Often there were wearying debates, which almost always ended with capitulation to him. The fundamental problem was this: the war in the east was producing terrible acts of cruelty committed by the Russians against German injured soldiers and prisoners of war; by its very nature partisan warfare was unrestricted. But for a country which was claiming so loudly to be the saviour of western civilisation it would have been more fitting to have insisted on the most rigid maintenance of traditional discipline and military honour.

Where troops or their individual commanders had spontaneously reacted with violence then it would normally have been up to their superiors, even by establishing courts martial, to establish whether the proper scale of reprisals had been exceeded. Hitler went exactly the opposite way: he normalised what would otherwise have been occasional, and under certain circumstances pardonable, acts of

* See Nuremberg Document PS-508, a minute reference WFSt./Op.(L) dated 21st November, 1942, among Dr. Nelte's papers; the report sent in by Captain von Liliensk-joeld, intelligence officer of the Fifth Air Group (Norway).

violence and made terrorism the order of the day. Once again one is forced to ask whether the Chief of Hitler's military chancellery was obliged to go along with all this. Certainly he was not. But Hitler would never have permitted this field-marshal, who had become so indispensable to him in so many ways, to go. Several times Keitel demanded to be posted elsewhere, but each time in vain.

The more fiercely the war was prosecuted, the more the so-called 'Severity Orders' multiplied. There still remain several accusations which were unjustly brought forward against Keitel, but which also illuminate the difficult position of the Chief of the High Command.

It proved impossible, but not for lack of effort on the prosecution's part, to implicate the field-marshal in having planned or even ordered the murder of two of France's leading generals, General Weygand and General Giraud. It was in fact the Giraud case—in 1942 the general had managed to escape from Königstein fortress near Dresden—that had called Hitler's suspicious attention to what seemed in his view to be certain shortcomings in the prisoner-of-war system.* It was a fact that in this field the old customary military proprieties were still observed. Among the files of Keitel's defence counsel are references to one case where the Munich secret state police authorities had complained about the commander of the prisoners of war in Military District VII, Bavaria; the latter, Major-General von Saur, was accused of impeding the work of a special squad of secret state police working in the POW's camps to single out the communists, Jews and intellectuals among the Soviet prisoners for 'special treatment', in other words for liquidation.

As far as prisoners of war were concerned, the OKW only had purely ministerial and supervisory functions. In any case, the air force and the navy maintained their own camps. But particularly after General Giraud's escape, Hitler's distrust had been awakened and it was nourished by the SS Reichsführer, who recommended that the prisoner of war system should be supervised by the police authorities, a demand that was impossible in international law.

It happened that on the night of 25th March, 1944, eighty Royal Air Force officers made an escape attempt from Stalag Luft III at Sagan in Silesia, a prisoner of war camp of about twelve thousand men; among the eighty were a number of Belgian, French, Greek, Norwegian, Polish and Czech volunteers who had been serving with the R.A.F. They had dug a tunnel under the barbed wire

* This is based on file on the Sagan incident among the Nelte papers, and a file on POWs; also on Nuremberg Document R-178 (Von Saur case).

to freedom. Four of them were captured in the tunnel itself, while the other seventy-six won an illusory freedom. Three of them were never traced again, while fifteen were picked up at once in the ensuing manhunt and returned to camp; this, thanks to Keitel's intervention, saved their lives. Eight more fell at once, or soon after, into the hands of the secret state police, but were spared the fate of the remaining fifty officers who were picked up again at various locations in the Reich and shot, a crime which was laid at Keitel's feet at Nuremberg.

Mass escapes like that were a *cause célèbre* in the services; the finger was pointed at the camp commandant, Colonel Friedrich-Wilhelm von Lindeiner-Wildau, and he was relieved of his command for negligence of duty and sentenced to a period of fortress confinement by the Central Air Force Court. At the midday war conference at Berchtesgaden on 25th March, 1944, the SS Reichsführer zealously reported the escape of eighty British air force officers from Camp Sagan, and willingly depicted the consequences; the *Landwacht*, a paramilitary auxiliary police formation, would have to be alerted and that would cost millions of manhours and so on.

Hitler's reaction was immediate: the escapees were to be turned over to the police, and he added the outrageous afterthought that they were to be shot. Even those who had already been picked up were to be turned over to Himmler. Keitel replied sharply that that was a violation of the Geneva convention; all prisoners of war were after all servicemen, and according to their traditional code of honour escape attempts were virtually an unwritten obligation on them. According to Keitel, Hitler abided stubbornly by his own decision: 'Himmler, don't you let the escaped airmen out of your hands again.'

This time the field-marshal stuck to his guns, but his only achievement was the concession that the airmen who had been picked up already and were back in camp would not be turned over to the Reich's supreme chief of police. For the fifty other officers he could do nothing, and between 6th April and 18th May, 1944, they were all shot.

After this incident, he himself summoned the OKW's Inspector-General for Prisoner of War Affairs, Major-General von Graevenitz, and his prospective successor, Colonel Adolf Westhoff, the head of the Inspector-General's general office, and talked very angrily to them about the affair. Both of the officers were deeply dismayed by the implications, as they knew full well that the summary execution of prisoners of war for trying to escape represented a breach of international law which might well bring unpredictable consequences for our own prisoners of war.

After the war, Westhoff gave his own version of the affair to an American interrogator, Colonel Curtis L. Williams, who wrote an exaggerated report on the interrogation which gave the impression that Keitel had actually demanded that the escaped officers were to be shot. But a careful review of the evidence, and Major-General Westhoff's testimony in court proved it impossible to blame Keitel for the execution of the fifty R.A.F. officers. As far as Keitel is concerned, both the Sagan case and the earlier charge of having planned to have Weygand and Giraud assassinated lack any kind of substance, as do the accusations that he ordered the tattooing of Soviet prisoners and prepared for the waging of bacterial warfare against the Soviet Union.

A further accusation which has to be examined, of a similar nature, is the charge that the Chief of the High Command recommended the application of lynch law against the so-called Allied 'terror fliers', and had paved the way for orders to that effect. The whole lynch-law complex, and the peculiar problems presented by the Allied area bombardment policies, provide a useful example of the unique position of the officer at the Führer's headquarters, and of the need to exercise extreme caution in judging many apparently well-documented crimes of the Third Reich; often it will be found that the sole purpose of the central figures was to create a paper war around certain questions and prosecute this paper war for as long as was necessary for the whole matter to be dropped and filed, because Hitler had either forgotten all about it or had become interested in new problems.*

The question of whether one ought to, and indeed could, emulate the terrorism of the 'terror fliers' first arose in Hitler's mind early in the summer of 1944 in view of the virtually complete air superiority of the Allied bomber squadrons and long-range fighter escorts over the Reich. Once again, Hitler wanted to re-fashion what had previously been isolated and spontaneous acts of violence by the enraged local populations of blitzed cities against Allied airmen who had been shot down and were as prisoners of war in the protective custody of German troops, into a specific and systematic programme of deterrence. Hitler's proposal greatly embarrassed Keitel and

* For the question of the treatment of Allied airmen, see folder III/17 among Nelte's papers (lynch law), and Colonel (G.S.) Herbert Büchs's testimony at Nuremberg, IMT, Vol. XV.

Jodl: members of the enemy air forces were servicemen and were only carrying out orders when they released their bombloads over German city areas or when they tried to paralyse the complex arteries of the German armaments industry, the traffic networks, by low-level machine-gunning attacks. Were not the members of the 'anti-aircraft regiment' responsible for launching V-1 flying bombs at London just as guilty of terrorist tactics? Where would this war end?

Field-Marshal Keitel and Colonel-General Jodl advised that the concept of 'terror flier' ought first to be clarified in the light of international law. Hitler was indignant. The field-marshal then proposed that initially an ultimatum ought to be issued to the enemy countries, with warnings of reprisals to follow. Hitler grew even more indignant; perhaps he recalled Keitel's suggestion that at least they ought to issue an ultimatum to Stalin before their attack on the Soviet Union. These generals, he said, were too 'unpractical'; he wanted deterrence by 'terrorism'.

The only hope now lay in prevaricating by prolonging the debate. The following procedures were put forward in the lengthy debate that followed:

1. Court-martialling the 'terror fliers'.
2. Turning the 'terror fliers' over to the police.
3. Releasing the 'terror fliers' to the tender mercies of the populace and lynch law, as both the Party and the Führer wished.

The field-marshal was later called to account for some of the marginalia on the various memoranda: he had noted, for example: 'Courts martial? That won't work.' In his own view only low-level strafing attacks with some attempt at aiming at targets could properly be termed 'terror attacks'. But in such instances there were only two outcomes: either the attack succeeded and the airman flew off, or he crashed and was killed. The field-marshal commented further: 'If one is to permit lynch law, it will be hard to establish guidelines.' That was the decisive point: the Chief of the High Command, the Chief of the OKW's operations staff and the normally reigning Commander-in-Chief of the Air Force, Reichsmarschall Göring, were as one in this: in this case there was and could be only one answer, they could never agree to lynch law. But they were obliged to prevaricate endlessly until the matter was finally dropped, and on this occasion the field-marshal did agree to such tactics, although he normally strove for the utmost propriety in his dealings.

There were lengthy discussions, involving the Reich Foreign Secretary and the Chief of the Reich Main Security Office, Kalten-brunner; there is on record an extensive correspondence dating from June 1944, involving Keitel and the Chief of Air Staff General Korten, in which they tried first of all to define what was meant by 'terror flier'. In a telegram dated 15th June, 1944 to Göring's adjutant, Keitel went into some detail with these terminological definitions, saying that one could consider only certain cases for 'special treatment' (in other words for turning over to the security service and execution) and these would be attacks on the civilian population, on individuals and on assemblies of individuals; firing on German airmen descending by parachute; machine-gun attacks on passenger trains, civilian and field hospitals and hospital trains.* Keitel asked in his telegram for *Herr Reichsmarschall's* agreement, satisfied that the latter would find sufficient new matters to raise.

Keitel's defence counsel asked him outright: 'Was such an order ever issued?' Keitel replied: 'No order was ever issued on this matter, and Hitler never returned to the question. He went out shortly afterwards to visit the eastern front and then, after 20th July, 1944, nobody mentioned anything about the affair any more.'

No order was ever issued. Only in one detail was Keitel mistaken: as was testified at Nuremberg by Major (G.S.) Herbert Büchs, the Air Staff Officer attached to the Chief of the military operations staff, Jodl, during March 1945 the question was raised once again at a bunker conference in Berlin, over which the last shadows were already lengthening; Hitler, after some prodding by the head of the party chancellery Martin Bormann, issued an order to Kalten-brunner that all 'bomber crews already arrived' and all bomber crews 'arriving' in the future were to be turned over to the security service by the Air Force and 'liquidated by the security service'.

After the Führer's conference, Büchs jumped on Keitel and said: 'The Führer's order is crazy.' Keitel replied: 'That may well be.' Büchs stressed that the Air Force would be keeping its banner clean, it would not execute the order. Keitel explained that Hitler did not want to sign such orders, so that it would all get hooked onto the OKW all the time: 'I am to be the devil who issues such orders.'

Later, Major Büchs was telephoned by Reichsmarschall Göring, asking him: 'Tell me, is Hitler quite out of his mind now, then?' The conversation ended with the Reichsmarschall saying: 'That's

* See Nuremberg Document PS-729, a memorandum signed by Keitel, reference number OKW Nr. 771793/44 g.K.Chefs. II Ang.F.St.Qu. (Verw. 1): 'Treatment of enemy terror fliers'.

all quite crazy, it can't be done.' Apart from Field-Marshal Keitel, General Koller, the Chief of the Air Force Operations Staff, was also against the 'lynch order', and it was never actually issued.

* * *

The struggle against such 'special orders', the conflict between one's judgment and the sheer impossibility of allowing one's judgment full play, and the necessity of launching paper wars in order to establish one's dutifulness while all the time trying to prevent or at any rate to modify totally illegal and dishonourable orders occupied by no means all of the time at the Führer's headquarters. But in the rarified atmosphere of Security Zone I of the Wolf's Lair it did have a strange effect on the officers brought together in Hitler's name to direct the affairs of the armed forces, and the effect grew more pronounced as each incident was followed by the next. To all this was now added the recognition that a normal victory in the traditional, Old Prussian sense was now out of the question, while it was equally impossible to establish a normal peace by negotiations and concessions, not only because of Hitler's whole character and attitude but because of the rigid demands for unconditional surrender formulated by the enemy nations. For senior officers like Keitel, who had been through both the defeat of 1918 and the 'peace' of Versailles this was a situation fraught with uncertainty.

The two most senior officers within this security zone, Field-Marshal Keitel and Colonel-General Jodl, were its prisoners, overwhelmed day after day by the enormous bureaucratic machinery of a war waged by eighty million Germans with an army of millions of soldiers, by the deskwork and the hourlong 'war conferences' which were in themselves microcosms of Nazi party conventions complete with speeches by the Führer. They were permanently overworked, like the directors of some vast industrial giant, and constantly exposed to Hitler's extraordinary ability to awaken false hopes in men and inspire their 'faith' in him. But as the flood tide of defeat rose and the crisis worsened, they were equally overwhelmed by the oppressive feeling that this one man alone might still find some way out; after all, he had survived so many crises before.

Keitel's basic attitude did not alter by one whit. He considered it his duty to associate himself publicly with the Führer's express orders, whatever bitter or even insulting exchanges might have preceded them, and thanks to his brusque insistence that these were 'the Führer's orders', he gave the impression to the worried frontline commanders protesting against them that he was just an 'amplifier' for Hitler's intentions. This above all was the cause of his extraordinary unpopularity among the General Staff; after the war he found no advocates among these latter, one-time comrades who now cursed his name and called him everything from 'Yes-Keitel' to 'the nodding ass'. But nobody was eager to lever Keitel out of office and take it upon himself; nor did Hitler believe that doing one's duty as a soldier was express proof of 'faith'; and he was probably never completely able to get over a certain lack of confidence in Keitel.

* * *

When the time-bomb detonated in the guest barracks, the so-called teahouse at the Wolf's Lair headquarters, shortly after 12.30 p.m. on 20th July, during the midday war conference, the last bastions which Keitel had sought to maintain were finally torn down. Colonel-General Jodl, who suffered head injuries in the blast, has described how Field-Marshal Keitel (also lightly wounded) carefully and solicitously helped the Führer, who had been only slightly scratched, out of the wrecked barracks; if one considers how cold had been the relations between Keitel and Hitler, it must have been a strange scene. According to the testimony of one of the Reichstag stenographers attached to the Führer's headquarters Hitler afterwards privately commented that it was only after this that he realised that Keitel was 'reliable' after all.

The bomb had been placed by Colonel Count Claus von Stauffenberg, a staff officer who had lost an eye while fighting with an armoured division in Tunisia. Keitel had originally introduced him to Hitler during conferences on reserve issues. It has been testified of Hitler that after Stauffenberg's first appearance he asked who this one-eyed Colonel was: he found Stauffenberg sinister.

Keitel had no insight into the world in which this desperate and aristocratic revolutionary of such high ideals and grim determination had moved and thought; the only quality in him that he found impressive in retrospect was a quality which he termed 'fanaticism'. The possibility that there could be an officers' revolt, a revolt in which aristocrats had been cast in the leading rôles, was unimaginable to Keitel.

During early 1943, Keitel was informed of the Oster case; it involved one of his own departments. Major-General Hans Oster, head of the central office of the OKW's Foreign Military Intelligence branch, was accused of having wrongly placed persons on the reserved list and indirectly of currency offences as well. But he was in fact guilty of far more: he was the chief of staff of a secret conspiracy against Hitler which never came to fruition. Like Stauffenberg, Oster had been body and soul a revolutionary, just as Schulze-Boysen of the '*Rote Kapelle*' had been in his own way. And like the latter he believed any means were justified provided they brought about Hitler's overthrow, for he considered Hitler to be the nation's destroyer. The political objectives of Oster and Schulze-Boysen were diametrically opposed to each other, but just as the latter had not hesitated to supply military Intelligence to the Bolsheviks, Oster did not hesitate to inform his friends in the west of, for example, the date of Hitler's invasion of France and the Netherlands in advance of the actual event.

The field-marshal only understood sufficient of the affair to see that it was apparently an embarrassment which had probably emerged from the kind of involved business which it was their Intelligence service's duty to transact. When a judge advocate informed Keitel during the course of the affair that he believed he could furnish him with evidence that Admiral Canaris, the head of the Foreign Military Intelligence branch, was guilty of nothing less than high treason, he handled him roughly as only Keitel could: how dare he suggest that one of the OKW's departmental heads was guilty of high treason? German admirals did not do such things. He threatened the unfortunate officer with a court martial and the allegations were hastily withdrawn; Oster himself was quietly pensioned off.*

Even when Admiral Canaris was arrested after the 20th July bomb plot and thrown into a concentration camp, the field-marshal still refused to believe he could be guilty in any way; he gave the admiral's family financial support. In the same way he refused to believe anything wrong of General Thomas, the head of his Military Economy branch, who was arrested at the same time. It was not departmental pride which inspired this disbelief in him; Keitel was literally too naïve an officer to believe that anybody he had known for years on end could have been playing a double game.

On the afternoon of 20th July, Colonel-General Fromm, Stauffenberg's superior, telephoned Keitel from Berlin to ask whether it was true that the Führer was dead? Keitel replied in the negative: it was true there had been an attempt on the Führer's life, but he

---

* Based on a folder among Dr. Nelte's papers, entitled 'General Thomas File: the Oster case'.

was only slightly wounded. And he asked where Fromm's chief of staff, Colonel Stauffenberg, was. The germs of suspicion were already there.

Next to Keitel, Colonel-General Fromm, an enemy of long-standing, was the biggest figure on the Armed Forces organisational scene. That very afternoon he was relieved of his command, a move he had not expected, particularly as he had originally been arrested by the conspirators in Bendlerstrasse; his successor was SS Reichsführer Heinrich Himmler. Keitel had lost the last great battle for control of the army and armed forces. He had always seriously believed he must hold on if only to prevent the SS from coming to power, but that was what had happened now. Keitel has repeatedly and insistently come back to one point in notes written for his defence counsel: it would never have occurred to him to have acted as the conspirators did. For him Hindenburg's words had always been emblazoned across his banner: 'Loyalty is the mark of honour'. And at Nuremberg, in his hour of misfortune, the words were doubly important to him.

That was why, while the Führer welcomed Mussolini to the Wolf's Lair, Keitel zealously set about countering all the orders for the *coup d'état* which had late that afternoon finally gone out to the Military District commanders. It has been said that this was a *coup d'état* by telephone and teleprinter; in the same way the *coup d'état* was crushed by telephone. For several hours that evening Keitel could and did issue orders again for the first time since his years at Bremen, and those were the hours that decided Germany's fate.

*   *   *

After the Hitler bomb plot, Field-Marshal Keitel wrote his first will, dated 2nd August, 1944; it expressly observed that he had escaped death in the bomb plot only by a miracle. He laid down in his will that Helmscherode, his main estate, should pass on to his eldest son; and he mentioned the £20,000 gift Hitler had made him on his sixtieth birthday, a sum which he had deposited untouched in his Bank in Berlin.

Keitel himself has described the end of the Third Reich in his *Memoirs*. In his final chapter of *Memoirs*, it is noticeable how little talk there is of any remaining concrete hopes; there could be no further hope of a diplomatic solution. In its stead the field-marshal tried to the very last to maintain the figure of Hitler as the supreme leader of the Reich, although Hitler himself was already determined to die in the battle of Berlin and was interested in diplomacy no

267

longer. The field-marshal probably had the impression that only one man could end the war now, and that was Hitler himself: if the Führer went, the Reich might crumble into anarchy. That Hitler might evade his ultimate responsibility by committing suicide was a possibility of which he never dreamed. It was because of his preoccupation with the prospect of the total collapse of law and order, if the worst came to the worst, that he was desperately worried about losing touch with the Führer's bunker beneath the Reich Chancellery in Berlin, even during the OKW's hazardous flight to Mecklenburg; it was a terrible blow when he learned it was no longer possible to fly in to Berlin.

On the other hand this final scene awakened the true soldier which had slumbered within him. The hands of the clock were standing at midnight, and there was not much more commanding to be done, but the field-marshal won back his independence, drove out to the front line, directed, gave orders, sent back commanders who seemed to have lost their head into the battle, and tried everything to accomplish the relief of Berlin. He refused to see how far the fighting spirit of the eastern armies had been ground away in almost four years of terrible fighting, how great had grown their naked fear of the Russians with their indescribable ravaging, their hordes of tanks and artillery divisions. The impetus of 1940 and 1942 was long spent, and the will to resist even more markedly consumed. Strict orders alone were no longer enough; only new squadrons of aircraft and fresh armoured divisions with full fuel tanks and munition racks could still have achieved something. But these the field-marshal could not supply, for there were none.

Then it was as though his long nightmare had come to an end: the news came that Hitler was dead. He realised that the war had to be ended.

Without doubt Field-Marshal Keitel was a changed man as, two weeks after Hitler's death, he was led off into captivity as a prisoner of war; but even as a 'war criminal' at Nuremberg he did not seek to save his own skin but only to expiate the actions of the German armed forces.

* * *

At the International Military Tribunal at Nuremberg, despite his outward lack of liberty as a prisoner and the often difficult conditions of prison life, the field-marshal was at last a free agent again after his long years as an officer dependent on a man he found so profoundly despotic. That he would be found guilty, whatever he might bring up in his own defence, he had realised as soon as he set eyes on the indictment, which was handed him on 19th October, 1945. The world was up in arms against him, against the Germans, after five and a half years of a terrible war with its terrible crimes against all natural law. He was no longer concerned to haggle and bargain for his own skin; his main objective was to establish his honour, and not only his own personal honour: he believed that it was his duty to uphold the honour of all German troops, because he was too honest not to admit to himself that he had frequently proved inadequate in his defence of the traditional concept of Prussian military honour; in addition to that, he wanted to make his own contribution to establishing historical truth. This and nothing more was what he endeavoured at Nuremberg.

On 1st October, 1946, the International Military Tribunal found him guilty on all four counts of the indictment: conspiracy to wage a war of aggression; waging a war of aggression; war crimes, and crimes against humanity. He was sentenced to death by hanging, and this sentence was executed on 16th October, 1946.

Notes

2: *The Blomberg-Fritsch Crisis, 1938.*

Colonel-General Wilhelm Heye (*page 36*) (1869–1946) Chief of the *Reichswehr's* Army Directorate (*Heeresleitung*) from 1926 to 1930.

Colonel-General Wilhelm Adam (1877–1949), Chief of the Troop Office from 1930 to 1933, as a Lieutenant-General; from 1935 to 1938 he was commandant of the Military Academy.

Lieutenant-Colonel (G.S.) (later Colonel-General) Kurt Zeitzler of the national defence department was chief of the Army General Staff from September 1942 to June 1944; he was relieved of his post on 20th July, 1944.

No details of the quarrels between Keitel and Beck, both of them poles apart in character, have hitherto come to light. All that is known is Beck's memorandum on the supreme command of the Armed Forces, dated 9th December, 1935 ('The Commander-in-Chief of the Army and his Immediate Adviser').

General Halder was at the time a lieutenant-general and commanding officer of the 7th infantry division. He was entrusted with the direction of the armed forces' manoeuvres and posted as Chief Quartermaster II to the General Staff in the autumn of 1937.

The appearance of a company of war correspondents at the manoeuvres (*page 38*) is explained by the fact that the units later to become famous as *Propaganda-Kompanien* were being tried out for the first time.

Lieutenant-General Erich Hoepner, the chief of staff to Rundstedt, later commander-in-chief of the Fourth Tank Army; in January 1942 he was dismissed the army by Hitler for 'disobedience'. He was involved in the 20th July, 1944, conspiracy; he was condemned to death on 8th August, 1944, and hanged.

Colonel-General Gerd von Rundstedt (1875–1953) Commander-in-Chief of the First Army Group.

Major-General Oshima (*page 40*) was the Japanese military attaché in Berlin and later the Japanese ambassador; he was a disciple of the Japanese army, which aspired to a military treaty with Germany.

General Hans von Seeckt (1866–1936) was from 1922 to 1936 Chief of the Army Directorate; he visited China in 1933 and then again from 1934 to 1935, ending up as President Chiang-Kai-Shek's 'general adviser'.

Marshal Chiang-Kai-Shek was president of China from 1929 to 1949.

General Alexander von Falkenhausen, the German military adviser, was recalled from China in 1938; from 1940 to 1944 he was military commander of Belgium and northern France.

Lutz, Count Schwerin von Krosigk, was Reich Minister of Finance from 1932 to 1945; Kung Hsiang-hsi was the Chinese Finance Minister.

The activity of the German military advisers to Chiang-Kai-Shek in China did not end until 1938.

Field-Marshal Keitel has not referred at all to Hitler's conference with the service Commanders-in-Chief and the Reich Foreign Secretary on 5th November, 1937, in which Hitler, according to Hossbach's minutes of the meeting, dwelt upon a possible outbreak of war.

Major Georg von der Decken was killed in action as a colonel in 1945. General (ret.) Erich Ludendorff had been the Chief Quartermaster General of the Army

Notes

General Staff in the First World War, from 1916 to 1918; his state funeral took place on 24th December 1937 in Munich. Von Blomberg was promoted to *Generalfeldmarschall* on 20th April, 1936. Blomberg's wedding took place on 12th January, 1938.

The Chief of Berlin Police (*page 43*), SA-General and Cavalry captain (ret.) Wolf-Heinrich, Count von Helldorf (1896–1944) probably had his first interview with Keitel on 23rd January, 1938; Blomberg returned from Eberswalde to Berlin on 24th January, 1938, the day on which the Blomberg-Fritsch crisis began. Blomberg's interview with Keitel must have taken place on 26th January, 1938; Jodl noted in his diary: '26th January: 12.00 noon, General Keitel informs me on his word of honour that the *Generalfeldmarschall* has been overthrown'. Keitel's description tends to support the statement by Captain Fritz Wiedemann (who at the time of the crisis was Hitler's personal adjutant) that in 1938 Göring had been aspiring to the Supreme Command of the Armed Forces in order to become the real 'second man' in the State.

Keitel's first interview with Hitler on the crisis (*page 46*) must have been on 26th January.

Hjalmar Schacht (to whom Keitel wrongly refers in his original text as being 'Minister of Finance' as well as President of the Reichsbank) occupied the latter post from 1933 to 1939; from 1934 to 1937 he was additionally Reich Minister of Economics. It is clear that the name 'Keitel' meant nothing to Hitler at this time, for according to Hossbach, (*page 131*) he announced that he wanted to have a talk with 'this General von Keitel'.

Hossbach's (*page 47*) memoirs reveal nothing of any animosity towards Keitel in his period as adjutant to the Führer. Keitel, on the other hand, not without reason, thought Hossbach was a strong-man and champion of Beck's policies who had somehow managed to work himself into a strong position at Hitler's side.

Franz Gürtner (1881–1941) had been Reich Minister of Justice since 1932 in the Cabinets of von Papen, Schleicher and Hitler. The document that Hitler showed Keitel can only have been a legal opinion by Gürtner on the file on Fritsch which had been cooked up by the secret state police authorities. The interview between Hitler and Colonel-General von Fritsch took place, on Colonel Hossbach's insistence, as early as the evening of 26th January, 1938.

Hitler's version of the 'recognition of Fritsch' told to Keitel (*page 48*) was not accurate.

There is evidence that Keitel was alive to the possibility that there had been an intrigue against the body of the Armed Forces; Jodl noted in his diary on 3rd February the remarks made by Schacht to the effect that the whole thing was obviously an SS intrigue aimed against the Armed Forces command. But Jodl drew no conclusions from this.

On page 50 Keitel referred originally to von Brauchitsch as being in command of an 'armoured group being raised in Leipzig'; this has been corrected to the 'Fourth Army Group'.

Dr. Hans Heinrich Lammers had been Secretary of State and Head of the Reich Chancellery since 1933, a Reichsminister without Portfolio.

The major Cabinet reshuffle accompanying the crisis (*page 51*) brought Joachim von Ribbentrop to the German Foreign Office in place of Freiherr von Neurath, while the latter was appointed President of a purely paper body, the Privy Cabinet Council, which never once met.

The memorandum handed to Keitel by Blomberg must have been the one composed by Lieutenant-General von Manstein.

Reinhard Heydrich, a retired naval lieutenant, was head of the Reich security service and chief of the Reich Main Security Office from 1939 until 1943 when he was murdered.

On the subject of Keitel's comments that nobody was eager to replace him as Chief of the OKW (*page 53*) Vice-Admiral Leopold Bürkner recorded that he

271

Notes

'never met one officer during the whole war who would have been prepared voluntarily to take over the thorny office of Chief of the OKW'.

Generalfeldmarschall Milch has testified at Nuremberg that Blomberg was the only senior soldier who was in a position to resist Hitler, and who had done so very often: 'This resistance could not be kept up by the men around Hitler later on. They were too weak for that. That is probably why he chose them.'

3: From Austria to the end of the French Campaign, 1938–1940.

Friedrich Hossbach had been simultaneously departmental head of Central Office of the Army's General Staff and armed forces adjutant to the Führer.

Admiral Karl Dönitz (born 1892) was promoted Grand-Admiral and Commander-in-Chief of the German Navy in January 1943, in succession to Grand Admiral Raeder.

There were in fact a number of personnel changes in the War Office: the chief of army personnel, General von Schwedler; the Chief Quarter-master of the Army General Staff, Lieutenant-General von Manstein; and the armed forces adjutant Colonel Hossbach were all relieved of their posts. In addition, three commanding generals—von Leeb, von Kleist, and von Kressenstein—were dismissed. All of them were officers who were disinclined to meet Hitler's requirements (with which Brauchitsch had concurred) that they should associate the armed forces more closely with National Socialist doctrines.

Keitel's brother (*page 55*) was Major-General Bodewin Keitel, Chief of Army Personnel from 1938 to 1942. Keitel's account of the outcome of the Fritsch trial and the part played by Göring is very one-sided; the credit for Fritsch's acquittal is largely due to his defence counsel, Count von der Goltz. Keitel had not realised in 1946 that Hitler himself was one of the first to exploit the smear campaign against Fritsch. The demands for Fritsch's rehabilitation, summarised by General Beck, Admiral Canaris and Colonel Hossbach, were: Fritsch's complete and public rehabilitation; an announcement of the reasons for his original dismissal and a review of the leadership of the SS and of the Secret State Police headquarters; Himmler, Heydrich, Dr. Best and a number of others were to be dismissed.

Keitel's description of General Beck's activities are not accurate. To Keitel, it was unthinkable for a soldier in a responsible position to express conscientious opposition to his superiors. In 1938 Beck recorded his views: 'A highly placed soldier would be deficient in greatness and would be failing to recognise his duty if at times like these he looked at his duties and functions only in the restricted sense of the military role he had been given to perform; exceptional circumstances demand exceptional methods . . .' As for Colonel Hossbach, he was not so much 'deeply embittered' (*see* Keitel, *page 56*) as gravely worried about developments; Keitel had insisted upon his removal from Hitler's entourage as a dangerous champion of Beck's ideas.

Keitel's reference to the 'loss' of Brauchitsch (*page 56*) is an allusion to the latter's removal at his own request from the post of Commander in Chief of the Army during the crisis of the battle for Moscow on 19th December, 1941. Hitler himself then became C.-in-C. of the Army.

Kurt Edler von Schuschnigg (born 1897), Federal Austrian Chancellor, from 1934 to 1938.

General von Reichenau, Commander-in-Chief of the Fourth Army Group (Leipzig). Air Force General Hugo Sperrle commanded the Condor Legion in Spain and was Commander in Chief elect of the Third Air Group (Munich).

Guido Schmid had been Austrian Secretary of State for Foreign Affairs since 1936.

Notes

Lieutenant-General Max von Viebahn was chief of the OKW's embryo operations staff from February to April 1938. General Fedor von Bock was commander in chief of the Eighth Army, which was standing by to enter Austria.

Nothing is known of a 'telephone conversation' (*page 59*) between Hitler and Mussolini at this time; on 13th March Hitler sent Mussolini a telegram from Linz: 'Duce, I will never forget you for this. Adolf Hitler.'

Arthur Seyss-Inquart was Federal Austrian Chancellor for two days from 11th to 13th March, 1938, before the union. From 1940 to 1945 he was Reich Commissioner for the Netherlands.

Friedrich, Count von der Schulenburg (*page 60*) (1865–1939), a former artillery general and member of the National Socialist Party with an honorary rank in the SS.

Colonel-General Freiherr von Fritsch (*page 61*) was acquitted on 13th March, 1938. On Canaris, Keitel wrote that he had always been 'a riddle and a book with seven seals'. In this case, Keitel's mistrust was unjustified; the prosecution witness had been executed without a court hearing.

On 5th May, 1938, General Beck had on his own initiative composed a memorandum on 'Thoughts on the Military and Political Position of Germany.' In view of Britain's attitude, Beck held that a political alliance against Germany would be a likely outcome of the Czech developments; he warned against belligerent actions and stressed that Germany could never win a European war. The 1937 memorandum referred to had originally been drafted by Lieutenant-General von Manstein and was newly tabled by the C.-in-C. Army on 7th March, 1938.

Dr. Fritz Todt (*page 64*), Air Force Major-General and Inspector-General of German road construction, was entrusted with the construction of the West Wall in 1938; in 1940 he became Reichminister of Armaments and Munitions. Pioneer-General Foerster was responsible for the construction of fortifications, not the General Staff.

Keitel's chronology is a bit obscure at this point (*page 65*). Beck himself read out his memorandum of 16th July, 1938, to the commanding generals in the presence of Brauchitsch early in August. In July, Beck had tried verbally to convince Brauchitsch of the dangers of the 'SS and gangster-ocracy'. All this therefore refers, not to the memorandum of 5th May, 1938, but to yet a third memorandum of Beck; its predecessor had been a memo of 3rd June, 1938, in which he had expressed the view that even if the Czech campaign were to be successful, Germany would lose the major war and he turned sharply against the existing 'anarchy' in the leadership of the armed forces. On 18th August, 1938, Beck asked the C.-in-C. Army to relieve him of his office as Chief of General Staff. On 27th he handed over to his successor General Halder. His final discharge from the army followed on 31st October, 1938. Despite the Führer's categoric refusal to post Beck elsewhere (*page 65*), Beck was earmarked for the war command of Third Army Group until the time of his final discharge. There are two possible reasons for Keitel's bitter tirade: firstly, in Keitel's view, Beck refused to take seriously the plans which Keitel and Jodl had worked out for the reform of the services' command structure; secondly, Beck had a faculty for cool and considered judgement which Keitel had often observed to his own discomfort. Beck certainly did not 'make common cause' with Germany's enemies (*page 66*). Beck has recorded that the concepts of revolution and mutiny must find no place in the German soldier's dictionary, but in contrast to Keitel, he did consider it to be part of the soldier's duty to dabble in politics.

The visit paid by British Prime Minister Sir Neville Chamberlain to the Berghof took place on 15th September, 1938.

Lieutenant-General Karl-Heinrich von Stülpnagel acted as Chief Quartermaster under Halder. A close friend of Beck, he had already been initiated in the secret plans to prevent Hitler starting a new war.

The Münich talks referred to (*page 70*) were on 29th September, 1938.

Notes

Edouard Daladier was French Prime Minister; André François-Poncet was French Ambassador to Berlin. Czechoslovakia—not represented at these Münich talks—was obliged to agree to the cession of the Sudeten land on 30th September. General Ritter von Leeb had been relieved of his post as C.-in-C. Second Army Group during the Fritsch crisis. General Adam himself asked to be relieved of his post. He had already been dismissed from the Troop Office because of his negative attitude to National Socialism.

General Erwin von Witzleben (1881–1944) commanded the Third Army Corps in Berlin; in October he succeeded Adam as C.-in-C. Second Army Group; he was deeply involved in the September crisis and the plan for a coup d'état. He was hanged after the Bomb Plot of 1944.

The OKW 'Directive for Deployment and Battle' referred to by Keitel (*page 75*) is an allusion to the 'Directive to the Armed Forces, 1939–1940'. Part II set the objective of readiness by 1st September, 1939, to destroy 'Poland's defence potential' if relations with Poland were to deteriorate. There was in other words a very offensive 'defensive purpose'.

Colonel Rudolf Toussaint was commander of the army district of Bohemia and Moravia from 1944 to 1945. Emil Hacha (1872–1945) was President of the Czech Republic from 1938 to 1939; 1939 to 1945 he was President of the Government of the Bohemian and Moravian protectorates.

Joachim von Ribbentrop was German Foreign Secretary from 1938 to 1945. The reference to the Witkowitz region (*page 79*) is explained thus: during the Sudetenland crisis of 1938, Poland had annexed the Olsa region.

The 'independent Slovak state' (*page 87*) had declared its independence of the Czecho-Slovak federation and had accepted the protection of the Reich; Josef Tiso became Prime Minister; Ferdinand Durczansky became Foreign Secretary and Deputy Prime Minister; Voytech Tuka became Minister of the Interior.

Marshal Joseph Pilsudski (1867–1935) controlled Polish diplomacy from 1926. Colonel Joseph Beck (1894–1944) was Polish Foreign Secretary from 1932 to 1939.

General Johannes Blaskowitz was commander-in-chief of the Eighth Army in Rundstedt's Army Group South.

That Hitler had *asked* for Stalin's military intervention (*page 98*) has not hitherto been revealed. The Red Army began its invasion of Eastern Poland on 17th September, 1939, in order, as the Soviets officially claimed, to safeguard the western frontiers of the U.S.S.R.

No documents relating to this first attempt by Keitel to resign (*page 100*) have come to light after the war; they were probably destroyed with Hitler's private papers in 1945. Keitel's repeated requests to be sent to the front have been confirmed by Colonel General Jodl among others.

That there *were* lapses in discipline among the German troops (*page 102*) is shown by the extra regulations drawn up in November 1939 and April 1940.

Keitel's insistence on Hitler's authorship of the tactical plan of attack on France (*page 103*) is more than the facts would seem to warrant. The latter had—in line with his own ideas—developed a plan to mass a second armoured attacking force in the middle of the front with Sédan and the Ardennes as the general direction of its thrust; this plan only took detailed shape in the draft of Lieutenant-General von Manstein, then chief of staff to Army Group A (Keitel: Army Group Centre). Hitler admittedly undertook to work to this plan and probably began to regard it as his. Tank-General Heinz Guderian commanded the Nineteenth Army Corps; General Paul von Kleist was commander in chief of the 'armoured group' subordinate to Army Group A.

Vidkun Quisling (*page 104*) headed the Norwegian government during the occupation; he was also Reich Commissioner. Keitel exaggerated the operation as purely naval; the Army General Staff was not called in, but the operation could not have been executed without the Air Staff.

Notes

Josef Terboven (1898–1945), a former bank clerk, became Gauleiter of Essen; from 1940 to 1945 he was Reich Commissioner for Norway and committed suicide in 1945.

Keitel's description of the courier to the Queen of the Netherlands refers to Captain Kiewitz's mission (*page 106*). Kiewitz was not arrested; the Dutch government refused to allow him to enter the country. Adolf Freiherr von Steengracht was Under-Secretary at the German Foreign Office from 1943 to 1945.

Admiral Canaris was not the 'traitor' in this instance, though he may have known that Colonel Oster had passed information to the Dutch military attaché in Berlin. The Dutch chief of Intelligence did not believe that the warnings were genuine because he thought that no German staff officer would betray his country in this way.

Marshal Henri Philippe Pétain was French Prime Minister at the time and headed the new French government at Vichy.

4: Prelude to the attack on Russia, 1940–1941.

Marshal Graziani was Italian Commander-in-Chief, Libya, in succession to Marshal Italo Balbo, who had been shot down by his own anti-aircraft guns. The Innsbruck Conference took place on 14th and 15th November, 1940.

Colonel Freiherr von Funck was commander of the 5th light infantry division; he left for Libya on 15th January, 1941, after his division had been detailed to act as a 'blocking force' in north Africa.

The whereabouts of the important *memorandum* (*page 122*) are not known. It can be assumed that it was burnt, either with Hitler's private papers or with those of the OKW operations staff. His version here can be compared with his statement at Nuremberg: "At that time, as has been briefly discussed here by the Foreign Secretary, I wrote a personal memorandum containing my thoughts on the subject, I should like to say, independently of the experts working in the General Staff and the Armed Forces operations staff, and wanted to present this memorandum to Hitler. I decided on that method because, as a rule, one could never get beyond the second sentence of a discussion with Hitler; he took the words out of one's mouth."

Molotov (*page 123*) visited Berlin on 12th to 13th November, 1940. Keitel's reference to Stalin purging his military 'elite' (*page 124*) refers to the execution in June 1937 of Marshal Tukhachevsky and a series of other senior generals who had for the most part been participants in the close collaboration with the German *Reichswehr*, and to Stalin's subsequent purge of the Red Army's officer corps.

The Führer's meeting first with Pétain and then with General Franco took place in October, 1940 (Keitel: 'Early in September'). Pierre Laval was at the time the French Prime Minister. Franco and Hitler met on 23rd October, 1940, at Hendaye (Keitel: 'Andechnel(?)'), on the Spanish frontier. Serrano Suñer was the Spanish Foreign Secretary from 1939 to 1941.

Mussolini's letter to Hitler announcing his plan to attack Greece (*page 126*) reached the German Führer on 25th October, 1940, at Yvoir, south of Namur. The instigator of the plan was not the Italian Foreign Secretary, Count Ciano, but Mussolini himself. Hitler, in his now well-known table-talk in the Berlin bunker in 1945, even went so far as to say that Mussolini's 'encore' in Greece was the reason why he, Hitler, had lost the war: it was the beginning of the end.

Keitel's reference to the 'Vienna Award' (*page 128*) concerns the agreement reached on the delimitation of the frontier between Hungary and Roumania on 30th August, 1940. The King who went into exile from Roumania (*page 128*) was King Carol II, who abdicated in favour of his son Michael on 6th September, 1940. The new Head of State was General Jon Antonescu, Chief of the General

Notes

Staff, who had been declared *'Condocaturul'* (Head of State) two days earlier, keeping this office under King Michael until 23rd August, 1944. King Boris III (King of Bulgaria from 1894 to 1943) was the son-in-law of King Victor Emanuel III of Italy.

Yugoslavia joined the Axis Pact on 25th March, 1941 (*page 131–2*), the Yugoslav Prime Minister Zvetkovic signing on behalf of his country and aligning his country thereby with the German Reich, Italy and Japan.

Air-Force General Wolfram Freiherr von Richthofen was at the time commanding general of the Eighth Air Corps. General Vigon was chief of the Spanish Secret Service. The plan of attack for *Felix*, the Spanish campaign, provided for the operation of the Forty-Ninth Army Corps under infantry General Kübler, and Richthofen's Eighth Air Corps. Field-Marshal von Reichenau was to be placed in overall command. There is no doubt that Admiral Canaris did not exhort Franco to comply over Gibraltar. In any event, Spain was in no position to fight a war and nobody knew that better than General Franco. Hitler did not—as Keitel assumes—want only transit permission for his troops, but also a military alliance between Spain and the Reich; it was simply the law of survival that compelled the Spanish to keep out of the affair, and it was this that General Franco made plain to Canaris on 7th December, 1940.

The conference at which Halder outlined plans for the attack on Russia (*page 134*) was probably the Führer conference of 3rd February, 1941. The subsequent conference at the end of March' was on 30th March, 1941, in Berlin.

Keitel's reference to that clause of the 'Directions' referring to Himmler (*page 136*) is explained by the content of the OKW's 'Directions'; according to these, SS-Reichsführer Heinrich Himmler was entrusted with 'special' duties of the autonomous nature appropriate when war broke out between two 'diametrically opposed ideologies'. So the formulation of these 'special duties', the basis for the later activities of the 'special operations' units of the Security Service, had commenced even before Hitler's address of 30th March, 1941! Hitler's Decree on Liability to Courts Martial in the *Barbarossa* area was circulated on 13th May, 1941; according to this, excesses committed by German troops were not necessarily to be punished if they were committed against the civil population.

In both cases (i.e. the 'Commissar' and the 'Liability to Court Martial' orders) the orders were indisputably 'OKW-orders'.

Keitel wrongly wrote 'Zimowice' for Zvetkovic (*page 138*). General Zimowic was the leader of the military *Putsch* in Belgrade on 27th March, 1941, by which Prince-Regent Paul of Yugoslavia and his Prime Minister Svetkovic were overthrown. Demetrius von Sztojay (text: 'Sztoyay') was the Royal Hungarian Minister in Berlin.

For Hungary the position was not entirely as Keitel saw it in his recollections (*page 140*). She was being obliged to abandon the Imperial Administrator's chosen course of non-intervention in the war.

Tank-General Erwin Rommel (*page 142*) was C.-in-C. of the German Africa Corps in Libya, comprising one light infantry and one armoured division. Keitel's description of the battle for Crete has been drastically edited, as it contained little of consequence.

Josip Broz-Tito (*page 143*), the present Head of State in Yugoslavia, was at the time leader of the communist partisan groups in southern Serbia, Bosnia and Herzegovina; Keitel's accusations against the security forces of the Italian Ninth Army in the Balkans are unjustified; they may well occasionally have sought to establish contacts with the Serbian (anti-communist) Chetniks, but they never supported Tito.

The conference held by Hitler in the 'middle of June' (*page 144*) prior to the attack on Russia was in fact on 14th June, 1941.

Keitel refers (*page 144*) to a Christmas 1945 memorandum: no such document has been located among the private papers of Dr. Nelte. But clear insight into

Notes

Hitler's fearful blunders is given by those of the Field-Marshal's numerous memoranda that have survived.

Colonel-Generals Heinz Guderian and Hermann Hoth (*page 150*) were the Commanders-in-Chief of the Second and Third Armoured Groups, which had been allocated to Army Group Centre. Field-Marshal Fedor von Bock was Commander-in-Chief of Army Group Centre until 18th December, 1941. It should be noted that every major armoured advance required a definite pause after a certain time if the equipment was not to become totally unserviceable.

The *Nacht-und Nebel* (Cover of Darkness) decree (*page 153*) was the OKW's order dated 7th December, 1941, re: 'Prosecution of Punishable Acts Committed against the Reich or the Occupation Forces': this basically stipulated the death sentence for non-Germans committing punishable offences against the Reich or the occupation forces. If the trial and execution were not carried out as speedily as was desired in the occupied territories, the wrongdoers were to be transported to the Reich. Courts martial would be considered only if particular military interests demanded it. The only information permitted on the whereabouts of the deportee would be that he had been *sub judice*, and that no further information could be given as the matter was *sub judice*. Hence the term 'Cover of Darkness'. The 'Commando Order' was somewhat similar, dated 18th October 1942: 'British sabotage troops and their accomplices' taking part in 'commando raids' in Europe or in Africa—even if they were soldiers in uniform—were to be ruthlessly 'wiped out to the last man in the fighting or when attempting to escape'; prisoners were not to be spared. Individual commandos falling into the hands of the armed forces—either as agents or as saboteurs—were to be turned over to the Security Service. Commanders and officers failing to comply with this order would be called to answer before courts martial.

Apropos Keitel's protest that the main orders in the Russian campaign were not initiated by the OKW, the fact remains that the orders that transgressed international law, for example the 'Commissar Order', were circulated by Hitler not via the War Office but via the OKW. Colonel-General Ritter von Schobert was C.-in-C. of the Eleventh Army; he was killed in action on 12th September, 1941.

Lieutenant-General Erik Heinrichs was Chief of the Finnish General Staff. Colonel-General Nikolaus von Falkenhorst was Commander-in-Chief of the German Army in Norway. Marshal Carl Gustaf Freiherr Mannerheim was the Commander-in-Chief of the Finnish armed forces.

General Franz Szombathelyi ('Strombathelyi') became Chief of the Royal Hungarian General Staff in 1941. Keitel's Budapest visit (*page 157*) was probably at the end of January 1942; Keitel's original text has been amended. The nine light infantry divisions and one armoured division (mobile corps) went into action on the southern part of the eastern front as the Second Hungarian Army, under Colonel-General Gustav Jany, from April 1942 to February 1943; but Keitel's pledges to provide modern equipment could not be honoured as German tank and anti-tank gun production could not even meet the demands of the German forces. Horthy, whom Keitel terms 'the old gentleman', was at the time 74 years old.

During the encirclement action at Vyasma-Bryansk—the first phase of the German autumn assault on Moscow, lasting from 2nd to 20th October, 1941, 600,000 Russian prisoners of war were taken. Field-Marshals von Rundstedt and Ritter von Leeb (*page 160*) were Commanders-in-Chief of Army Groups South and North respectively; von Leeb (*page 162*) was at his own request relieved of his command on 16th January, 1942, and went into enforced retirement; his successor was Colonel-General Georg von Küchler. As can again be established here (*page 162*), Keitel (writing without access to documentary material) has confused the timing of the events: on 7th December, 1941, the Japanese attacked Pearl Harbour and the American Pacific Fleet; on 11th December, 1941, the German Reich and Italy declared war on the United States. But in fact, while the command

Notes

crisis on the eastern front did begin on 3rd December, 1941, with von Rundstedt's removal from command of Army Group South, all Hitler's subsequent steps were *after* Japan's entry into the war.

Halder claims that on 19th December, 1941, the day of Brauchitsch's dismissal, Hitler told him: "Anybody can do what little operational commanding there is to be done. The job of the Commander-in-Chief of the Army is to see to the national-socialist training of the Army. I know of no general able to do that in the way I have in mind. So I have decided to take over supreme control of the Army myself."

5: The Russian Campaign, 1941–1943.

Field-Marshal Keitel completed this section of his *Memoirs* on 30th September, 1946, and sent them to his counsel, Dr. Nelte, with a covering note which read: 'Enclosed is a description of Hitler's leadership of the Army as its Commander-in-Chief from 19th December, 1941, covering the period up to the winter of 1942–1943. This will supplement my testimony and amplify the descriptions I gave both at the Trial and during my interviews with you.'

The Reichstag session on Japan's entry into the war (*page 166*) was on 11th December, 1941 (Keitel: '9th December').

Hitler's 'first order to the eastern front' during the winter crisis was the 'Halt Order' already referred to; it was dated 16th December, 1941, and called for 'fanatical resistance'. Three times in his original manuscript Keitel mistakenly writes 'Field-Marshal von Bock', where it has now been corrected to 'von Kluge'; the Hoepner (Keitel: 'Hoeppner') affair had occurred at the turn of the year, 1941–1942; General Erich Hoepner's reprimanding was on 8th January, but the command of Army Group Centre had already been transferred to Field-Marshal von Kluge on 18th December, after Bock had been advised to go on leave to recover his shattered health. General Hoepner himself had been Commander-in-Chief of the Fourth Tank Army (ex-4th armoured group); on 8th January, 1942, he was discharged from the armed forces for withdrawing sections of his front, an action which had been unavoidable, but which he took on his own responsibility. He was a leading conspirator in the 20th July, 1944, bomb plot, and he was executed on 8th August, 1944.

Colonel-General Adolf Strauss (*page 167*), Commander-in-Chief of the Ninth Army, was relieved of his post on health grounds on 15th January, 1942. Engineer-General Foerster was commanding general of the Sixth Army Corps and *persona non grata* with Hitler who had already (unjustifiably) had him dismissed once in 1938, from the position of Inspector of Fortifications.

Keitel's manuscript originally puts the year of Todt's death (*page 168*) as 1941; he has frequently written 1941 instead of 1942 in the following pages, and each time it has, of course, been corrected.

For Hitler's summer offensive, see Führer's Directive No. 41, 'Operation Blue', dated 5th April, 1942; Field-Marshal von Reichenau had died on 17th January, 1942, as the result of a heart attack suffered at the headquarters of the Army Group South at Poltava.

The Roumanian army was never fitted out with modern German equipment to any great extent; as for the French equipment, it had already shown its inadequacy in 1940. King Michael I of Roumania (born 1921) had ruled since 6th September, 1940; he was forced to abdicate by the Soviet's Union on 30th December, 1947. Queen Helene of Roumania (born 1896) had been the wife of King Michael's father, King Carol II; their marriage was dissolved in 1928. After her son's accession to the throne she assumed the style of 'Queen Mother'. Helene Lupescu became the morganatic wife of ex-king Carol II in 1947.

Notes

The operation in which Hitler 'intervened' (*page 177*) to scoop victory from the jaws of defeat was the second battle of Kharkov in May 1942, during which the Russian attempt to strike at the Germans as they advanced ended with a decisive defeat for Marshal Timoshenko; but it was not Hitler, as Commander-in-Chief of the Army, but his C.G.S., General Halder, who had reached the right conclusions here; Hitler merely authorised them.

Hitler's visit to Army Group South (*page 179*) must have been on the 4th or 5th July, 1942. Colonel-General Maximilian Freiherr von und zu Weichs a.d. Glon took over as Commander-in-Chief of Army Group B (ex-South) on 15th July, 1942, commanding it until 12th February, 1943. Army Group A had been formed from parts of Army Group South, the Seventeenth Army and the First and (sometime) Fourth Tank Armies, together with Roumanian and Czechoslovakian units. Field-Marshal Wilhelm List was Commander-in-Chief of Army Group A from 15th July, 1942, until 10th September, 1942. He was never given a new command. His Army Group A was directed personally by Hitler as Commander-in-Chief of the Army from Vinnitsa until 22nd November, 1942. General Konrad (Keitel: 'Conrad') was commanding general of the Forty-Ninth Mountain Corps.

It is probable that there was more to Hitler's angry outburst (*page 181*) than just this difference of opinion at Stalino; this was his first realisation that the capture of the Caucasus oil fields was out of the question, and it was this that Hitler had, during his visit to the headquarters of Army Group South at Poltava on 1st June, 1942—before the offensive—declared to be the prerequisite of its successful conclusion.

General Georg Thomas (*page* 183) was head of the Economic Warfare department of the OKW from 1st October, 1942, onwards.

Colonel-General Halder was dismissed his office as Chief of the Army General Staff on 24th September, 1942, and given no new command; after 20th July, 1944, he was arrested.

Keitel's revelation of Rommel's earlier illness (*page 185*) throws new light on the reasons for Rommel's being in Germany at the time of the British counter-offensive in October, 1942. His deputy, General Georg Stumme, was killed in action at the onset of the second battle of El-Alamein. Keitel included in his original manuscript his views on the north African campaigns, which have been omitted as of no consequence.

In his original text, Keitel put the date of the Russian counter-offensive (*page 185*) as December, 1942; in fact the counter-offensive in the Stalingrad area was launched on 19th November, 1942. As far as is known to the editor from verbal descriptions of the war conferences late in November, 1942, Keitel failed at the time to make any outspoken proposal for a break-out attempt to the west.

8: *The Last Days under Adolf Hitler, 1945.*

The General Krebs (*page 198*) was infantry General Hans Krebs, entrusted with the command of the Army General Staff between 29th March and 30th April, 1945; he died or committed suicide in Russian captivity in about May, 1945.

Keitel's adjutant was Air Force Major Gerhard von Szymonski; Lieutenant-General Paul Winter was chief of the OKW's central office; Ferdinand Schörner had been a Field-Marshal since 1st March, 1945, and commanded Army Group Centre (ex-A) from January to May, 1945. The tank General Walter Wenck had been chief of the operations division and then the 'command group' in the War Office from July 1944 to February 1945, when he suffered an automobile accident; since 10th April, 1945, he had been C.-in-C. of the newly-raised Twelfth Army. Colonel-General Guderian had been Chief of the General Staff from July 1944

Notes

to March 1945, when he had been sent on permanent leave by Hitler after violent disputes. Keitel's description (*page 200*) of the weakness of the senior commanders when faced with Hitler can be compared with General Wenck's statement that he probably thought there was some prospect of success for the attack on Berlin, but he was far too clever not to realise after a very few days that his only function now would be to establish an escape route to the west for the encircled remnants of the Ninth Army.

Colonel-General Gotthard Heinrici (*page 201*) had been C.-in-C. of the Vistula Army Group fighting in the region from north of Berlin to the Pomeranian coast of the Baltic from 1st March, 1945.

Field-Marshal Keitel does not refer to Hitler's 'collapse' witnessed by several officers on the 22nd April, and expressly referred to by Major-General Christian (chief of Air Force operations staff) together with the news that Hitler was having his personal papers burnt. Vice-Admiral Voss, the Admiralty's representative in the Führer's headquarters made a similar comment later.

General Koehler was commanding general of the Thirtieth Armoured Corps, and had his headquarters at Wiessenburg to the south-west of Belzig.

Hitler's story to Keitel of 'peace negotiations with England' (*page 206*) was of course a downright lie.

SS-General Steiner (*page 208*) had been C.-in-C. of the Eleventh Tank Army, and then of the 'Steiner' Army Group formed to create a mobile reserve. Steiner himself was very short of manpower; Field-Marshal Keitel was suffering from the same brand of optimism for which he had earlier castigated General Wenck! In Berlin Steiner had been pressed to mount his attack on the capital, but he had rejected the attack as hopeless. He wrote: 'At 5.00 a.m. on 22nd April, Field-Marshal Keitel again endeavoured to bring me round to this idea, but he did it without any inner conviction and probably only from an innate sense of duty.' Keitel was unable when writing his manuscript to recall the name of Rathenow, and just wrote 'X-town' each time.

Colonel-General Robert Ritter von Greim (*page 124*) had previously been AOC-in-C. the Sixth Air Group (Eastern Front); he had been flown into Berlin by the aerobatic pilot Hanna Reitsch on 26th April; Hitler promoted him to Field-Marshal and named him Supreme Commander of the German Air Force in Göring's place. In his original manuscript, Keitel implied that Greim shot himself in the leg when his plane landed in Berlin, but, according to General Koller, the field-marshal was shot through the foot by rifle fire just as the plane came in to land. Greim committed suicide in May, 1945.

Göring asked for Hitler's agreement to his taking over complete control of the leadership of the Reich (on the basis of the Succession-to-the-Führer Act of 29th June, 1941) on 23rd April; he intended to fly to General Eisenhower's headquarters the next day to take up negotiations; by signal that evening, Hitler forbade Göring's projected assumption of authority over the Reich, and on the 24th Göring and Koller were arrested by the SS for treason.

According to Keitel's reckoning the visit to Heinrici (*page 215*) would have been on 26th April, but there is no doubt that it was on the 28th. The phrase 'To have to abandon Steiner's attack . . .' (*page 216*) originally read 'to have to abandon Heinrici's attack . . .'—clearly a slip of the pen by Keitel. (There was never any suggestion of Heinrici delivering any attack, while all their hopes had been pinned on the success of that by Steiner.) General Hasso von Manteuffel was C.-in-C. of the Third Tank Army.

At this stage of the narrative, Keitel's memory put the dates one day earlier than was actually the case; all the dates have been corrected in the printed text to avoid confusion.

Field-Marshal Busch (*page 225*) had been C.-in-C. North-West since 15th April.

SS-Lieutenant-General Hermann Fegelein had been the SS-Reichsführer's representative at the Führer's headquarters; he was married to Grete Braun (Eva

Notes

Braun's sister) and was thus Hitler's brother-in-law. He was executed on Hitler's orders, as the Führer harboured private suspicions that he had been planning to slip out of Berlin in plain clothes, and he was aware of the secret talks that had taken place at the end of April between the SS-Reichsführer and a representative of the Swedish Red Cross, Count Bernadotte.

The telegram from Bormann (*page 226*)—'Testament in force . . . etc.'—reached Grand-Admiral Dönitz at 10.15 a.m. on 1st May. The telegram added that Bormann would endeavour to report to Dönitz personally as soon as possible; it was not to be made public until then. The first of the two telegrams mentioned by Keitel (original manuscript slightly incorrect) was signed 'Goebbels. Bormann' and reached Plön at 3.18 p.m. on 1st May. It continued: 'Testament of 29th April confers the office of Reich President on you.' It added a list of Ministers.

In his description of the Flensburg-Mürwick interlude (*page 228*), Field-Marshal Keitel ignored the controversy over whether he should remain Chief of the OKW. One general (of whose identity the Editor of this book is aware) told Jodl he refused to work any longer under Keitel. At first Colonel-General Jodl answered him very curtly and ordered him out of the room; but later he had him called back and commiserated with him that he fully understood his views, as he, Jodl, had 'suffered' enough himself in the six years he had worked with him.

Jodl later quoted a view expressed by Dr. Lehmann: 'Lehmann once said on this point that Keitel is brave enough to take on a lion in bare-fisted combat; but faced with Hitler he is as helpless as a babe.' To which Jodl commented: 'His own will-power was not very strongly developed, and inferior to the unusually marked will-power of the Führer.' In the early phase of the war Keitel had indeed often put up a 'very energetic opposition' to Hitler, but then he had become resigned, especially when Hitler began to get aggressive and insulting. In fairness to Keitel one is obliged to point out that Colonel-General Jodl can hardly be said not to have become equally resigned himself.

Colonel-General Karl Hilpert was the C.-in-C. of the Courland Army Group; he died in Russian captivity in 1949. Lieutenant-Colonel (G.S.) Ulrich de Maiziere was in the operations division of the Army in the combined OKW-operations-staff-plus-Army-General-Staff. General Franz Böhme was C.-in-C. of the German Twentieth Army in Norway.

It is not clear why Keitel repeatedly speaks of a 'preliminary treaty'. The surrender of the German armed forces had already been signed in the Allied headquarters at Reims; it was merely that the Russians insisted on the repetition of the ceremony in Berlin. The American general who broke the news to Keitel that he was to consider himself as a prisoner of war (*page 234*) was Major-General Rooks: 'Keitel made no comment on the disclosure, but merely explained that he had put his signature to the Instrument of Unconditional Surrender and was well aware of the consequences now . . .'

Lieutenant-General John von Freyend, one of Keitel's companions into captivity (recorded by Keitel in his agitation as Lt.-Col. 'von John') was the senior adjutant to the Chief of the OKW.

Index

282

Index

Flensburg, 228, 229, 233, 234
Florence, 126
Foerster, Pioneer-General, 75, 167
Fontaine, Lisa *see* Keitel, Lisa
France and the French, 22, 25, 40, 63, 71,
  73, 74, 75, 85, 91, 93, 94, 98, 99, 100,
  103, 108–118, 121, 125, 126, 131, 132,
  133, 137, 148, 152, 168, 181, 192, 241,
  246, 253, 254, 255, 256, 259, 266
Franco, Gen., 125, 126, 133
François-Poncet, André, 40, 71
Frankfurt-on-Oder, 75, 196, 199
Freyend, Lt. Col. von, 234
Friedeburg, Admiral von, 43, 228, 230
Fritsch, Col.-Gen. Freiherr Werner von,
  16, 19, 20, 21, 22, 23, 24, 25, 26, 27,
  35, 37, 45, 46–52, 55, 56, 61, 96, 97
Fromm, Col.-Gen., 266, 267
Funck, Col.-Gen. Freiherr von, 120, 127
Funk, Air Staff Engineer, 96, 199
Fürstenberg, 208, 209, 217
Fürstenwalde, 191
Fuschl, 85, 122

Galicia, 159
Gandersheim, 12
Gandin, Gen. Antonio, 127, 258
Gatow, 209, 210, 213
Gdynia, 96
Geneva, 18, 135, 260
Gercke, Gen., 176, 177
Gibraltar, 121, 132, 133, 134
Giraud, Gen., 259, 261
Gisevius, Dr. Hans Bernd, 46, 47, 51
Godesberg, *see under* Bad Godesberg
Goebbels, Dr. Joseph, 197, 226, 241
Goldap, 190
Göring, Reichsmarschall Hermann, 24, 38,
  43, 44, 45, 46, 47, 48, 49, 50, 55, 62,
  64, 71, 79, 80, 85, 94, 113, 118, 119,
  136, 142, 145, 155, 175, 178, 180, 181,
  189, 197, 198, 202, 207, 213, 214, 224,
  262, 263
Gotha, 201
Göttingen, 13
Graevenitz, Maj.-Gen. von, 260
Graziani, Marshal, 120, 127
Great Britain, *see under* British
Greece, 126, 127, 128, 129, 139, 141, 142,
  160, 259
Greim, Col.-Gen. von, 213, 214, 215, 223,
  224, 225
Grille, The Führer's Yacht, 67
Gruhn, Erna *see* Blomberg, Erna von
Grunewald, 106
Guderian, Gen. Heinz, 65, 150, 151, 167,
  199, 200
Guhr, Dr., 18
Gumbinnen, 190
Gürtner, Minister of Justice, 47, 48, 50

Hacha, President Emil, 78, 79, 80, 81, 83
Hague, The, 106, 135

Halder, Col.-Gen. Franz, 37, 38, 65, 66,
  67, 69, 89, 90, 91, 99, 100, 102, 111,
  134, 139, 146, 156, 157, 163, 164, 165,
  166, 179, 180, 181, 182, 183, 184, 244
Halle, 198
Hamburg, 106, 187, 201
Hammerstein, Gen. von, 19
Hanover, 11, 13, 16, 244
Hansen, Gen., 129, 156
Harz, Region of, 199, 201
Hase, Gen. von, 192
Heinrichs, Gen., 156
Heinrici, Gen., 201, 208, 209, 213, 215,
  216, 217, 218, 219, 220, 229
Heligoland, 104
Helldorf, Count von, 43, 44, 46
Helmscherode, 12, 13, 14, 23, 41, 76, 83,
  119, 154, 267
Hendaye, 125
Henderson, Sir Nevile, 40, 90, 91
Herzegovina, 253
Hewel, Minister Walter, 79
Heye, Gen., 36
Heydrich, SS-Gen. Reinhard, Protector,
  52, 62, 255
Hildesheim, 119
Hilpert, Gen. 229
Himmler, Reichsführer Heinrich, 52, 136,
  181, 197, 208, 214, 215, 220, 223, 225,
  226, 227, 229, 230, 241, 250, 251, 252,
  260, 267
Hindenburg, Field Marshal von, 17, 18,
  19, 267
Hindenberg, Gen. von, 19
Hitler, Adolf, 15, 17, 18, 19, 20, 21, 22, 25,
  27, 28, 29, 30, 35–53, 54–119, 120–
  164, 165–186, 189, 190, 192, 193, 194,
  196–226, 227, 235, 236, 241, 243, 244,
  245, 246, 247, 248, 249, 250, 252, 253,
  254, 255, 256, 257, 258, 259, 260, 261,
  262, 263, 264, 265, 266, 267, 268
Hoepner, Col.-Gen., 38, 166, 167
Holland, 97, 99, 106, 222, 225, 253, 255,
  266
Holste, Gen., 204, 205, 206, 208, 209, 210,
  212, 213, 216, 217, 219, 223
Horthy, Admiral Nikolaus von, 128, 129,
  139, 140, 141, 158
Hossbach, Gen., 27, 47, 49, 54, 56, 190
Hoth, Col.-Gen. Hermann, 150
Hotz, Lt. Col., 255
Hradshin, 81
Hungary, 128, 129, 130, 138, 139, 140, 155,
  156, 157, 158, 159, 174, 175, 176,
  182
Huntziger, Gen., 112, 113, 125

Ironside, Field Marshal Sir Edmund, 37
Italy and the Italians, 36, 37, 88, 89, 106,
  111, 112, 114, 120, 121, 126, 128, 130,
  131, 134, 137, 139, 141, 142, 143, 155,
  159, 160, 174, 176, 182, 185, 188, 190,
  199, 202, 206, 215, 227, 253, 257, 258

284

Index

Index

Volchov, River, 162
Volga, 174, 185, 186
Voronezh on Don, 172, 174, 178, 179, 182
Vyasma, 151, 160, 162

Waizenegger, Major, 107
Waren, 222
Warlimont, Col., 74, 92, 123, 144
Warsaw, 84, 91, 94, 95, 96, 97, 98
Warta, River, 75
Weichs, Field-Marshal Freiherr von, 180
Weidling, Gen., 221
Weimar, 18, 26, 29, 201
Wenck, Gen., 199, 200, 201, 202, 203, 204, 206, 207, 208, 210, 216, 218, 219, 223
Wenge, Col., Freiherr von der, 14
Westhoff, Col. Adolf, 260, 261
Westphal, Lt. Gen., 244
Westphalia, 100
West Wall, The, 65, 71, 73, 74, 86, 94, 97, 98, 132
Wetzell, Lt. Gen., 16
Weygand, Gen., 259, 261
Wietersheim, Gen. von, 87

Wilhelm II, Kaiser, 15, 16, 29
Williams, Col. Curtis L., 261
Winter, Lt. Gen. August, 203, 215, 229
Winter, Lt. Gen. Paul, 251
Wismar, 224
Witkowitz, 79
Wittenberg, 210
Witzleben, Field Marshal von, 73, 192, 193, 247
Wolfenbüttel, 13
Wolff, Otto and Company, 40
Wolff-Wusterwitz, Gen. von, 160
Wülfel, 13
Wunsdorf, 203

Yugoslavia, 128, 131, 132, 137, 138, 139, 140, 141, 143

Zeitzler, Lt. Gen., 36, 81, 108, 183, 184
Zhukov, Marshal G. K., 230, 231, 232, 233
Zoppot, 96, 99
Zossen, 89, 100, 156, 196
Zvetkovic, Prime Minister of Yugoslavia, 138

288